FIGHTING FEDERAL WRITS OF HABEAS CORPUS

FIGHTING FEDERAL WRITS OF HABEAS CORPUS
EXPERIENCED HABEAS ATTORNEYS EXPLAIN THE DETAILS OF FEDERAL WRITS

Caitlin Dukes & Aaron Spolin

Library of Congress Catalog Card No. 2023915788

ISBN 9798857615935

Spolin & Dukes P.C.
11500 W. Olympic Blvd., Suite 400
Los Angeles, CA 90064

TABLE OF CONTENTS

Chapter 4

APPROPRIATE ARGUMENTS

Chapter 5

ARGUMENTS THAT SHOULD NOT BE RAISED IN A

Chapter 6

CLAIMS OF ACTUAL INNOCENCE

Chapter 1
OVERVIEW

A. The Basics

Many people have heard of a petition for writ of habeas corpus, but few know the mechanics of it. This book is presented to educate about what is often referred to as the "Great Writ." Writs of habeas corpus have complex and detailed procedural rules. Writs of habeas corpus also have complex requirements for the types of arguments that can be made and the types of arguments that cannot be made.

We, the authors of this book, hope to share some of the experience we have obtained handling federal writs throughout the country. Aaron Spolin is a former Assistant District Attorney and the author of <u>Witness Misidentification in Criminal Trials</u>. Caitlin Dukes is a former Deputy District Attorney with a resume that includes work in state and federal government. Both of us currently serve as partners at a law firm that exclusively handles criminal appeals and habeas writs. Therefore, our approach to federal writs is not merely academic; we live and breathe these cases on a day-to-day basis.

This book serves to organize and simplify the rules for the benefit of the lay person and for the benefit of other attorneys. The book is presented as a general guide to federal writs of habeas corpus. It is not presented as legal advice and should not be construed as such. A person who wishes to fight a federal writ of habeas corpus is well advised to seek out an attorney with experience handling these types of cases, as federal writs are often complex and a challenge to win.

Our own experience handling federal writs throughout the country has demonstrated to us the importance of procedural rules. A strong case "on the merits" can and will be denied if important procedural rules are violated. Even a well-supported federal writ for a truly innocent client will generally be denied if it is *one day* late, if the parallel state court filings were improperly done, or for any number of other rule violations. Therefore, knowledge is power when it comes to federal writs of habeas corpus.

So what exactly is a federal writ of habeas corpus? *Habeas corpus* is a Latin phrase that roughly translates to "bring a body before the court." A writ, in general, is an order from a higher court to a lower court, government agency, or government official. A writ of habeas corpus is, therefore, an order from the court to the government official who is acting on behalf of the state to incarcerate the defendant. This person is typically the warden of the prison where the defendant is incarcerated. A writ of habeas corpus requests that the court order the warden to bring the defendant to court in order to argue the issues that are raised in the petition for writ of habeas corpus. A petition for writ of habeas corpus argues that the conviction was improper and unlawful.

Writs of habeas corpus have been around for hundreds of years, and the writ is codified in the Constitution. "The Privilege of the Writ of Habeas Corpus shall not be suspended, unless when in Cases of Rebellion or Invasion the public Safety may require it."[1]

In 1830, Chief Justice John Marshall of the United States Supreme Court wrote, "The writ of habeas corpus is a high prerogative writ, known to the common law, the great object of which is the liberation of those who may be imprisoned without sufficient cause."[2] In 1948, the Supreme Court began a decision with, "The writ of habeas

---

[1] There have been a few times in history when the writ of habeas corpus was suspended. Abraham Lincoln suspended the writ of habeas corpus during parts of the Civil War. The reader who wants to learn more about this is directed to David L. Martin, "When Lincoln Suspended Habeas Corpus," *American Bar Association Journal* 60, no. 1, 99–102 (1974).

George W. B. Bush also suspended the writ of habeas corpus to incarcerate individuals in Guantanamo Bay. In *Boumediene v. Bush*, 553 U.S. 723 (2008), the Supreme Court struck down President Bush's law, holding that the attempt to deny a writ of habeas corpus to the prisoners in Guantanamo Bay was unconstitutional.

[2] *Ex parte Watkins*, 28 U.S. 193, 202 (1830). Tobias Watkins filed a petition for habeas corpus inquiring into the legality of his confinement in a jail in Washington County, District of Columbia.

corpus has played a great role in the history of human freedom. It has been the judicial method of lifting undue restraints upon personal liberty."[3] Later in that decision, the Court wrote, "The primary purpose of a habeas corpus proceeding is to make certain that a man is not unjustly imprisoned. And if for some justifiable reason he was previously unable to assert his rights or was unaware of the significance of relevant facts, it is neither necessary nor reasonable to deny him all opportunity of obtaining judicial relief."

An old Florida Supreme Court case summarizes the importance of writs of habeas corpus. "The procedure for the granting of this particular writ is not to be circumscribed by hard and fast rules or technicalities, which often accompany our consideration of other processes. If it appears to a court of competent jurisdiction that a man is being illegally restrained of his liberty, it is the responsibility of the court to brush aside formal technicalities and issue such appropriate orders as will do justice. In habeas corpus, the niceties of the procedure are not anywhere near as important as the determination of the ultimate question as to the legality of the restraint."[4]

Unfortunately, over the last few decades, the government and the courts have retreated from the view that the procedural rules are less important than whether someone is being illegally restrained. What the Florida court called "technicalities" are indeed very important to the ability to file and argue a writ of habeas corpus in federal court. This retreat makes it all the more important to be aware of the rules and requirements of a writ of habeas corpus.

Consequently, this book can be viewed as the "dos and don'ts" of a federal writ of habeas corpus. Since the subject matter of this book is about *federal* writs, the book is really the second part in a series about writs. The first part in the series (or really the first 50 parts) would be a book about filing a writ of habeas corpus in each state court. Every state has its own rules and requirements for how an

---

[3] *Price v. Johnston*, 334 U.S. 266 (1948).
[4] *Anglin v. Mayo*, 88 So.2d 918 (Fla.1956).

individual who was convicted may seek to argue that his or her conviction and incarceration are unlawful.

One significant limitation of federal writs is that the defendant, almost always, must have argued the specific issues in the state court before he or she will be allowed to argue the issues in federal court. Another limitation of federal writs is that they must be premised on violations of *federal* law. While there may be some flexibility in the types of arguments that may be included in a state writ of habeas corpus, a federal writ needs to be grounded in one or more of the Amendments to the Constitution. Because of this, a significant mistake by an attorney becomes "ineffective assistance of counsel," which is a violation of the Sixth Amendment. Similarly, the exclusion of a member of the jury for racial reasons becomes a violation of the Fourteenth Amendment's Equal Protection clause.

There are two central components to a federal writ: the procedural rules and the substantive requirements. This book is organized around these. Our hope is that the lay reader will be able to assist his or her attorney, or his or her family member, in considering whether to file a writ of habeas corpus and in filing the best possible writ that may be filed. Our hope also is that the attorney will have a better and deeper understanding of federal writs of habeas corpus and how they can be used as a method to achieve justice for his or her clients.

B. How to Submit a Successful Writ of Habeas Corpus

There is no recipe that guarantees success in a writ of habeas corpus. There is no formula that always works, and there is no way to predict whether a writ of habeas corpus will be successful or not. A defendant can, however, maximize his or her chances of success. To maximize the odds of a successful writ of habeas corpus, a defendant should focus on three areas: (1) complying with the procedural rules, (2) making the strongest legal arguments possible, and (3) appealing to the judge's sense of justice and fair play.

Procedural Rules

A petition for writ of habeas corpus must follow the procedural rules. This means that it must be filed before any deadlines pass. A petition that is filed late stands little chance of success. The petition must also be filed after the issues have been exhausted in state court. A petition that is filed in federal court before the state court has had a chance to review the issues also stands little chance of success. These are two of the most important procedural rules and will be addressed at length in future chapters.

Strong Legal Arguments

Legal arguments are the foundation of a writ of habeas corpus. A well-crafted petition supported both by the facts of the case and by strong legal arguments stands a far greater chance of success than a haphazard and disorganized petition. A good petition will cause the judge to think that there is merit to the claims. It takes a great deal of time and effort and legal knowledge to present strong legal arguments.

As we will see later, there is usually only *one* chance to file a writ of habeas corpus. This is known as the rule against successive writs. In a defendant's writ, the defendant must include *all* arguments that he or she wishes to raise. Knowing the possible arguments, too, requires a great deal of legal knowledge.

A substantial part of this book addresses the arguments that are appropriate for a writ of habeas corpus. The list of arguments is not exhaustive, but it does contain many of the more common arguments that are found in writs of habeas corpus. The reader is cautioned that the law changes. Every year, the courts clarify, expand, and restrict the protections of the federal Constitution. Therefore, the list of arguments and the cases that support them, as presented later, are subject to change. The court may apply the Constitution to new situations or may restrict how it previously applied the Constitution to certain situations. Consequently, everything contained in this book should be double checked before definitively relying on it.

Appeal to the Judge's Sense of Justice and Fair Play

Judges are people. Prosecutors are also people. Nobody wants to see an innocent person in jail, and nobody wants to see someone incarcerated due to significant infringements on that person's constitutional rights. For example, a reasonable judge does not want to see a defendant found guilty at trial because the defendant's attorney did a poor job in representing his or her client.

Thanks to television, the Miranda warning has entered the vocabulary of the average person. We have all seen a TV show where the police arrest a character and tell him or her, "You have the right to remain silent. Anything you say may be used against you in a court of law. You have the right to an attorney. If you cannot afford an attorney, the state will provide one for you." If a suspect confesses to a crime without having been given a Miranda warning and his or her attorney does not try to suppress the confession, the attorney will then have rendered ineffective assistance of counsel.

If this defendant files a writ of habeas corpus, he should focus on justice and fair play. It is *unjust* for him to have been found guilty due to his attorney's mishandling of the Miranda warning issue. In the interests of justice and fair play, the conviction must be vacated. Appealing to the judge's sense of justice and fair play does not mean writing one sentence about this subject. It means organizing the petition for writ of habeas corpus in the best possible way so that the reader—meaning the judge and, to a lesser extent, the prosecution—will understand the injustice that occurred to the defendant. The feeling of injustice may be conscious, or it may be subconscious. The tone of the writ should, therefore, be shaped by the appeal to the judge's sense of justice and fair play.

C. An Archetypical Example of a Writ of Habeas Corpus

In the previous section, we briefly noted an example of a person whose Miranda rights were violated. We will discuss violations of Miranda rights in depth later in this book. For now, we present an archetypical case of a writ of habeas corpus that involves a violation of a defendant's Miranda rights.

In one case, the police believed that Kevin James was a suspect in a shooting and brought him to the police station for questioning. After two hours of questioning, Mr. Jones told the police, "I don't want to talk no more." Mr. Jones had invoked his Miranda right to remain silent ("you have the right to remain silent"). When a suspect tells the police that he does not want to talk, the police officers must stop asking questions. However, despite Mr. Jones's clear invocation of his right to remain silent, the police continued with their questions. Eventually, Mr. Jones made some incriminating statements. He was arrested, tried and convicted of murder, and sentenced to 75 years to life in prison.[5]

Subsequently, Mr. Jones argued on appeal that his Miranda rights had been violated. The California state court thought that Mr. Jones had not been clear in invoking his right to remain silent and affirmed the conviction. If not for the existence of a federal writ of habeas corpus, Mr. Jones's case would have ended, and he would be sitting in jail for 75 years to life.

This, however, is not where Mr. Jones's story ends. He filed a petition for writ of habeas corpus in federal court to review whether his constitutional rights had been violated. To the federal court, it was very clear that Mr. Jones's rights had been violated. The Court held, "By continuing to interrogate Jones after he had invoked his right to remain silent, officers violated *Miranda*—which means the government cannot use against Jones anything he said after his invocation."

In the final paragraph, the Court summarized its decision as follows:

> The Supreme Court has repeatedly made clear that when a suspect simply and unambiguously says he wants to remain silent, police questioning must end. Under any reasonable

---

[5] *Jones v. Harrington*, 829 F.3d 1128 (9th Cir. 2016).

interpretation of the facts, Jones simply and unambiguously invoked that right. Clearly established Supreme Court law required the suppression of Jones's interrogation. The state shall either release Jones or grant him a new trial.

This case illustrates an important point about federal writs of habeas corpus—state courts sometimes get it wrong about the law. This is why there is a procedure for filing a writ of habeas corpus in federal court. This case also illustrates a second principal about writs of habeas corpus—a defendant must be diligent in pursuing his case. If Mr. Jones had given up after the state court affirmed his conviction, he would have been incarcerated with a sentence of 75 years to life.

After his conviction was vacated, Mr. Jones was re-tried for the murder, and the jury deadlocked. He was tried another time, and that jury found him guilty. He was sentenced to 10 years plus 50 years to life. He appealed the conviction, and the state court of appeals reversed the conviction. According to California records, Mr. Jones pleaded no contest to voluntary manslaughter in 2020 and received a 21-year sentence. Presumably, Mr. Jones had many years of credits to apply toward his sentence since he was first arrested in late 2003.

With this introduction in mind, we now turn to the details of the writ of habeas corpus.

Chapter 2
OVERVIEW OF REQUIREMENTS

A. Introduction

A few things must happen before a defendant can file a writ of habeas corpus in federal court. First, a defendant must be convicted in a state court. The defendant will then appeal the conviction, which is then affirmed by the state appellate court. The defendant may also seek review in the state supreme court, which is denied. At this point, some defendants may file a writ of habeas corpus in federal court. Other defendants, however, must first file a writ of habeas corpus in state court before filing in federal court. This will all be explained later in this book in Chapter 7 Exhaustion of Claims in State Court.

The federal codes have two different sections for a writ of habeas corpus:

- 28 U.S.C. § 2254—the statute for when a person in state custody challenges his or her conviction; and
- 28 U.S.C. § 2255—the statute for when a person in federal custody challenges his or her conviction.

This book will mainly focus on writs filed in federal court by those who are in state custody (28 U.S.C. § 2254).

B. The "In Custody" Requirement

To file a writ of habeas corpus in federal court, the defendant must be "in custody." This requirement is found in 28 U.S.C. § 2254(a), which states:

> The Supreme Court, a Justice thereof, a circuit judge, or a district court shall entertain an application for a writ of habeas corpus in behalf of a person *in custody* [emphasis added] pursuant to the judgment of a State court only on the ground that he is in custody in violation of the Constitution or laws or treaties of the United States.

There was a time when being in custody was understood in its literal sense. A defendant had to be under physical restraint in order to file a writ of habeas corpus. This did not, however, mean that a defendant had to be chained down or something of the sort. It basically meant that the defendant had to be in jail.

Beginning in 1963, the Supreme Court provided a broad definition of "custody." "Custody" includes someone who is on parole because "the custody and control of the Parole Board involve significant restraints on petitioner's liberty . . . which are in addition to those imposed by the State upon the public generally."[6] It also includes someone who is not physically in jail but who has been convicted and is waiting for his or her sentence to commence.[7] Additionally, it includes someone who filed a writ of habeas corpus while he was incarcerated but was subsequently released from jail before the court could adjudicate the writ.[8]

In one case, a defendant was sentenced to 3 years for drug charges and then 25 years to life for murder. After serving the drug sentence, the defendant filed a writ of habeas corpus, seeking to challenge the drug charges. The issue, however, was that the writ was filed after the defendant had finished the portion of the sentence for the drug charges. Nonetheless, the Court held that "we view consecutive sentences in the aggregate, not as discrete segments." Therefore, the defendant was permitted to file a writ of habeas corpus related to the drug sentence.[9]

C. The "In Violation of the Constitution" Requirement

To file a writ of habeas corpus in federal court, the defendant must argue that his or her custody is in violation of federal law. This requirement is found in 28 U.S.C. § 2254(a), which again states:

---

[6] *Jones v. Cunningham*, 371 U.S. 236 (1963).
[7] *Hensley v. Municipal Court*, 411 U.S. 345 (1973).
[8] *Carafas v. LaVallee*, 391 U.S. 234 (1968).
[9] *Garlotte v. Fordice*, 515 U.S. 39 (1995).

The Supreme Court, a Justice thereof, a circuit judge, or a district court shall entertain an application for a writ of habeas corpus in behalf of a person in custody pursuant to the judgment of a State court only on the ground that he is in custody *in violation of the Constitution or laws or treaties of the United States* [emphasis added].

Practically, this means that the person must argue that his or her incarceration is in violation of the Constitution. The bulk of this book will focus on addressing the various types of constitutional violations that are more common. A non-exhaustive list of potential violations that are available to be argued in a writ of habeas corpus includes the following:

- The Fifth Amendment prohibits double jeopardy and Miranda violations.
- The Sixth Amendment requires a speedy trial, the right to confront witnesses, and effective assistance of counsel. Effective assistance of counsel is an extremely broad category. Later, we will discuss many types of situations where a defendant received ineffective assistance of counsel.
- The Sixth Amendment also provides a right to self-representation and the right to a unanimous jury verdict.
- The Eighth Amendment protects against cruel and unusual punishment.
- Other sections of the Constitution require fairness. The prosecutor must act in a fair way, and the judge cannot be biased. For example, the prosecution cannot remove a member of the jury pool for racial reasons. The prosecution must also turn over all exculpatory information to the defendant.

The Supreme Court has been very clear that "federal habeas corpus relief does not lie for errors of state law."[10] In one case, a lower

---

[10] *Lewis v. Jeffers*, 497 U.S. 764 (1990).

federal court granted a writ of habeas corpus because "evidence was 'incorrectly admitted . . . pursuant to California law.'" In other words, the California court did not follow the California evidence rules. The Supreme Court highlighted that "it is not the province of a federal habeas court to reexamine state-court determinations on state-law questions. In conducting habeas review, a federal court is limited to deciding whether a conviction violated the Constitution, laws, or treaties of the United States. 28 U.S.C. § 2241."[11]

This issue frequently comes up both in the Supreme Court and in federal circuit courts.[12] The fact that this issue often comes up shows the importance of submitting a well-drafted writ of habeas corpus. Sometimes, there is a thin line between arguing that a conviction was obtained in violation of a state law and that a conviction was obtained in violation of a federal law. Sometimes, a violation of state law can be reframed as a violation of the Constitution. A writ of habeas corpus must be clear that a federal right was violated.

D. The One-Year Deadline

The deadline to file a writ of habeas corpus, sometimes referred to as a "statute of limitations" or just the "limitations" period, is quite short. In 1996, Congress passed the Antiterrorism and Effective Death Penalty Act of 1996 (AEDPA), which was signed into law by President Clinton. This legislation adopted a one-year limitations

---

[11] *Estelle v. McGuire*, 502 U.S. 62 (1991).

[12] *See, e.g.*, *Wilson v. Corcoran*, 562 U.S. 1 (2010) ("Federal courts may not issue writs of habeas corpus to state prisoners whose confinement does not violate federal law. Because the Court of Appeals granted the writ to respondent without finding such a violation, we vacate its judgment and remand."); *Santone v. Fischer*, 689 F.3d 138 (2d Cir. 2012); *Cuero v. Cate*, 827 F.3d 879 (9th Cir. 2016); *Smith v. Davis*, 927 F.3d 313 (5th Cir. 2019).

period for the filing of a writ of habeas corpus, with only limited exceptions.[13]

While the one-year statute of limitations seems relatively straightforward, it is not. There are many questions that complicate the application of the limitations period, including:

- When does the one-year period begin?
- If there are multiple claims, is it possible that each claim begins on a different date?
- What happens if a writ is filed after the one-year deadline? Will the writ automatically be dismissed?
- Are there any situations in which it is okay to file a writ after one year?
- What if there are circumstances in which it would be manifestly unfair to dismiss a writ that was filed after the deadline? May the Court consider the claims made in the writ?

These are some of the questions that will be addressed in Chapter 3 about deadlines. For now, the important thing to remember is that a writ of habeas corpus should be filed as quickly as the circumstances allow.

E. Exhaustion

The general rule is that only claims that were "exhausted" in state court may be brought to federal court. Typically, to exhaust a claim, one must seek review of that claim in the highest state court available. In California, for example, a claim must be presented to the California Supreme Court before a defendant can file a writ of habeas corpus in federal court. Arguments may be exhausted during the appellate process or by filing a writ of habeas corpus in state court. Under both scenarios, the claim would have to be taken to the highest court in the state. Though the concept of exhaustion seems straightforward, it can

---

[13] *See* 28 U.S.C. § 2244(d)(1).

be somewhat complicated. We devote a whole chapter to it later in this book.

F. Is There a Right to an Attorney for the Filing of a Writ of Habeas Corpus?

There is long-standing precedent that a defendant has a right to counsel for filing an appeal. Yet, this precedent has never been extended to having counsel appointed to file a writ of habeas corpus. In *Pennsylvania v. Finley*, the Supreme Court held,

> We have never held that prisoners have a constitutional right to counsel when mounting collateral attacks upon their convictions . . . and we decline to so hold today. Our cases establish that the right to appointed counsel extends to the first appeal of right, and no further.[14]

One limitation of *Finley* is noted by a subsequent Supreme Court decision. In *Coleman v. Thompson*, the Court noted that there may be an exception in "those cases where state collateral review is the first place a prisoner can present a challenge to his conviction," though the Court avoided answering this question.[15] In 2012, the Supreme Court once again declined to answer the question.[16] One type of claim that typically can only be raised in a writ of habeas corpus is a claim of ineffective assistance of counsel. Should a defendant be entitled to have an attorney appointed for a writ of habeas corpus in order to argue ineffective assistance of counsel? This is the question that the Court in *Coleman* declined to answer, thereby leaving the following general rule in place: The state and federal government is not required to provide an attorney for a writ of habeas corpus.

---

[14] 481 U.S. 551 (1987) (citing *Johnson v. Avery*, 393 U.S. 483, 488 (1969).
[15] 501 U.S. 722 (1991).
[16] *Martinez v. Ryan*, 566 U.S. 1 (2012) (holding a procedural default will not bar a federal habeas district court from hearing ineffective assistance of counsel of trial counsel if there was no counsel or ineffective counsel in the initial review collateral proceeding).

Despite this rule, 8 U.S.C. § 3006A authorizes the appointment of counsel "[w]henever the United States magistrate judge or the court determines that the interests of justice so require." This applies to a "financially eligible person." Rule 8(c) of the Federal Rules Governing Section 2254 Cases in the United States District Courts provides that, "If an evidentiary hearing is warranted, the judge must appoint an attorney to represent a petitioner who qualifies to have counsel appointed under 18 U.S.C. § 3006A." For this decision, the courts generally look to the complexity of the issues.[17]

---

[17] *See, e.g., Wardlaw v. Cain*, 541 F.3d 275 (5th Cir. 2008); *Luna v. Kernan*, 784 F.3d 640 (9th Cir. 2015).

Chapter 3
THE ONE-YEAR DEADLINE TO FILE A WRIT OF HABEAS CORPUS IN FEDERAL COURT

A. Introduction

Generally speaking, federal writs of habeas corpus have a strict one-year deadline, as detailed below. While there are exceptions to this rule, judges tend to enforce the one-year requirement.

In *Keeney v. Tamayo-Reyes*, 504 U.S. 1 (1992), the Supreme Court wrote:

> Habeas corpus is not an appellate proceeding, but rather an original civil action in a federal court. It was settled over a hundred years ago that "[t]he prosecution against [a criminal defendant] is a criminal prosecution, but the writ of habeas corpus . . . is not a proceeding in that prosecution. On the contrary, it is a new suit brought by him to enforce a civil right."[18]

As such, a writ of habeas corpus must comply with the federal laws that were enacted for habeas claims. Unfortunately, the federal law has certain procedural rules that make it challenging for an incarcerated individual to file a federal writ of habeas corpus. This chapter will discuss one such procedural rule for federal writs of habeas corpus—the deadline, sometimes referred to as a "statute of limitations" or just the "limitations" period. To determine the limitations period, one must determine when the period starts, when it ends, and if anything exists to "toll" (pause) the limitations period. In short, this chapter will focus on how to calculate the deadline for filing a writ of habeas corpus.

---

[18] 504 U.S. 1, 14 (1992) (citing *Browder v. Director, Dept. of Corrections of Ill.*, 434 U.S. 257, 269 (1978); *Ex parte Tom Tong*, 108 U.S. 556, 559–560 (1883)).

The information provided in this chapter (as is true for the other chapters of this book) should not be construed as legal advice and is solely intended to provide information to the reader. The information is also subject to change. The courts continuously update and amend the rules concerning the calculation of the deadline to file a federal writ of habeas corpus. With that, we will begin with the one-year deadline to file a federal writ of habeas corpus.

B. The One-Year Deadline

Before 1996, "there was no formal limit on the time for filing a habeas corpus petition pursuant to 28 U.S.C. § 2254. Delayed filing of a petition was a basis for dismissal only if the appellant knew or could have known the grounds for the petition earlier and if the state demonstrated 'that the delay prejudiced [it] in its ability to respond to the petition.' *Ross v. Artuz*, 150 F.3d 97, 99 (2d Cir. 1998) (internal quotations and citation omitted)."[19]

In 1996, Congress passed the Antiterrorism and Effective Death Penalty Act of 1996 (AEDPA), which was signed into law by President Clinton. The purpose of the AEDPA was, in the words of President Clinton, "to streamline Federal appeals for convicted criminals sentenced to the death penalty."[20] In his very next sentence, President Clinton clarified what he meant by stating, "For too long, and in too many cases, endless death row appeals have stood in the way of justice being served." With these words, President Clinton made clear that the AEDPA would, in some ways, limit the right of a defendant to file a federal writ of habeas corpus.

In his remarks, President Clinton noted a potential criticism with the AEDPA and articulated brief reasons why the potential

---

[19] *Bennett v. Artuz*, 199 F.3d 116, 118 (2d Cir. 1999).
[20] https://www.govinfo.gov/content/pkg/PPP-1996-book1/html/PPP-1996-book1-doc-pg630.htm.

problem was not an actual problem in his opinion.[21] President Clinton made no mention of another significant limitation for filing a writ of habeas corpus that was introduced by the AEDPA—the one-year deadline.

AEDPA provides that a federal writ of habeas corpus must be filed within one year.[22] A petition that is not filed within one year will be dismissed.[23] Due to the strict one-year deadline, much ink has been spilled to determine when the time period to file starts and ends.

For example, in *Gonzalez v. Thaler*, the issue facing the Supreme Court of the United States was whether the petitioner's writ of habeas corpus was timely filed.[24] Gonzalez, proceeding as a pro se petitioner, argued that his right to a speedy trial had been violated. The Supreme Court did not focus on the underlying facts of the claim and only noted "the nearly 10-year delay between his indictment and trial."[25]

Gonzalez filed his writ on *January 24, 2008*. He argued that his one-year deadline expired shortly after this date, so his petition was timely filed. The Supreme Court, agreeing with the lower courts, held that the one-year limitation period expired on *December 17, 2007*, and

---

[21] The issue was whether the AEDPA changed the standard for granting a writ of habeas corpus. This will be addressed later in the book. President Clinton predicted that "the Federal courts will interpret these provisions to preserve independent review of Federal legal claims and the bedrock constitutional principle of an independent judiciary." It turns out that he was very wrong.

[22] *See* 28 U.S.C. § 2244(d)(1).

[23] The exceptions to this rule will be discussed later.

[24] *Gonzalez v. Thaler* (2012) 565 U.S. 134 (Petitioner Rafael Gonzalez was convicted of murder in Texas state court).

[25] The right to a speedy trial is protected by the Sixth Amendment, which sets forth: "In all criminal prosecutions, *the accused shall enjoy the right to a speedy and public trial*, by an impartial jury of the state and district wherein the crime shall have been committed, which district shall have been previously ascertained by law, and to be informed of the nature and cause of the accusation; to be confronted with the witnesses against him; to have compulsory process for obtaining witnesses in his favor, and to have the assistance of counsel for his defense." U.S. Const. amend VI [emphasis added].

dismissed his petition. Gonzalez, therefore, was not able to have his Sixth Amendment claim heard by the federal courts, regardless of the fact that there had been a ten-year delay between his indictment and his trial!

Gonzalez v. Thaler highlights the importance of timely filing a federal writ of habeas corpus. It also raises many of the questions that will be addressed in the following sections, including when does the one-year limitation period begin? This was the actual issue in *Gonzalez*. Gonzalez claimed that his one-year period began at a later point in time, and the state of Texas claimed that it began at an earlier point in time. Another question is whether the one-year period may be paused ("tolled"). An unraised question in *Gonzalez* is what happens when the one-year limitation period is over? Is there any way to get around it?

The case also raises some policy questions that will not be addressed but that are significant: Is it fair to deny a pro se litigant a chance at federal review because the petition was filed a few weeks late? What about if the facts clearly show that he was denied a right to a speedy trial since his trial occurred 10 years after his indictment? What if there are two potential times to start counting the one-year period, and the petitioner filed a writ within one-year of the later date?

These questions are food for thought but illustrate a fundamental principle of the AEDPA—file the writ as quickly as possible.

C. When Does the Clock Start Running?

Since the limitation period is one year, the key question is when does the clock start running to file a federal writ of habeas corpus. The AEDPA lists four dates for when the clock starts running, which are quoted below:

(A) the date on which the judgment became final by the conclusion of direct review or the expiration of the time for seeking such review;

(B) the date on which the impediment to filing an application created by State action in violation of the Constitution or laws of the United States is removed, if the applicant was prevented from filing by such State action;

(C) the date on which the constitutional right asserted was initially recognized by the Supreme Court, if the right has been newly recognized by the Supreme Court and made retroactively applicable to cases on collateral review; or

(D) the date on which the factual predicate of the claim or claims presented could have been discovered through the exercise of due diligence.[26]

28 U.S.C. § 2244(d)(1)(A)—The Date That the Judgment Became Final

The most common date to start running the clock is the date that the judgment became final. Though the meaning of section A appears simple, appearances can be deceiving. Saying that the limitations period begins when the judgment becomes final begs the question: When is a judgment final? In the *Gonzalez* case, cited earlier, the Texas Court of Appeals issued a "mandate" on *September 26, 2006*. A mandate is a document that serves as official notice of the appellate decision. In Texas, the issuance of a mandate is what makes the appeal final. Yet, the time Gonzalez had to seek review in the Texas Court of Criminal Appeals expired on *August 11, 2006*. Which of these two dates, then, starts running the clock to file a federal writ? Is it August 11, 2006, or is it September 26, 2006? In the *Gonzalez* case, the writ was filed within one year of September 26, 2006, but was filed after one year of August 11, 2006. The U.S. Supreme Court held that the clock began to run on August 11, 2006, so the writ was not timely and was dismissed.

Nine years before the *Gonzalez* case, the Supreme Court addressed a related issue in *Clay v. United States* as follows:

---

[26] 28 U.S.C. § 2244(d)(1)(A)–(D).

> When a defendant in a federal prosecution takes an
> unsuccessful direct appeal from a judgment of conviction, but
> does not next petition for a writ of certiorari from this Court,
> does the judgment become "final" for post-conviction relief
> purposes (1) when the appellate court issues its mandate
> affirming the conviction, or, instead, (2) on the date, ordinarily
> 69 days later, when the time for filing a petition for certiorari
> expires?[27]

Though the *Clay* case occurred only a few years after the passage of
the AEDPA, the Supreme Court commented that the issue of when the
clock starts to run was "a narrow but recurring question." There was a
split in the federal courts about the answer. The Fourth and Seventh
Circuits held that the clock runs from the moment the appellate court
issues its mandate, while the First, Third, Fifth, Ninth, Tenth, and
Eleventh Circuits held that the limitations period runs from when the
time to seek review in the U.S. Supreme Court expires.

The Supreme Court agreed with the six circuit courts, stating,
"[f]or the purpose of starting the clock on § 2255's one-year limitation
period, we hold, a judgment of conviction becomes final when the
time expires for filing a petition for certiorari contesting the appellate
court's affirmation of the conviction."[28]

Therefore, the answer to when the clock starts running on a
federal writ of habeas corpus is the date on which a petitioner can no
longer file a writ of certiorari with the Supreme Court. Pursuant to the
rules of the Supreme Court, a writ of certiorari must be filed "within
90 days after entry of the judgment" or "within 90 days after entry of
the order denying discretionary review."[29]

In New York, for example:
> Once the New York Court of Appeals denies leave to appeal, a
> petitioner has ninety (90) days in which to file a petition for a

---

[27] *Clay v. United States*, 537 U.S. 522 (2003).

[28] *Id.*, 525.

[29] Rules of the Supreme Court of the United States, Rule 13.

writ of certiorari with the United States Supreme Court seeking review of the state court's decision. Thus, a New York defendant's conviction becomes final ninety (90) days after the New York Court of Appeals denies leave to appeal.[30]

Practically, this means the following:

- A Defendant Who Files a Writ of Certiorari in the U.S. Supreme Court—If a defendant seeks to appeal a conviction to the U.S. Supreme Court by filing a writ of certiorari, the one-year period to file a federal writ of habeas corpus starts to run from when the Court denies the writ or issues a decision.

- A Defendant Who Files a Petition for Rehearing in the U.S. Supreme Court—If the Supreme Court denies a defendant's writ of certiorari, a defendant may choose to file a petition for rehearing.[31] Nonetheless, the one-year period begins on the date that the petition for writ of certiorari is denied, not from the date that the petition for rehearing is denied.

  - In *United States v. Aguirre-Ganceda*, 592 F.3d 1043 (9th Cir. 2010), the Ninth Circuit Court of Appeals held that the petitioner's writ of habeas corpus was filed after the one-year deadline when the petitioner filed his petition for writ of habeas corpus within one year of the denial of his petition for rehearing but after one year of the denial of his writ of certiorari.

  - In 2015, the Second Circuit (covering New York, Connecticut, and Vermont) became the ninth circuit to adopt the rule that "the statute of limitations runs from the denial of certiorari, not from the denial of rehearing of the certiorari petition."[32]

---

[30] *Tripathy v. Schneider*, 473 F. Supp. 3d 220, 228 (W.D.N.Y. 2020) (citation omitted).
[31] Rule 44. https://www.law.cornell.edu/rules/supct/rule_44.
[32] *Rosa v. U.S.*, 785 F. 3d 856 (2d Cir. 2015).

- The courts rely on Supreme Court Rule 16.3, which states that when a petition for certiorari is denied, "the order of denial will not be suspended pending disposition of a petition for rehearing except by order of the Court or a Justice."
- <u>A Defendant Who Appeals to Highest Court in the State but Does Not File a Writ of Certiorari in the U.S. Supreme Court</u>— A defendant who seeks to appeal his or her conviction in the highest state court in his or her state (i.e., the state's Supreme Court) has 90 days from the date of the state court's denial, or 90 days from the date that the state Supreme Court enters a judgment, to seek a writ of certiorari from the U.S. Supreme Court.
  - This is the holding in *Clay v. United States*, cited earlier.
- <u>No Appeal/Appeal to the Appellate Court (not the state Supreme Court)</u>—If a defendant does not appeal a conviction or appeals a conviction to the appellate court but not to the state's Supreme Court, the deadline to file a federal writ of habeas corpus depends on when the conviction becomes "final." Below is a sample list of dates on which a conviction becomes final. These deadlines are subject to change and must be double (and triple) checked by anyone considering whether to file a writ of habeas corpus.
  - <u>California</u>:
    i. A felony conviction in the lower court becomes final 60 days after sentencing.[33]
    ii. A Court of Appeal decision becomes final after 40 days. *See Smith v. Duncan*, 297 F.3d 809, 815 (9th Cir. 2002) ("Under California law, Smith's conviction became final on January 20, 1998—forty (40) days after the California Court of Appeal filed its opinion.").
  - <u>New York</u>:

---

[33] Cal. Rules of Court, Rule 8.308(a).

i. A conviction in the lower court becomes final 30 days after sentencing. *See Restrepo v. Kelly*, 178 F.3d 634 (2d Cir. 1999) ("A person convicted of a crime in New York state has a right to appeal the conviction within 30 days after the imposition of the sentence. *See* N.Y. Crim. Proc. Law § 460.10(1)(a) (McKinney 1994). A defendant who fails to appeal within that time defaults his right to appeal.").

ii. A conviction becomes final in the appellate division after 30 days. *See Sparks v. Graham*, No. 6: 18-cv-06840-MAT (W.D.N.Y. July 9, 2019) ("When a habeas petitioner does appeal his conviction to the intermediate state appellate court but does not seek leave to appeal an adverse decision by that court to the New York State Court of Appeals, the conviction becomes final thirty days from the Appellate Division's decision.").

iii. If a defendant files a motion to extend time to appeal to the Court of Appeals, the one-year limitation period to file a writ of habeas corpus still begins 30 days after the appellate court's decision. *See Bethea v. Girdich*, 293 F.3d 577, 579 (2nd Cir. 2002).

iv. In New York, the time to appeal to the Court of Appeals begins when a defendant is served with a notice of the entry of the decision and is "[w]ithin thirty days after service upon the appellant of a copy of the order sought to be appealed."[34] Nonetheless, there are courts that start counting the 30 days from the date of the appellate decision, not from the date of notice of entry.[35]

---

[34] CPL § 460.10(5)(a).

[35] *See M.P. v. Perlman*, 269 F. Supp. 2d 36 (E.D.N.Y.2003) ("Petitioner was convicted on May 6, 1998. His conviction was affirmed by the Appellate Division on April 12, 1999. He did not seek leave to appeal the Appellate Division's decision from the New York Court of Appeals. His conviction therefore became final on May 12, 1999, which was 30 days after his conviction was affirmed by the Appellate

- Texas:
    i. A defendant has 30 days to file a notice of appeal.[36] A conviction is considered "final," for AEDPA purposes, 30 days after the sentence is imposed. A defendant who loses on appeal has 30 days to file a Petition for Discretionary Review with the Texas Court of Criminal Appeals.
- NOTE: There is a separate requirement that a petitioner must exhaust state remedies before filing a writ of habeas corpus in federal court. (This will be explained at length in a later chapter). Very briefly, a defendant must appeal to the highest court in his or her state before he or she may file a federal writ. For the above examples where a defendant did not seek to appeal the conviction to the state's supreme court, the defendant likely will have to pursue his or her claims in state court before proceeding with a federal writ of habeas corpus.

Given the technical requirements of the one-year statute of limitations, courts must calculate the exact dates that the limitations period begins and ends. In *Waldrip v. Hall*, 548 F.3d 729 (9th Cir. 2008), the court wrote out a list of the relevant dates:

- October 16, 2001—Conviction affirmed by state court of appeals

---

Division."). *But see Velasquez v. Ercole*, 878 F. Supp. 2d 387 (E.D.N.Y. 2012) ("When a defendant fails to appeal a decision of the New York Supreme Court, Appellate Division, the conviction becomes final thirty days after the service of Notice of Entry."). *See also Singh v. Dept. Of Corr. Svcs.*, No. 13-CV-1158 (JFB) (E.D.N.Y. 2014) ("More than two years later, petitioner was served with a Notice of Entry informing him that his conviction had been affirmed by the Appellate Division. The date of service of the Notice of Entry was June 21, 2010. Petitioner's time to appeal expired thirty days later, on July 21, 2010, and on that date his conviction became final.").

[36] Tex. R. App. P. 26.2(a)(1).

- October 31, 2001—Habeas petition filed in state court of appeals (by Waldrip's state appellate counsel)
- November 13, 2001—Habeas petition denied by state court of appeals
- November 26, 2001—Conviction final (40 days after conviction affirmed by state court of appeals when no petition for review was filed with state supreme court)
- March 14, 2002—Habeas petition filed in state superior court (by Waldrip pro se)
- March 28, 2002—Habeas petition denied by state superior court
- December 11, 2002—Habeas petition filed in state supreme court (by Waldrip's state appellate counsel)
- January 14, 2003—Supplement to habeas petition filed in state supreme court (by Waldrip pro se)
- June 18, 2003—Habeas petition denied by state supreme court
- July 16, 2003—Habeas petition deemed filed in federal district court.[37]

The Court then determined that the defendant had waited 1 year and 233 days to file his federal writ of habeas corpus, and was able to "toll" only 215 days. That meant that the writ was filed 18 days too late. The court denied the writ. This, once again, serves to illustrate the crucial point that a federal writ of habeas corpus must be filed as soon as possible.

28 U.S.C. § 2244(d)(1)(B): The Date That the Impediment to Filing Was Removed

The second date that the clock starts running is "the date on which the impediment to filing an application created by State action in violation of the Constitution or laws of the United States is removed, if the

---

[37] *Waldrip*, 548 F.3d 729, 735.

applicant was prevented from filing by such State action." This section has a narrow application and applies to situations where state action prevented a defendant from knowing about the one-year statute of limitations. For example, if a prison law library does not contain a copy of the AEDPA, courts have suggested, but not definitively concluded, that this may be an impediment to the filing of a timely writ of habeas corpus.[38]

If, however, an inmate argues that the impediment occurred because the law library did not have resources in his or her native language, the court will likely reject this argument. In *Then v. Griffin*, No. 17-CV-3681 (MKB) (E.D.N.Y. 2018), the federal court in the Eastern District of New York rejected a claim that an inmate was impeded from filing a writ because the law library did not contain any legal materials in Spanish. The law library had a copy of the AEDPA in English only. The Court cited other federal courts that rejected similar claims.

Nonetheless, a lack of native language could be used to support a "tolling" claim, which will be addressed below. Both the Ninth Circuit and the Second Circuit have suggested that "equitable tolling" could be available to someone who does not speak English and has limited materials available in the prison law library in the language that the petitioner speaks.[39]

---

[38] *See Egerton v. Cockrell*, 334 F.3d 433, 438 (5th Cir. 2003); *Whalem/Hunt v. Early*, 233 F.3d 1146 (9th Cir. 2000) (en banc); *Moore v. Battaglia*, 476 F.3d 504 (7th Cir. 2007).

[39] *See Mendoza v. Carey*, 449 F.3d 1065 (9th Cir. 2006); *Diaz v. Kelly*, 515 F.3d 149 (2d Cir. 2008). In both cases, the petitioner spoke Spanish. In *Mendoza*, the court held, "[b]ecause Mendoza alleged that he lacks English language ability, was denied access to Spanish-language legal materials, and could not procure the assistance of a translator during the running of the AEDPA limitations period, he has alleged facts that, if true, may entitle him to equitable tolling."

In *Diaz*, the court held, "[w]e conclude that English language deficiency can warrant tolling of the AEDPA limitations period, but that Diaz and Tan have failed to allege circumstances establishing the due diligence required to warrant tolling."

Another example of the state impeding a defendant's ability to file a writ of habeas corpus occurs when the state "without justification, refuse[s] to rule on a constitutional claim that has been properly presented to it."[40] This rarely occurs. In *Dubrin v. California*, the court found that the state "wrongly told Dubrin that he was ineligible for state habeas relief because he was no longer 'in custody,' and refused to reach the merits of his claims."[41]

28 U.S.C. § 2244(d)(1)(C): A Retroactive Constitutional Right

New constitutional rules usually do not apply retroactively.[42] This means that new constitutional rules do not usually apply to someone whose conviction is already final. The Supreme Court identified a complicated rule to determine when a new constitutional rule might apply:

> First, the court must determine when the defendant's conviction became final. Second, it must ascertain the legal landscape as it then existed and ask whether the Constitution, as interpreted by the precedent then existing, compels the rule. That is, the court must decide whether the rule is actually "new." Finally, if the rule is new, the court must consider whether it falls within either of the two exceptions to non-retroactivity.[43]

The two exceptions to non-retroactivity are: (1) "rules forbidding punishment of certain primary conduct or to rules prohibiting a certain category of punishment for a class of defendants because of their status or offense" and (2) "watershed rules of criminal procedure

---

The "due diligence" requirement means that a petitioner must show that he or she tried his or her best to file a writ of habeas corpus. This will be elaborated on below.
[40] *Dubrin v. California*, 720 F.3d 1095 (9th Cir. 2013) (citing *Lackawanna Cnty. Dist. Attorney v. Coss*, 532 U.S. 394 (2001)).
[41] *Dubrin v. California*, 720 F.3d at 1099.
[42] *Teague v. Lane*, 489 U.S. 288 (1989).
[43] *Beard v. Banks*, 542 U.S. 406 (2004).

implicating the fundamental fairness and accuracy of the criminal proceeding."[44]

If there is a new constitutional rule that the Supreme Court has held to be retroactive, then a defendant has one year from the Supreme Court decision to file a writ.

28 U.S.C. § 2244(d)(1)(D): The Date That the Factual Predicate Could Have Been Discovered with Due Diligence

If new evidence is discovered, the statute of limitations begins to run when the evidence "could have been discovered through the exercise of due diligence, not when it actually was discovered."[45] What is required is "reasonable diligence," not "maximum diligence." A court may also consider subjective circumstances. One court held that a case was discoverable with due diligence when the case became available in the prison library, not when the decision was issued.[46] Essentially, in determining when the defendant could have become aware of the new evidence, the court considered the fact that a defendant was incarcerated.

One claim that falls under this section is the discovery of new evidence that shows actual innocence. In one case, the lower court dismissed a federal writ of habeas corpus because it was filed 5 days too late. The appellate court held that a hearing was necessary to determine when an inmate could have discovered the new scientific evidence that demonstrated his innocence.[47] In that case, the Ninth Circuit issued a sharp refutation of the State's argument that the limitations period had passed, stating, "The state's circular argument

---

[44] *Id.*, 416–17.

[45] *Ford v. Gonzalez*, 683 F.3d 1230 (9th Cir. 2012).

[46] See *Easterwood v. Champion*, 213 F.3d 1321, 1323 (10th Cir. 2000).

[47] *Souliotes v. Evans*, 622 F.3d 1173 (9th Cir. 2010). Petitioner George Souliotes, a California state inmate, filed a writ of habeas corpus in the Eastern District of California in 2005 challenging his 2000 convictions for three counts of murder by arson. Souliotes filed the writ seeking to prove his innocence based on the results of a new fire testing method that had just been discovered in 2005.

points out the obvious—that an innocent defendant is aware of his innocence from the time he is convicted—and it is not helpful."

Another example is ineffective assistance of counsel. A claim for ineffective assistance of counsel, based on new evidence that counsel should have uncovered, runs from the date that the new evidence could have been discovered. In *Hasan v. Galaza*, 254 F.3d 1150 (9th Cir. 2001), a defendant knew about a possible jury tampering issue, and his attorney did not investigate. Later, the defendant learned that the person attempting to tamper with the jury was "in a long-term romantic relationship" with a prosecution witness. The court held that, even if the defendant knew about the tampering at an earlier date, it was only when the defendant discovered the romantic relationship that the defendant could assert a claim for being prejudiced by his counsel's errors. The court remanded the case to determine "when with the exercise of due diligence Hasan could have discovered the relationship between" the prosecution witness and the person who tried to tamper with the jury.

If a defendant challenges a denial of parole, the initial date of denial is the "factual predicate" for when a defendant should have known about a federal claim, even if the defendant first files writs of habeas corpus in state court.[48]

A Writ with Multiple Claims

If a writ has multiple claims, the court will examine whether each individual claim was timely filed.[49] The result, then, is that the same writ may contain some timely claims and some untimely claims. A petitioner must be prepared to apply each section of 28 U.S.C. § 2244(d)(1) to each claim filed in the federal writ.

---

[48] *Redd v. McGrath*, 343 F.3d 1077 (9th Cir. 2003).
[49] *Souliotes*, 622 F.3d at 1180 ("We adopt the reasoning in Fielder and hold that § 2244(d)(1) requires consideration of the appropriate triggering date for each claim presented in the application.").

D. Will a Writ That Was Filed Too Late Be Automatically Dismissed?

If a writ of habeas corpus is filed after the deadline has passed, the State will typically file a motion to dismiss. What happens if the State does not do so? Does the State waive the limitations defense? In 2001, the Second Circuit addressed these questions. After concluding that the statute of limitations for AEDPA claims is an "affirmative defense," meaning that it could be waived if it is not asserted by the State, and after noting that "[g]enerally, courts should not raise *sua sponte* nonjurisdictional defenses not raised by the parties," the court held that the AEDPA is an exception to the rule.[50]

The court reasoned that the AEDPA is not just about a defendant and a state:

> The AEDPA statute of limitation promotes judicial efficiency and conservation of judicial resources, safeguards the accuracy of state court judgments by requiring resolution of constitutional questions while the record is fresh, and lends finality to state court judgments within a reasonable time. Like the other procedural bars to habeas review of state court judgments, the statute of limitation implicates the interests of both the federal and state courts, as well as the interests of society[51]

The Fifth Circuit (Texas) and the Ninth Circuit also follow this rule.[52] Even if the State does not move to dismiss an untimely writ, the court may do so on its own authority. The court, however, must give notice to the petitioner, who will have an opportunity to argue that the writ was timely filed.

---

[50] *Acosta v. Artuz*, 221 F.3d 117 (2d Cir. 2000).

[51] *Id.*

[52] *See Kiser v. Johnson*, 163 F.3d 326, 329 (5th Cir. 1999) and *Herbst v. Cook*, 260 F.3d 1039 (9th Cir. 2001).

E. The "Prison Mailbox" Rule

A prisoner's writ of habeas corpus is considered to be filed when the petition is handed over to prison authorities to be mailed. This rule was set by the Supreme Court.[53] The Supreme Court reasoned that "prisoners cannot take the steps other litigants can take to monitor the processing of their" filings and cannot "ensure that the court clerk receives and stamps their" filings. They also "cannot personally travel to the courthouse" and are limited in their ability to call the courthouse. "Worse, the *pro se* prisoner has no choice but to entrust … prison authorities whom he cannot control or supervise and who may have every incentive to delay." Therefore, since a prisoner is "unskilled in law, unaided by counsel, and unable to leave the prison," the Supreme Court adopted the "prison mailbox" rule.

There are two requirements for this rule to apply: (1) the petitioner cannot be represented by counsel (i.e., the petitioner is *pro se*), and (2) the petition is handed over to the prison authorities before the one-year statute of limitations has passed.[54] It is important that the petition be given over to be mailed to the *clerk of court*, or whoever accepts legal filings in the court system. If the petition is given over to be mailed to another party, the "prison mailbox" rule will not apply.[55]

In one case, a district court refused to apply the "prison mailbox" rule because the petition was delivered by another inmate on behalf of the petitioner/inmate. This was reversed on appeal. The Circuit Court held that "the mailbox rule applies when a pro se habeas petitioner gives his petition to a third party to mail from within the prison." When this happens, the third party must deliver the petition to the prison authorities prior to the one-year limitation period.[56]

The prison mailbox rule is codified in Rule 3(d) of the Rules Governing Section 2254 Cases and Section 2455 Proceedings:

---

[53] *Houston v. Lack*, 487 U.S. 266 (1988).
[54] *Stillman v. LaMarque*, 319 F.3d 1199 (9th Cir. 2003).
[55]*Id.* (citing *Paige v. U.S.*, 171 F.3d 559 (8th Cir. 1999)).
[56] *Hernandez v. Spearman*, 764 F.3d 1071 (9th Cir. 2014).

A paper filed by an inmate confined in an institution is timely if deposited in the institution's internal mailing system on or before the last day for filing. If an institution has a system designed for legal mail, the inmate must use that system to receive the benefit of this rule. Timely filing may be shown by a declaration in compliance with 28 U.S.C. § 1746 or by a notarized statement, either of which must set forth the date of deposit and state that first-class postage has been prepaid.

F. Statutory Tolling

Before we begin the subject of statutory tolling, a brief recap is necessary. An inmate has one year from when his or her judgment became final to file a writ of habeas corpus in federal court. We have noted the different scenarios for calculating when the one-year period begins. As most people are likely aware, the court can sometimes be a bit slow in deciding cases. What happens, then, if a petitioner files a writ in state court and, from the state court to the appellate court and the state's supreme court, only learns that his writ was denied two years (or more) after his or her judgment became final? Can this petitioner file a federal writ of habeas corpus, or has the time passed to do so? On the one hand, the one-year limitation period is over. On the other hand, the inmate was required to "exhaust" all claims in state court before reaching federal court.[57] It would hardly be fair to require an inmate to exhaust all claims in state court before filing a writ in federal court and then deny the federal writ because it was filed too late. This is where the concept of "tolling" fits in.

What Is Tolling? An Introduction

Tolling is the concept by which the court "pauses" the one-year deadline for filing a writ in federal court. The court essentially counts

---

[57] More on this later.

the number of days that a writ of habeas corpus is pending in state court and extends the one-year limitation by that number. Specifically, 28 U.S.C. § 2244(d)(2) states:

> The time during which a properly filed application for State post-conviction or other collateral review with respect to the pertinent judgment or claim is pending shall not be counted toward any period of limitation under this subsection.

The phrase "properly filed" is important and implies that tolling is not available for a claim that was "improperly filed" in state court. The statute also uses the word "pending." The courts interpret both words as a limit to the concept of tolling. We will return to this in the next section.

While the concept of tolling may appear simple, it is not. There are two types of tolling—statutory tolling and equitable tolling. In this section, we will focus on statutory tolling. We will focus on equitable tolling in the next section.

Statutory Tolling

Statutory tolling means the time that is tolled pursuant to a statute, in this case pursuant to 28 U.S.C. § 2244(d)(2) (cited above). There are some significant limitations to this rule. To understand the limitations, one must closely read the statute. As noted, 28 U.S.C. § 2244(d)(2) requires that a writ of habeas corpus be *properly* filed in state court, and the writ must be *pending*. Courts interpret these words to mean that the writ of habeas corpus must have been filed according to the state's rules. "Tolling, however, is not appropriate for a petition that is untimely under state law, because such a petition is considered neither properly filed nor pending."[58] This is because an untimely writ that was filed in state court was not *properly* filed.

---

[58] *Campbell v. Henry*, 614 F.3d 1056 (9th Cir. 2010) (citations omitted). *See also Nedds v. Calderon*, 678 F.3d 777 (9th Cir. 2012) ("A petitioner who unreasonably delays in filing a state habeas petition would not be granted the benefit of statutory

The problem with this understanding is that states often do not have firm and clear deadlines to file a writ of habeas corpus. In California, there are no "fixed statutory deadlines to determine the timeliness of a state prisoner's petition for habeas corpus. Instead, California directs petitioners to file known claims as promptly as the circumstances allow."[59] A petitioner "has the burden of establishing the absence of 'substantial delay.' Substantial delay is measured from the time the petitioner or counsel knew, or reasonably should have known, of the information offered in support of the claim and the legal basis for the claim."[60]

If there has been a "substantial delay" in filing the petition, the petitioner must explain "good cause" for the delay. Generally, an ongoing investigation into other claims that may be included in the writ of habeas corpus is considered to be "good cause." Willful ignorance is usually not considered to be "good cause."[61]

In New York, arguments that could be raised in a federal writ are typically raised in a CPL 440 motion (the functional equivalent of a state writ of habeas corpus). There is no deadline to file a CPL 440 motion, though the court may deny the CPL 440 motion if a defendant waits too long to assert his or her rights. For example, in *People v. Hanley*, 255 A.D.2d 837 (3rd Dept. 1998), the court denied a CPL 440 motion when the defendant delayed for three years before seeking to vacate the judgment.

In Texas, there is also no official deadline to file a state writ of habeas corpus, but a court may deny a writ that was filed too long after a conviction. In 2013, the Court of Criminal Appeals wrote:

> We, however, also reaffirm that "we have no desire to impose upon defendants the requirement that claims for relief be asserted within a specified period of time," but will continue to

---

tolling because the petition would not be considered "pending," or "properly filed," within the meaning of § 2244(d)(2)") (citations omitted).

[59] *Walker v. Martin*, 131 S. Ct. 1120, 1142 (2011) (citation omitted).

[60] *In re Robbins*, (1998) 18 Cal.4th 770, 780, 77 Cal.Rptr.2d 153, 959 P.2d 311.

[61] *See In re Douglas* (Ct. App. 2011) 200 Cal. App. 4th 236, 132 Cal. Rptr. 3d 582.

apply laches as a bar to relief when an applicant's unreasonable delay has prejudiced the State, thereby rendering consideration of his claim inequitable.[62]

In that case, the Court stated some of the factors to be considered, "such as the length of the applicant's delay in filing the application, the reasons for the delay, and the degree and type of prejudice resulting from the delay."

Therefore, the federal requirement that a state writ be timely filed in order to toll the one-year federal limitation can be confusing, given that states do not set strict deadlines for the filing of state writs of habeas corpus. Practically, this means that a state writ of habeas corpus should be filed as quickly as possible. Otherwise, a petitioner may find himself embroiled in a dispute regarding whether his federal petition was timely, as the government will argue that the petitioner waited too long to file a writ in state court and that the time should not be tolled.

Another ramification of this rule is that state writs filed in the state appellate court and state supreme court must be filed within a reasonable time of the denial of the writ in the superior court. This ramification is for states, such as California, where a petitioner must file a *new writ* in the appellate court. For these states, "Only the time period during which a round of habeas review is pending tolls the statute of limitation; periods between different rounds of collateral attack are not tolled."[63] For states that require the petitioner to file an *appeal* from a lower court's denial, this ramification is not relevant.

When a writ is filed in state appellate court within a reasonable time of the lower court's denial, the entire period is tolled. Until 2020, the Ninth Circuit federal court held that the appellate filing must be

---

[62] *Ex parte Perez*, 398 S.W.3d 206, 212-14 (Tex.Crim.App.2013).

[63] *Banjo v. Ayers*, 614 F.3d 964 (9th Cir. 2010).

made within either 30–45 days[64] or 30–60 days.[65] In 2015, the Ninth Circuit certified a question to the California Supreme Court about how many days may pass between the filing of a superior court writ and an appellate writ in order for the period to be tolled.[66] In that case, a petitioner waited 66 days between the denial of his writ in the superior court and his filing of a new writ in the California appellate court, and then waited 91 days after his writ was denied in the appellate court before filing a writ in the California Supreme Court. The federal district court held that the Petitioner waited too long, so the time in between the filing of his state writs was not tolled. The Federal appellate court certified the question to the California Supreme Court to answer the question about how long a petitioner may wait between filing a writ in the next court.

The California Supreme Court answered the question and held that, "[a] new petition filed in a higher court within 120 days of the lower court's denial will never be considered untimely due to gap delay."[67] Therefore, applying this rule, a gap of 120 days between petitions in California will result in the writ of habeas corpus being considered "pending" for the entirety of the time period. The whole time period is then considered tolled.

Bottom Line—in California, file a state writ as soon as possible, and do not wait more than 120 days to file the writ in the appellate court/supreme court. The best thing is to file the state writs as soon as possible, but file it before 120 days to avoid any possible issues that may arise.

---

[64] *Carey v. Saffold*, 536 U.S. 214 (2002) (noting that other states have a 30–45-day rule for appealing denials of writs).
[65] *Evans v. Chavis*, 546 U.S. 189 (2006) (holding that the petition to the appellate court was not timely, since it was not filed "within 30 or even 60 days after the lower court (the California Court of Appeal) had reached its adverse decision").
[66] See *Robinson v. Lewis*, 795 F.3d 926 (9th Cir. 2015).
[67] *Robinson v. Lewis,* 9 Cal.5th 883, 901 (2020).

How To Know If the State Writ Was Denied on Timeliness Grounds

If a state writ is not timely, then it does not toll the statute of limitations. How does one know if his or her state petition was denied on timeliness grounds? For starters, if the court writes that the writ is denied because it is not timely, then the writ is denied on timeliness grounds. What if the court simply denies the writ, including citations to a few cases? This scenario is common in California. Since "a habeas petitioner may skip over the lower courts and file directly in the California Supreme Court, that court rules on a staggering number of habeas petitions each year,"[68] and it may not always spell out the precise reason that a writ was denied.

The rule is that, if the court cites to *Clark* and *Robbins*, then the writ was denied on timeliness grounds, but if the court cites to *In re Swain* and *Duvall*, the writ was denied because not enough facts were pleaded to state a valid claim.[69] If the court gives no indication as to why it denied a state writ of habeas corpus, the federal court will review the record and reach its own determination about the timeliness of the state writ.[70] If the state writ is timely, then the time that it is pending will be tolled.

What Happens When Some Claims Are Timely and Some Are Not?

When some claims are timely asserted in state court, the writ is considered to be timely filed, and the statute of limitations will be tolled. In *Campbell v. Henry*,[71] the petitioner asserted 23 claims of constitutional violations. The government argued that the one-year limitation period was not tolled because the state petition was not timely filed. To recap, the one-year limitation period is tolled only when a writ is *timely* filed in state court.

---

[68] *Walker v. Martin*, 562 U.S. 307 (2011).
[69] *Curiel v. Miller*, 830 F.3d 864 (9th Cir. 2016).
[70] *See Robinson v. Lewis*, 795 F.3d 926 (9th Cir. 2015). *See also Curiel v. Miller*.
[71] 614 F.3d 1056 (9th Cir. 2010).

In this case, however, the state court concluded that *one* of the 23 claims was timely asserted. Because of that, the court held that the state writ tolled the federal statute of limitations for *all* claims in the federal writ. The court looked to the word "judgment" that appears in 28 U.S.C. § 2244(d)(2) and held that it means "any application for relief from a conviction or sentence that is properly filed in state court will toll the statute, whether or not it includes any claim present in the federal petition." The court concluded that "the one timely claim in Campbell's state habeas petition was sufficient to toll the AEDPA statute of limitations with regard to any and all claims in her federal petition."

When Does the Tolling Begin? The Prison Mailbox Rule (Again)

Earlier, we referred to the "prison mailbox" rule. For a *pro se* petitioner, a petition is considered to be timely filed when delivered to the prison authorities for filing with the court. The same rule applies to tolling the statute of limitations. Tolling begins when the state petition is delivered to prison authorities to file with the court.[72]

In *Campbell*, the Ninth Circuit pointed out that the District Court "inadvertently" failed to apply the prison mailbox rule. "Under the mailbox rule, a prisoner's pro se habeas petition is deemed filed when he hands it over to prison authorities for mailing to the relevant court."[73] Courts sometimes do make obvious mistakes, and a petitioner should not be afraid to advocate on his or her own behalf. In *Campbell*, the Ninth Circuit reversed the lower court and remanded the case to the District Court to consider the merits of the writ of habeas corpus.

---

[72] *See Campbell v. Henry.*
[73] *Id.*, 1058–59.

When the Gap Between the Superior Court Filing and the Appellate Court Filing Is Greater Than 120 Days

What happens if a petitioner files a writ in the superior court, the writ is denied, and the petitioner waits more than 120 days to file the writ in the appellate court? Normally, in this scenario, the period between the lower court's denial and the filing in the appellate division will not be tolled. There is, however, an exception if good cause exists for the late filing.

In *Maxwell v. Roe*,[74] the petitioner filed a state writ, which resulted in a hearing on the issue raised. After the superior court denied the writ, the petitioner filed a writ in the appellate court over one year later. The hearing in the superior court spanned two years and produced a record that "filled ten volumes and thousands of pages." The Ninth Circuit held that "based on the need to review the voluminous record, to conduct legal research of complex claims, to address the Superior Court's lengthy decision, to incorporate the findings of the two-year evidentiary hearing, and to redraft the original habeas corpus petition, Maxwell's delay was reasonable in this case." The court also noted that the new writ was not simply a re-filing of the old writ, stating that "the petition spans over 160 pages and cites to the evidentiary hearing record, the reporter's transcript, and exhibits from the evidentiary hearing over 500 times."

This case, however, has extreme facts, and it is rare that a court will consider a year-long delay to be part of the statutory tolling period. Absent comparable facts, a petitioner should not rely on this case to toll his or her statutory limitations period.

Statutory Tolling Is Not Available for a Writ That Is Filed in Federal Court

What happens if a petitioner mistakenly files a claim in the federal court before exhausting his or her claims in the state courts? Only a

---

[74] 628 F.3d 486 (9th Cir. 2010).

writ for an "exhausted" claim may be filed in the federal court. If a claim is not exhausted, the federal court will usually dismiss the writ. However, as is obvious, the process of filing a federal writ and the dismissal of the writ will take time, anywhere from a few weeks to a few months (if not longer). What happens, then, to the one-year limitations period while the federal writ is pending?

The Supreme Court answered this question in *Duncan v. Walker*.[75] In this case, the Supreme Court held that "§ 2244(d)(2) does not toll the limitation period during the pendency of a federal habeas petition."[76]

In *Duncan*, the petitioner's federal petition was dismissed more than nine months before the statute of limitations expired, and the petitioner did not file a state petition in that time. It is often said that bad facts make bad law, and this is a good example of that expression. Courts routinely cite to *Duncan* for the holding that the "filing of a petition for federal habeas corpus relief does not toll AEDPA's statute of limitations."[77] Even though there exists "potential for unfairness to litigants who file timely federal habeas petitions that are dismissed without prejudice after the limitation period has expired … we are convinced that § 2244(d)(2) does not toll the limitation period during the pendency of a federal habeas petition."[78]

G. Equitable Tolling

For a petitioner who does not qualify for statutory tolling, there is good news and bad news. The good news is that there is something called "equitable tolling," which may allow for an untimely habeas

---

[75] *Duncan v. Walker*, 533 U.S. 167 (2001).
[76] *Id.*, 181.
[77] *See, e.g., King v. Ryan*, 564 F.3d 1133 (9th Cir. 2009).
[78] *Duncan*, 533 U.S. at 181.

claim to be considered by the federal court. The bad news is that it is often difficult to qualify for equitable tolling.[79]

Equitable tolling is "highly fact dependent" and is "made on a case-by-case basis." Even though equitable tolling is done on a case-by-case basis, "courts of equity can and do draw upon decisions made in other similar cases for guidance. Such courts exercise judgment in light of prior precedent, but with awareness of the fact that specific circumstances, often hard to predict in advance, could warrant special treatment in an appropriate case."[80] What follows here is general guidance that must be adapted to the unique facts of each situation.

What Is Equitable Tolling?

We will begin with the basics of equitable tolling. Unlike statutory tolling, which is based on a *statute* (hence the name *statutory* tolling), equitable tolling is based on *equity* (hence the name *equitable* tolling). It was not always so clear that the one-year limitation period of the AEDPA could be tolled for equitable considerations. In 2010, after all the federal Courts of Appeals held that equitable tolling applies to the AEDPA, the Supreme Court agreed, stating, "Now, like all 11 Courts of Appeals that have considered the question, we hold that § 2244(d) is subject to equitable tolling in appropriate cases."[81]

Equitable tolling essentially means that the one-year limitation period of the AEDPA should be extended, in the interests of fairness. To qualify, a petitioner must prove "(1) that he has been pursuing his rights diligently, and (2) that some extraordinary circumstance stood in his way and prevented timely filing."[82]

Regarding the first prong, "reasonable diligence" is required. In *Holland*, the petitioner wrote numerous letters to his attorney,

---

[79] The Ninth Circuit has noted that the phrase "extraordinary circumstances" "necessarily suggests the doctrine's rarity." *See Waldron-Ramsey v. Pacholke*, 556 F.3d 1008 (9th Cir. 2009).

[80] *Sossa v. Diaz*, 729 F.3d 1225 (9th Cir. 2013).

[81] *Holland v. Florida*, 560 U.S.631 (2010).

[82] *Id.*

inquiring about the status of his state writ and requesting his attorney to timely file a writ in federal court. His attorney ignored all the letters. The petitioner also sent many letters to the state court in an attempt to learn the fate of his state petitions. Then, as soon as the petitioner learned (on his own) that the time to file a federal claim had expired, he wrote his own pro se claim and mailed it immediately.

Regarding the second prong, the Supreme Court rejected the view that only egregious cases count as "extraordinary circumstances." The government urged the court to accept "bad faith, dishonesty, divided loyalty, mental impairment or so forth on the lawyer's part" as examples of "extraordinary circumstances." Instead, the Supreme Court held that "serious instances of attorney misconduct" may be considered an extraordinary circumstance. Regular negligence is not an extraordinary circumstance and would not be grounds for equitable tolling.

Examples of Situations Where Equitable Tolling Was Applied

What follows are some examples of situations that may be considered extraordinary circumstances. This list is not intended to be all-inclusive of the cases that qualify. As mentioned above, for equitable tolling, each case is unique, and the factors in each case must be analyzed.

    a. **Attorney misconduct**—To qualify for equitable tolling, the misconduct would have to be something more than regular negligence.

    b. **Attorney abandonment**—"[A] client cannot be charged with the acts or omissions of an attorney who has abandoned him. Nor can a client be faulted for failing to act on his own behalf when he lacks reason to believe his attorneys of record, in fact, are not representing him."[83]

---

[83] *Maples v. Thomas*, 565 U.S. 266 (2012). In this case, the petitioner was represented pro bono by two attorneys from Sullivan and Cromwell. Both attorneys left the firm and failed to withdraw from the case. The petitioner, therefore, was

c. **Lack of attorney communication**—"Failure to inform a client that his case has been decided, particularly where that decision implicates the client's ability to bring further proceedings *and* the attorney has committed himself to informing his client of such a development, constitutes attorney abandonment."[84]

d. **Reliance on case that was overturned**—"A habeas petitioner who decides when to file his federal habeas petition by relying on Ninth Circuit precedent that is later overturned by the Supreme Court is entitled to equitable tolling."[85]

e. **Reliance on court order**—If a court grants an extension to file a federal writ of habeas corpus, an inmate is entitled to rely on the extension. In *Sossa v. Diaz*, Sossa filed a federal writ that stated "See Attached Petition" but forgot to attach the petition. The court denied the petition but gave Sossa 30 more days to file an amended petition. Sossa then requested and received an extension.

The court held, "We conclude that the magistrate judge's orders affirmatively led Sossa to believe that he had until June 9, 2008, to file his FAP. Sossa's reliance on these orders entitles him to equitable tolling of the statute of limitations from March 12, 2008, through June 9, 2008."

Similarly, a Fifth Circuit case held that "the district court's order granting him additional time for the express purpose of filing his petition at a later date was crucially misleading. Prieto relied on the district court's order in good faith and to his detriment when he filed his petition. As Prieto submitted his petition within the time expressly allowed him by the district court, he is entitled to equitable tolling."[86]

---

effectively left without counsel and was not receiving court notices, which were being sent to the attorneys who had abandoned the case.

[84] *Gibbs v. Legrand*, 767 F.3d 879 (9th Cir. 2014).

[85] *Nedds v. Calderon*, 678 F.3d 777 (9th Cir. 2012).

[86] *Prieto v. Quarterman*, 456 F.3d 511, 514-15 (5th Cir. 2006).

f. **Failure to receive required documents in time**—In *Grant v. Swarthmore*, Grant requested a "prison account statement" so that he could file his federal writ *in forma pauperis*. When he requested the statement, he had seven days remaining to file his federal writ of habeas corpus. He received the statement almost one month later. The court held that Grant was entitled to equitable tolling.

g. **Denial of access to law library**—In *Sossa*, Sossa alleged that he was not given access to the law library. He showed his due diligence by applying for a "priority legal user" status but was not given this status until a few days before his petition was due.

    Since the factual record was not developed, the court remanded the case for a hearing about the lack of access to the prison law library. The Court wrote, "If the evidence supports Sossa's allegations that prison conditions made filing the petition prior to the June 9 [*sic*] impossible, the prison's provision of last-minute access to the law library on June 7 does not undermine Sossa's claim to equitable tolling through June 11."

h. **Deprivation of legal materials**—A deprivation of an inmate's legal files may qualify an inmate for equitable tolling. In one case, the petitioner was temporarily transferred to another prison while he was being a witness in a different case, and his files were kept in storage in his original prison. He submitted proof that the prison policy was to not allow inmates who were temporarily transferred to take their legal papers with them. The court suggested that "the denial of his legal files for eighty-two days appears to satisfy the impossibility requirement as well," but remanded "for a more complete development of the record as it relates to the availability of equitable tolling."[87]

---

[87] *Lott v. Mueller*, 304 F.3d 918 (9th Cir. 2002).

Generally, a "temporary deprivation of an inmate's legal materials does not, in all cases, rise to a constitutional deprivation."[88]

i. **Mental Illness**—The Ninth Circuit held that "[w]here a habeas petitioner's mental incompetence in fact caused him to fail to meet the AEDPA filing deadline, his delay was caused by an 'extraordinary circumstance beyond [his] control,' and the deadline should be equitably tolled."[89]

As well, the Second Circuit held, "in order to justify tolling of the AEDPA one-year statute of limitations due to mental illness, a habeas petitioner must demonstrate that her particular disability constituted an 'extraordinary circumstance' severely impairing her ability to comply with the filing deadline, despite her diligent efforts to do so."[90]

The Ninth Circuit has adopted a two-part test to determine whether mental illness may serve as an equitable toll to the statute of limitations: "First, a petitioner must show his mental impairment was an 'extraordinary circumstance' beyond his control, see Holland, 130 S. Ct. at 2562, by demonstrating the impairment was so severe that either:

(a) petitioner was unable rationally or factually to personally understand the need to timely file, or
(b) petitioner's mental state rendered him unable personally to prepare a habeas petition and effectuate its filing.

Second, the petitioner must show diligence in pursuing the claims to the extent he could understand them, but that the mental impairment made it impossible to meet the filing

---

[88] *Vigliotto v. Terry*, 873 F.2d 1201, 1202–03 (9th Cir. 1989) (holding that a "three-day deprivation does not rise to constitutional proportions").
[89] *Laws v. Lamarque*, 351 F.3d 919 (9th Cir. 2003).
[90] *Bolarinwa v. Williams*, 593 F.3d 226, 231-32 (2d Cir. 2010).

46

deadline under the totality of the circumstances, including reasonably available access to assistance.[91]

The "Due Diligence" Requirement

In 2020, the Ninth Circuit Court of Appeals held that there are other requirements for equitable tolling. First, a petitioner "must show that he has been reasonably diligent in pursuing his rights not only while an impediment to filing caused by an extraordinary circumstance existed, *but before and after as well* [emphasis added], up to the time of filing his claim in federal court." Second, "it is only when an extraordinary circumstance prevented a petitioner acting with reasonable diligence from making a timely filing that equitable tolling may be the proper remedy."[92]

In *Smith*, even though the petitioner's attorney waited five months to inform him that his appeal had been denied, the petitioner waited one year to file his federal writ. The Court held that the petitioner was not reasonably diligent in pursuing his rights. The court even noted that it would have had no problem "where a petitioner is impeded by extraordinary circumstances from working on a habeas petition for two months, but after those circumstances are dispelled, uses the next 364 days diligently, files his petition, and has the entire two months during which the extraordinary circumstances existed equitably tolled." In this case, however, the petitioner could not show that "he had acted diligently but had not been able to file earlier."

A related requirement is that the petitioner must be "diligent in his efforts to pursue his appeal *at the time his efforts* [emphasis added] were being thwarted."[93] This requires "the petitioner to attempt to resolve the impediment preventing timely filing so that the courts can consider his petition as soon as possible."[94] In *Grant*, the court wrote,

---

[91] *Bills v. Clark*, 628 F.3d 1092 (9th Cir. 2010).

[92] *Smith v. Davis*, 953 F.3d 582 (9th Cir. 2020).

[93] *Gibbs*, 767 F.3d at 893 (citation omitted).

[94] *Nedds v. Calderon*, 678 F.3d 777 (9th Cir. 2012).

"Although it would probably have been possible for Grant to contact his counselor more often regarding his prison account certificate during the twenty odd days, two attempts were adequate under the circumstances." The court also cited many cases to support its holding:

> *Fue v. Biter*, 842 F.3d 650, 655 (9th Cir. 2016) (en banc) (holding that petitioner would be sufficiently diligent where he contacted the California Supreme Court only once in fourteen months regarding the status of his state petition); *Gibbs*, 767 F.3d at 890 (holding that a prisoner was "adequately diligent" when he wrote to his attorney three times over the course of seven months to find out if the state supreme court had ruled on his state petition); *Miles*, 187 F.3d at 1105, 1107 (holding that a prisoner was diligent where he waited over six weeks to re-submit a petition which prison officials never sent to the court). *See generally Rudin*, 781 F.3d at 1055 ("The diligence required for equitable tolling purposes is 'reasonable diligence,' not 'maximum feasible diligence.'" (quoting *Holland*, 560 U.S. at 653, 130 S. Ct. 2549).

Practice Tip

An inmate must follow up, to the best of his or her ability, whenever there is a delay in the case. Write letters, make phone calls (if possible), and ask questions. Document everything. Write down the date that the letter was mailed. Make a copy of the letter for your records. Write down who you spoke to in the prison about your filings, etc. This way, a petitioner will be able to show that he or she made a diligent effort in seeking to file a writ in the federal court.

H. Tolling for Claims of Actual Innocence

In 2013, the Supreme Court decided whether a claim of "actual innocence" may be filed after the one-year limitation period.[95] The

---

[95] *McQuiggin v. Perkins*, 569 U.S. 383 (2013).

Court noted many situations where claims of "actual innocence" overrides other impediments to the filing of a writ of habeas corpus in federal court, such as a claim of actual innocence raised in a "successive petition" or a claim of actual innocence with an undeveloped state record, and the petitioner "could obtain evidentiary hearings in federal court even if they failed to develop facts in state court." In fact, the court referred to claims of "actual innocence" as "the miscarriage of justice exception," based on previous Supreme Court decisions.

The Supreme Court rejected "the State's argument that habeas petitioners who assert convincing actual-innocence claims must prove diligence to cross a federal court's threshold" but held "that the Sixth Circuit erred to the extent that it eliminated timing as a factor relevant in evaluating the reliability of a petitioner's proof of innocence." The court essentially balanced two competing concerns: that the "fundamental miscarriage of justice exception is grounded in the 'equitable discretion' of habeas courts to see that federal constitutional errors do not result in the incarceration of innocent persons,"[96] and "the State's concern that it will be prejudiced by a prisoner's untoward delay in proffering new evidence."

The Court held that "untimeliness, although not an unyielding ground for dismissal of a petition, does bear on the credibility of evidence proffered to show actual innocence." What this means is that a petitioner cannot wait too long to file a claim of actual innocence, even though a claim of actual innocence is not subject to the one-year deadline of AEDPA.

The court also noted the difficulty in establishing claims of actual innocence. "[A] petitioner does not meet the threshold requirement unless he persuades the district court that, in light of the new evidence, no juror, acting reasonably, would have voted to find

---

[96] *Id.* (citing *Herrera v. Collins*, 506 U.S. 390 (1993)).

him guilty beyond a reasonable doubt."[97] This "standard is demanding and permits review only in the 'extraordinary' case."[98]

In *McQuiggin*, the Court concluded by again noting that "[t]he gateway should open only when a petition presents 'evidence of innocence so strong that a court cannot have confidence in the outcome of the trial unless the court is also satisfied that the trial was free of nonharmless constitutional error.'"[99]

Practice Tip

Claims of actual innocence should be investigated and filed as quickly as the circumstances allow.

I. "Stay and Abeyance" and the "Relating Back" Doctrine

Later, we will address the concepts of "exhausted" and "unexhausted" claims in detail. For now, an exhausted claim is a claim that was addressed in state court (on appeal or via a state writ of habeas corpus), and unexhausted claims are claims that were not addressed by the state court. The general rule is that only claims that were "exhausted" in state court may be brought in federal court. Typically, to exhaust a claim, one must seek review of that claim in the highest state court.

For many years, if a federal writ contained both exhausted and unexhausted claims, called a "mixed petition," the federal court would dismiss the writ. That left a petitioner with one of two options—forego the unexhausted claims and proceed in federal court with the exhausted claims, or have the federal petition dismissed so that the

---

[97] *Id.* (citing *Schlup v. Delo*, 513 U.S. 298 (1995)).

[98] *House v. Bell*, 547 U.S. 518 (2006).

[99] *McQuiggin* (citing *Schlup*, 513 U.S. at 298).

petitioner could go back to state court to exhaust all of the claims and then proceed with all of the claims in federal court.[100]

Once the AEDPA was passed, going back to state court carried a huge risk because the strict one-year deadline meant that there was often not enough time to exhaust the state claims. Even with statutory tolling, a petitioner would need to act extremely quickly to file a federal writ if the petitioner first needed to exhaust his claims in state court.

Stay and Abeyance

In response, the courts developed a procedure known as "stay and abeyance." For this procedure, a petitioner files his *exhausted* claims in federal court and asks the federal court the hold the petition in place while the *unexhausted* claims are filed in state court. After the state court reaches a decision on the unexhausted claims, the petitioner files an *amended* petition in federal court, which contains the previously unexhausted claims that are now exhausted.

While the Supreme Court held that "stay and abeyance" may only be used when there is "good cause for the petitioner's failure to exhaust his claims first in state court,"[101] the Ninth Circuit side-stepped this requirement. The Ninth Circuit held that a *mixed petition* must have good cause for a "stay and abeyance," but a petition that contains *only unexhausted* claims need not show "good cause" for the "stay and abeyance."[102]

What this means is that a "stay and abeyance" works in two distinct ways. One way is to ask the court to stay the *unexhausted* claims. To do this, "good cause" is necessary. The second way that "stay and abeyance" works is to ask the court to *dismiss* the

---

[100] Pursuant to the rule against "successive petitions," a petitioner cannot have the federal court consider some of his claims (the exhausted ones) and then later file a second writ of habeas corpus to consider his other claims (the unexhausted ones).

[101] *Rhines v. Weber*, 544 U.S. 269 (2005).

[102] *Jackson v. Roe*, 425 F.3d 654 (9th Cir. 2005).

unexhausted claims so that only fully exhausted claims are present, and then to ask the court to stay the *fully exhausted petition* so that the petitioner can seek to exhaust the rest of his claims in state court.[103]

There is a three-part procedure for a "stay and abeyance," as follows:

> (1) a petitioner amends his petition to delete any unexhausted claims; (2) the court stays and holds in abeyance the amended, fully exhausted petition, allowing the petitioner the opportunity to proceed to state court to exhaust the deleted claims; and (3) the petitioner later amends his petition and re-attaches the newly exhausted claims to the original petition.[104]

The "stay and abeyance," however, is not necessarily as good as it seems to be. In *King*, the Court pointed out that the "stay and abeyance" option resulted in the new claims being untimely:

> Because the *Kelly* procedure requires petitioners to dismiss their unexhausted claims and then attempt to add them back into the federal complaint later, the *Kelly* procedure, unlike the *Rhines* procedure, does nothing to protect a petitioner's unexhausted claims from untimeliness in the interim [emphasis added]. And *Duncan* and *Mayle*, taken together, make demonstrating timeliness of claims amended into federal habeas petitions after exhaustion often problematic."[105]

The *Rhines* procedure, in contrast, leaves the unexhausted claim pending in federal court but asks the court to pause the federal case so that the petitioner can exhaust the claims in state court. The unexhausted claims, consequently, are timely since they have been pending in the federal court from when the case was filed.

Therefore, a petitioner has one of two options, each of which having a procedural downside: the *Rhines* procedure, which requires a

---

[103] *See King v. Ryan*, 564 F.3d 1133 (9th Cir. 2009) (elaborating on this difference in procedural approaches).

[104] *Id.* (citing *Kelly v. Small*, 315 F.3d 1063 (9th Cir. 2003).

[105] *Id.*, 1141. We will address the *Duncan* and *Moyle* cases shortly.

showing of "good cause," or the *Kelly* procedure, which requires a showing of timeliness.

Relating Back

Rule 15(c)(1)(b) of the Federal Rules of Civil Procedure sets forth that "An amendment to a pleading relates back to the date of the original pleading when the amendment asserts a claim or defense that arose out of the conduct, transaction, or occurrence set out—or attempted to be set out—in the original pleading." In *Mayle v. Felix*, 545 U.S. 644 (2005), the Supreme Court held that an amended federal writ, filed after the one-year limitation period, "does not relate back (and thereby escape AEDPA's one-year time limit) when it asserts a new ground for relief supported by facts that differ in both time and type from those the original pleading set forth."

> There is a two-step process to determine if a claim "relates back" to another claim:
>
> First, we determine what claims the amended petition alleges and what core facts underlie those claims. Second, for each claim in the amended petition, we look to the body of the original petition and its exhibits to see whether the original petition set out or attempted to … set out a corresponding factual episode—or whether the claim is instead supported by facts that differ in both time and type from those the original pleading set forth.[106]

The reason the issue of relating back is so important, especially for "stay and abeyance," is because, for "stay and abeyance," an amended petition must be filed. If the amended petition is filed after the one-year limitation period of the AEDPA, then the new claims will be considered "timely" only if they "relate back" to the original claims. If the new claims are "related" to the previous claims, then they will be timely. If not, the new claims will be untimely.

---

[106] *Ross v. Williams*, 950 F.3d 1160 (9th Cir. 2020) (citations omitted).

Recall from earlier that, if a writ has multiple claims, the court will examine whether each individual claim was timely filed.[107] Also recall that a pending federal writ does not toll the statute of limitations.

Returning to *King*, the Ninth Circuit held that, while "a petitioner may invoke *Kelly*'s three-step procedure subject only to the requirement that the amendment of any newly exhausted claims back into the petition must satisfy *Mayle*," the petitioner in that case did not relate his nine unexhausted claims into his one exhausted claim. Therefore, the Court determined that the petitioner's nine unexhausted claims, which he went back to state court to exhaust, were all untimely.

Summary

If a petitioner has exhausted and unexhausted claims, the petitioner has the following four options:

(1) File a federal writ with the exhausted claims and forget about the unexhausted claims.

(2) Voluntarily dismiss the federal writ until the state claims are exhausted and then file the federal writ with all the claims.

(3) File a "mixed petition" with both claims and file a "stay and abeyance," asking the federal court to stay the federal writ. This requires a showing of "good cause."

(4) File a "mixed petition" and then amend the petition to delete the unexhausted claims and ask the court to stay the federal writ. Then, after exhausting the claims in state court, file an amended petition. The new claims, however, may face timeliness issues.

---

[107] *Souliotes*, 622 F.3d at 1180 ("We adopt the reasoning in *Fielder* and hold that § 2244(d)(1) requires consideration of the appropriate triggering date for each claim presented in the application.").

Practice Tip

Once again, the concepts of "relating back" and "stay and abeyance" teach that a petitioner must move quickly to assert federal rights. If not, the petitioner may be forced to face choices about how to proceed with his or her petition, each with a potential downside. To ensure that a federal writ is timely, and to obtain review by a federal court, a petitioner must act as quickly as possible.

Recall that when signing AEDPA into law, President Clinton predicted "that the Federal courts will interpret these provisions to preserve independent review of Federal legal claims and the bedrock constitutional principle of an independent judiciary." For the federal writ, courts do not "interpret these provisions to preserve independent review of Federal legal claims," and time is not on the petitioner's side.

J. Standard of Review

We end this chapter with a brief note about "standard of review." This is the standard that an appellate court (i.e., Circuit Court) will review the lower court's decision concerning the timeliness of a federal writ of habeas corpus. The Ninth Circuit reviews denials on a *de novo* basis.[108] The same holds true for the Fifth Circuit.[109] This means that the court looks "like new" at the lower court's decision and reaches its own decision, without according deference to the legal conclusions of the lower court.

K. Conclusion

We have seen that there is a one-year limitation period to file a writ of habeas corpus in federal court. The time starts to run from the date that the conviction becomes final and can be "tolled" (paused) during the

---

[108] *Cross v. Sisto*, 676 F.3d 1172 (9th Cir. 2012). The "court reviews the underlying findings of fact for clear error."

[109] *Starns v. Andrews*, 524 F.3d 612 (5th Cir. 2008).

time that a valid claim is pending in state court and can be tolled for equitable reasons. We reiterate that a petitioner must act *as quickly as possible* to ensure the timeliness of a writ of habeas corpus and, in the words of President Clinton, to "preserve independent review of Federal legal claims."

Chapter 4
APPROPRIATE ARGUMENTS

A. Introduction

For a federal writ, there are *procedural* requirements, and there are *substantive* requirements. Deadlines, which we previously discussed at length, are procedural requirements. An untimely writ of habeas corpus will be dismissed, but a timely writ of habeas corpus will not automatically be granted. One can think of it this way: A procedurally compliant writ of habeas corpus reserves the petitioner a spot at the table to argue that his or her federal rights were violated. A lack of compliance with the procedural rules means that the petition will not be heard. Simply being heard, however, is not the same as having the petition granted. For a writ of habeas corpus to be granted, the petitioner must present cogent, coherent, and compelling arguments about what rights were violated.

To present such arguments, a petitioner must generally do at least two things, and it is strongly recommended to do a third thing. First, a petitioner must cite the Constitution and relevant cases to explain the constitutional provisions that were violated.

Second, a petitioner must make a strong factual showing that his or her constitutional rights were violated. To do this, the petitioner must heavily rely on the facts of the case. This part is far more important than the first part. A federal writ will stand (or fall) mainly on the strength of the facts of the case. A strong presentation of facts, even with a weak citation to cases, is better than strong citation to cases with a weak presentation of the facts. A petitioner must show how the facts of the case correspond to a violation of federal rights. Essentially, a petitioner must take the facts of his or her case and apply the law to the facts.

Third, it is strongly recommended to locate cases with a similar fact pattern in which the court granted the habeas petition. Thus, the petitioner can point to analogous cases and use them as support for the writ of habeas corpus.

Alternatively, one may present cases with a weaker set of facts in which the court granted the habeas petition. One can argue something like, "In _____ v. _____, where the violation of the petitioner's right to effective assistance of counsel was not as egregious as the violation in this case, the court granted the petitioner's writ of habeas corpus. In this case, all the more, the court must grant the petitioner's writ of habeas corpus." Making an argument like this highlights the strength of the writ of habeas corpus and points out to the court that it would be incongruent for it to deny the writ of habeas corpus when the court previously granted other similar petitions.

We now turn to common arguments that are made in federal writs of habeas corpus. This chapter is presented to provide a background and general outline of the numerous violations of federal constitutional rights that make up a high percentage of writs that are filed. This information is presented as a starting point, not an ending point.

B. AEDPA's "Unreasonable" Standard for Writs of Habeas Corpus

In our chapter on deadlines, we wrote that President Clinton claimed that the AEDPA did not change the standard to use to determine whether to grant a writ of habeas corpus. He was wrong. "Under pre-AEDPA standards, both questions of law and mixed questions of law and fact are subject to *de novo* review, which means that a federal habeas court owes no deference to a state court's resolution of such legal questions (in contrast with post-AEDPA standards)."[110]

The AEDPA (28 U.S. Code § 2254(d)) changed this, instead requiring that the petitioner show that the state court's decision "resulted in a decision that was contrary to, or involved an

---

[110] *Clark v. Chappell*, 936 F.3d 944 (9th Cir. 2019).

unreasonable application of, clearly established Federal law, as determined by the Supreme Court of the United States," or that the petitioner's claim "resulted in a decision that was based on an unreasonable determination of the facts in light of the evidence presented in the state court proceeding."

The Supreme Court highlighted that "an unreasonable application of federal law is different from an incorrect application of federal law."[111] Therefore, "a federal habeas court may not issue the writ simply because that court concludes in its independent judgment that the relevant state-court decision applied clearly established federal law erroneously or incorrectly. Rather, that application must also be unreasonable."[112]

In *Lockyer v. Andrade*,[113] the Supreme Court referred to this standard as "objectively unreasonable." Initially, the Ninth Circuit understood the AEDPA standard to mean that the state court made a clear error.[114] The Supreme Court, however, rejected this test because it "fails to give proper deference to state courts by conflating error (even clear error) with unreasonableness." For a federal writ to be granted, the state court's decision must be *unreasonable.*

For example, the Fifth Circuit originally avoided providing a precise definition of "objectively unreasonable."[115] Now, the Fifth Circuit applies "a substantially higher threshold" than "incorrect or erroneous."[116]

Similarly, the Second Circuit wrote, "Some increment of incorrectness beyond error is required. We caution, however, that the increment need not be great; otherwise, habeas relief would be limited to state court decisions so far off the mark as to suggest judicial

---

[111] *Williams v. Taylor*, 529 U.S. 362, 410 (2000).

[112] *Id.*, 411.

[113] 538 U.S. 63, 76 (2003).

[114] *Van Tran v. Lindsey*, 212 F.3d 1143, 1152-54 (9th Cir. 2000).

[115] *See, e.g., Neal v. Puckett*, 286 F.3d 230, 246 n.14 (5th Cir. 2002).

[116] *Blue v. Thaler*, 665 F.3d 647, 654-55 (5th Cir. 2011).

incompetence. We do not believe AEDPA restricted federal habeas corpus to that extent."[117]

Later, however, in light of Supreme Court precedent, the Second Circuit walked back this test. The Second Circuit now applies the following test:

> An unreasonable application occurs when the state court correctly identifies the governing legal principle ... but unreasonably applies it to the facts of the particular case, so that the state court's ruling on the claim ... was so lacking in justification that there was an error well understood and comprehended in existing law beyond any possibility for fairminded disagreement.[118]

This test is based on the decision in *Harrington v. Richter*, 562 U.S.86 (2011). In that case, the Supreme Court noted the framework for 28 § 2254(d) as follows: "Under § 2254(d), a habeas court must determine what arguments or theories supported or, as here, could have supported, the state court's decision; and then it must ask whether it is possible fairminded jurists could disagree that those arguments or theories are inconsistent with the holding in a prior decision of this Court." The Court further noted, "[i]t bears repeating that even a strong case for relief does not mean the state court's contrary conclusion was unreasonable."

The Court summarized its holding as follows:

> As a condition for obtaining habeas corpus from a federal court, a state prisoner must show that the state court's ruling on the claim being presented in federal court was so lacking in justification that there was an error well understood and comprehended in existing law beyond any possibility for fairminded disagreement.

Therefore, not only must the petitioner have a meritorious case, but the state court's denial of the petitioner's arguments must have been "so

---

[117] *Monroe v. Kuhlman*, 433 F.3d 236, 246 (2d Cir. 2006).
[118] *Washington v. Griffin*, 876 F.3d 395 (2d Cir. 2017) (citations omitted).

lacking in justification that there was an error well understood and comprehended in existing law beyond any possibility for fairminded disagreement." This standard is highly deferential to the state court's determination. The "AEDPA thus imposes a highly deferential standard for evaluating state-court rulings and demands that state-court decisions be given the benefit of the doubt."[119]

There is, however, one exception to this standard. If the state court does not reach a decision regarding one of the issues in the case, then the federal court uses a *de novo* review and uses its own judgment to consider the issue. The federal court will use a *de novo* review, for example, when a claim has numerous elements and the state court denies the petition based on one of the elements without addressing the other elements. The federal court may then use its own judgment to analyze the other elements.

By way of a specific example, a claim of ineffective assistance of counsel has two parts—a petitioner must show that his attorney's conduct was deficient and that he was prejudiced by his attorney's deficient performance. If the state court determines that the attorney's conduct was proper, then it will deny the writ of habeas corpus. If the federal court determines that it was unreasonable for the state court to hold that the attorney's conduct was proper, then the federal court will use its own judgment to determine the second prong—whether the petitioner was prejudiced by the attorney's deficient conduct. Since the state court did not make a determination about prejudice, the federal court may make the determination. We will explain ineffective assistance of counsel at length later in this chapter.

In *Rompilla v. Beard*,[120] the state court denied an ineffective assistance of counsel claim, reasoning that the attorney's conduct was not deficient. Because of this, the state court made no finding about the prejudice prong of the claim. The federal court, however, found that the attorney's conduct was deficient. Since there was no state court

---

[119] *Renico v. Lett*, 559 U.S. 766 (2010) (citations omitted).
[120] 545 U.S. 374 (2005).

decision about prejudice, the federal court applied a *de novo* review to determine whether the attorney's conduct was prejudicial to the petitioner.

In *Rompilla*, the petitioner's attorney failed to investigate whether mitigating evidence existed in order to present the mitigating evidence in a death penalty hearing. "If the defense lawyers had looked in the file on Rompilla's prior conviction, it is uncontested they would have found a range of mitigation leads that no other source had opened up." The Supreme Court then granted the writ and ordered that "Pennsylvania must either retry the case on penalty or stipulate to a life sentence." In citing this case, we highlight that the federal court applied a *de novo* standard in determining whether the petitioner was prejudiced since the state court had not made a determination about prejudice.

On the other end of the spectrum, the Supreme Court recently reversed the granting of two writs of habeas corpus on the grounds that the federal court failed to apply the correct standard. In *Mays v. Hines*,[121] the Sixth Circuit effectively applied a *de novo* review and "focused on all the reasons why it thought [the witness] could have been a viable alternative suspect." The Supreme Court held that the Sixth Circuit was not deferential enough to the state court. The Supreme Court reversed the granting of the writ and held, "The Sixth Circuit had no reason to revisit the decision of the Tennessee court, much less ignore the ample evidence supporting that court's conclusion."

Similarly, in *Shinn v. Kayer*,[122] the Supreme Court reversed the Ninth Circuit's granting of a writ of habeas corpus. The Supreme Court explicitly criticized the Ninth Circuit for using a *de novo* standard of review. The Supreme Court held as follows:

> Under AEDPA, state courts play the leading role in assessing challenges to state sentences based on federal law. A state

---

[121] 141 S. Ct. 1145 (2021).
[122] 141 S. Ct. 517 (2020).

court heard Kayer's evidence and concluded that he failed to
show prejudice. The court below exceeded its authority in
rejecting that determination, which was not so obviously wrong
as to be beyond any possibility for fairminded disagreement.

In *Mays v. Hines*, the Supreme Court reaffirmed the standard for
federal writs of habeas corpus by stating that the state court "managed
to blunder so badly that every fairminded jurist would disagree."[123]
With this standard in mind, we will turn to common arguments that are
available for federal writs of habeas corpus. We will organize the
arguments Amendment by Amendment beginning with the Fourth
Amendment.

C. Fourth Amendment

Text of the Fourth Amendment

The Fourth Amendment provides:

> The right of the people to be secure in their persons, houses,
> papers, and effects, against unreasonable searches and seizures,
> shall not be violated, and no Warrants shall issue, but upon
> probable cause, supported by Oath or affirmation, and
> particularly describing the place to be searched, and the
> persons or things to be seized.[124]

A Writ of Habeas Corpus Generally Cannot Be Based on a Fourth Amendment Violation

The Fourth Amendment protects against unlawful searches and
seizures. This generally means that the government may not search
private property without a search warrant or without permission from
the owner (or someone who appears to have authority to give
permission for the search). If the police enter a private premise for a

---

[123] *Mays v. Hines*, 141 S. Ct. at 1149.
[124] U.S. Const. amend XIV.

search and seizure without warrant or permission, the evidence is usually not admissible in court.[125]

In 1976, the Supreme Court addressed whether a writ of habeas corpus may be based on an unconstitutional search and seizure in violation of the Fourth Amendment. In *Stone v. Powell*,[126] the Supreme Court held:

> [W]here the State has provided an opportunity for full and fair litigation of a Fourth Amendment claim, the Constitution does not require that a state prisoner be granted federal habeas corpus relief on the ground that evidence obtained in an unconstitutional search or seizure was introduced at his trial.

The rationale for this decision was a bit convoluted. The Court focused on the fact that the "exclusionary rule" is designed to prevent police officers from performing illegal searches and seizures. "The view that the deterrence of Fourth Amendment violations would be furthered rests on the dubious assumption that law enforcement authorities would fear that federal habeas review might reveal flaws in a search or seizure that went undetected at trial and on appeal." Therefore, based on the *Stone v. Powell* decision, a writ of habeas corpus *cannot* be premised on a violation of the Fourth Amendment.

The First Exception to the Stone v. Powell Rule

In *Stone v. Powell*, the Court left open the possibility of making a Fourth Amendment claim in a writ of habeas corpus when the petitioner was not provided with a "full and fair" opportunity to litigate the issue at trial. In practice, this exception does not apply very often. In some federal districts, all that is required is that there be a procedure in place to raise the Fourth Amendment claim. For example, in *Capellan v. Riley*,[127] the Second Circuit held that as long as there is

---

[125] A full discussion of the Fourth Amendment's protection against searches and seizures is beyond the scope of this chapter.
[126] 428 U.S. 465 (1976).
[127] 975 F.2d 67 (2d Cir. 1992).

a procedure in place to address the search and seizure claims, then the claims cannot be raised in a writ of habeas corpus.

The Ninth Circuit, on the other hand, focuses on whether the petitioner received a fair hearing on a motion to suppress the evidence. If, for whatever reason, the Court did not address the substance of the motion to suppress, then the petitioner did not receive a "full and fair" hearing and may, therefore, assert the Fourth Amendment claim in a writ of habeas corpus.[128]

Is the Stone v. Powell *Rule Still Valid After the Passage of the AEDPA?[129]*

We have noted how the AEDPA changed the rules and the standards of federal writs of habeas corpus. In *Newman v. Wengler*, the petitioner raised a novel argument that the AEDPA replaced the *Stone v. Powell* rule. The petitioner argued that, since 28 U.S.C. § 2254(d) states, "*any* [emphasis added] claim that was adjudicated on the merits," then the AEDPA must apply to Fourth Amendment claims.

The Ninth Circuit engaged in a lengthy literary analysis, which included a discussion about whether the AEDPA implies a "negative pregnant"—whatever the heck that is—to conclude that the *Stone v. Powell* rule is still in place. The Court then went on to determine if the petitioner received a full and fair opportunity to litigate his Fourth Amendment claim and, ultimately, denied the writ of habeas corpus.

The Second Exception to the Stone v. Powell *Rule—File a Writ of Habeas Corpus Based on Ineffective Assistance of Counsel for Counsel's Failure To Suppress the Evidence Seized*

A few years after the Supreme Court's holding in *Stone v. Powell*, the Supreme Court addressed a related issue. As we noted, a petitioner may not allege in a writ of habeas corpus that his or her Fourth

---

[128] *See, e.g., Anderson v. Calderon*, 232 F.3d 1053 (9th Cir. 2000). In *Good v. Berghuis*, 729 F.3d 636 (6th Cir. 2013), the Court summarizes each of the approaches.
[129] 790 F.3d 876 (9th Cir. 2015).

Amendment rights were violated. Could a petitioner allege instead that he or she received ineffective assistance of counsel (a violation of the Sixth Amendment) based on an attorney's failure to exclude evidence that was unlawfully seized according to the Fourth Amendment? Essentially, this would be a way around the *Stone v. Powell* decision. Instead of arguing a Fourth Amendment violation, the petitioner argues a Sixth Amendment violation based on a Fourth Amendment right. Would that work?

In *Kimmelman v. Morrison*,[130] the Supreme Court held that a claim for ineffective assistance of counsel (Sixth Amendment) may be made based on an attorney's failure to suppress evidence (Fourth Amendment). The Court explained that the Sixth Amendment and the Fourth Amendment are two different amendments with different rules that apply to each of the amendments. Therefore, the rule in *Stone v. Powell* does not apply to a Sixth Amendment claim for ineffective assistance of counsel. We will discuss this at length later in this chapter in the section about the Sixth Amendment and ineffective assistance of counsel.

D. Fifth Amendment

Text of Fifth Amendment

The Fifth Amendment provides that:

> No person shall be held to answer for a capital, or otherwise infamous crime, unless on a presentment or indictment of a Grand Jury, except in cases arising in the land or naval forces, or in the Militia, when in actual service in time of War or public danger; *nor shall any person be subject for the same offence to be twice put in jeopardy of life or limb; nor shall be compelled in any criminal case to be a witness against himself* [emphasis added], nor be deprived of life, liberty, or property,

---

[130] 477 U.S. 365 (1986).

without due process of law; nor shall private property be taken for public use, without just compensation.

Self-Incrimination and Miranda Rights

"Taking the Fifth" or "pleading the Fifth" has entered the everyday lexicon. When someone says this, he or she is usually refusing to answer a question to avoid getting into trouble. This phrase comes from the Fifth Amendment of the Constitution, which protects a person from being required to incriminate himself or herself. Through the Fifth Amendment, there is a constitutional right against self-incrimination.

A violation of one's right against self-incrimination may occur: (a) if a defendant is coerced into answering questions about a crime or (b) if a defendant is promised immunity in exchange for testimony, and the testimony is then used against the defendant in a later case. In the middle of 2021, Bill Cosby's *state* writ of habeas corpus was granted, and he was released from prison. One of his main arguments was that his right against self-incrimination was violated because he was promised immunity in exchange for his testimony in a civil action, and his testimony was later used against him in a criminal case.

In that case, the court wrote, "In accordance with the advice of his attorneys, Cosby relied upon D.A. Castor's public announcement that he would not be prosecuted. His reliance was reasonable, and it resulted in the deprivation of a fundamental constitutional right when he was compelled to furnish self-incriminating testimony."[131]

In *Dickerson v. United States*,[132] the Supreme Court provided a historical overview of the law regarding coerced confessions. "Over

---

[131] *Commonwealth v. Cosby*, 252 A.3d 1092 (Pa. 2021). William ("Bill") Cosby is an American actor and media personality. He was accused of raping multiple women over the span of decades. Most of these allegations were outside of the statute of limitations period for prosecution. However, he was later tried and convicted by jury in Montgomery County, Pennsylvania. The Supreme Court of Pennsylvania overturned his conviction holding his right to due process was violated.
[132] 530 U.S. 428 (2000).

time, our cases recognized two constitutional bases for the requirement that a confession be voluntary to be admitted into evidence: the Fifth Amendment right against self-incrimination and the Due Process Clause of the Fourteenth Amendment." Then, in the 1960s, "we held that the Fifth Amendment's Self-Incrimination Clause is incorporated in the Due Process Clause of the Fourteenth Amendment and thus applies to the States."

In the famous *Miranda* case, the Court addressed "the admissibility of statements obtained from an individual who is subjected to custodial police interrogation and the necessity for procedures which assure that the individual is accorded his privilege under the Fifth Amendment to the Constitution not to be compelled to incriminate himself."[133] The context is crucial: Miranda applies to custodial interrogations.

In *Miranda*, the Court was clear that a defendant may waive his or her Fifth Amendment right against self-incrimination. This may occur when a statement is voluntarily provided by the defendant, and the defendant is not coerced to make the statement.[134]

The Supreme Court had referred to *Miranda* warnings as a "prophylactic rule protecting the Fifth Amendment's privilege against self-incrimination."[135] This suggests that there is no inherent constitutional right to a *Miranda* warning, and the warning is in place to protect a suspect's privilege against self-incrimination. In *Dickerson*, the Court clarified that *Miranda* rights are an actual constitutional right—there is a constitutional right to remain silent.

A suspect invokes his or her *Miranda* rights by doing one of two things: either by asking for an attorney or by saying that he or she wants to remain silent.[136] If a suspect remains silent, without saying

---

[133] *Miranda v. Arizona*, 384 U.S. 436, 439 (1966).
[134] *Edwards v. Arizona*, 451 U.S. 477 (1981).
[135] *New York v. Quarles*, 467 U.S. 649 (1984).
[136] *Berghuis v. Thompkins*, 560 U.S. 370 (2010).

anything, and then begins to speak, the courts will likely find the statements to be admissible. The right must be unequivocally *invoked*.

An Example of a Successful Writ Premised on a Miranda Violation

Sometimes, *Miranda* cases are straightforward, yet it still takes a diligent petitioner to ultimately prevail on his or her claims. In *Garcia v. Long*,[137] Garcia was asked whether he wanted to talk to the police, and he said "no." After the police pressured him to say yes, he eventually relented and ultimately confessed to rape and other sexual crimes. He was subsequently sentenced to 35 years to life in prison.

Garcia's attorney sought to suppress his confession on the grounds that it was obtained in violation of Garcia's Fifth Amendment right against self-incrimination and that the confession was not voluntary since Garcia had told the police that he did not want to speak to them. The state trial court denied the motion to suppress, and the jury heard the three-and-a-half hour recorded confession. The California Court of Appeal agreed with the trial court and affirmed the conviction and sentence.

Garcia then filed a writ of habeas corpus in federal court. The federal district court granted the writ, and the Ninth Circuit Court of Appeals agreed. The Ninth Circuit viewed this as a straightforward case, stating, "We hold that any reasonable jurist would have to conclude that 'no' meant 'no.'"

In addressing the level of clarity that is required, the Supreme Court held that a suspect "must articulate his desire to have counsel present sufficiently clearly that a reasonable police officer in the circumstances would understand the statement to be a request for an attorney."[138]

Since Garcia's answer was clear—he said "no," which only has one meaning—the police were not allowed to ask follow-up questions to clarify the already clear answer. The police were supposed to have

---

[137] 808 F.3d 771 (9th Cir. 2015).

[138] *Davis v. United States*, 512 U.S. 452 (1994).

immediately stopped asking questions, but instead they continued. "The only reasonable reading of the record is that Garcia told the officers that he wanted to remain silent. Quite literally, however, the officers did not take 'no' for an answer." The Ninth Circuit Court of Appeals affirmed the granting of the writ of habeas corpus and ordered the State of California to either release Garcia or hold a new trial.

This case illustrates the importance of filing writs of habeas corpus in federal court. In *Garcia v. Long*, the state court concluded that Garcia's constitutional rights were not violated. It was only through Garcia's filing of a writ of habeas corpus in federal court that Garcia was able to vindicate his constitutional rights and to obtain ether a release or a new trial.

Another Example of a Successful Writ Premised on a Miranda Violation—"I don't want to talk no more, man"

To illustrate that *Miranda* violations are sometimes obvious, but that the state courts nonetheless deny the claim, in *Jones v. Harrington*,[139] Jones was being interrogated and told the police officer, "I don't want to talk no more, man." The officer continued questioning Jones, who ultimately gave incriminating statements to the police.

On appeal, the California appellate court decided that the phrase "I don't want to talk no more, man" was ambiguous and was not a clear statement that Jones did not want to talk to the police. Unlike the *Garcia* case, the federal district court (lower court) denied the writ of habeas corpus.

The Ninth Circuit Court of Appeals, however, held that Jones's statement was not ambiguous. It was a clear statement that Jones did not want to talk to the police. The continuation of the interrogation, therefore, was done in violation of Jones's Fifth Amendment rights. The Court concluded that:

> The Supreme Court has repeatedly made clear that when a
> suspect simply and unambiguously says he wants to remain

---

[139] 829 F.3d 1128 (9th Cir. 2016).

silent, police questioning must end. Under any reasonable interpretation of the facts, Jones simply and unambiguously invoked that right. Clearly established Supreme Court law required the suppression of Jones's interrogation. The State shall either release Jones or grant him a new trial.

This case, and the case discussed in the previous section, illustrate that a petitioner must be diligent and relentless in seeking to vindicate his or her constitutional rights. It was only when this case reached the Court of Appeals that the Court recognized that "I don't want to talk no more, man" is a clear statement that a suspect does not want to talk to the police.

The Prosecutor Cannot Comment About a Defendant's Right To Remain Silent

Generally, a prosecutor cannot comment about a defendant's silence, either as a way to show that the defendant is guilty or to impeach a defendant with his previous silence.[140] In *Hurd v. Terhune*,[141] the petitioner was convicted of first-degree murder and was sentenced to life in prison without parole. The petitioner then filed a writ of habeas corpus, arguing that his constitutional rights were violated because the prosecutor commented about his refusal to reenact the murder. In other words, the prosecutor commented on the defendant's silence.

The court granted the writ of habeas corpus, reasoning that the state court's decision was an unreasonable application of the law.[142] The court wrote:

As clearly established federal law prohibits the use of a criminal defendant's post-*Miranda* silence against him in court,

---

[140] *See Doyle v. Ohio*, 426 U.S. 610, 619 (1976) ("We hold that the use for impeachment purposes of petitioners' silence, at the time of arrest and after receiving Miranda warnings, violated the Due Process Clause of the Fourteenth Amendment.")
[141] 619 F.3d 1080 (9th Cir. 2010).
[142] Recall that the federal court may grant a petition for writ of habeas corpus only when it determines that the state court decision was an unreasonable application of the law. This was extensively discussed earlier.

a reasonable application of the law requires the government to establish that Hurd either waived his right to remain silent or never effectively invoked it. See Arnold, 421 F.3d at 866. Here, Hurd unambiguously invoked his right to silence when the officers requested that he reenact the shooting. Hurd responded to the officers' requests by saying, among other things, "I don't want to do that," "No," "I can't," and "I don't want to act it out because that—it's not that clear."

Double Jeopardy

The Fifth Amendment protects against double jeopardy and applies under three general circumstances: (1) A person cannot be prosecuted a second time for the same offense after being acquitted in the first trial; (2) a person cannot be prosecuted a second time for the same offense after being convicted in the first trial; and (3) a person cannot receive two punishments for the same crime.[143] We will discuss these situations in this section.

A Second Prosecution: Guilt, Innocence, and Mistrial

In 1896, the Supreme Court faced an interesting question. Three people were indicted for murder. Two of them were found guilty, and one of them was found not guilty. The guilty parties appealed, and the Supreme Court dismissed the indictment for being defective. When the government tried to indict all three defendants again, the case reached the Supreme Court—again. The Supreme Court held that the person who was found innocent could not be re-tried because that would violate his double jeopardy rights. The other two defendants, who were found guilty, could be re-tried.[144]

Not long after this decision, the Supreme Court held that a person who is found not guilty cannot have his not-guilty verdict reversed on appeal. To allow an appellate court to overturn a finding

---

[143] *Ohio v. Johnson*, 467 U.S. 493 (1984).
[144] *U.S. v. Ball*, 163 U.S. 662 (1896).

of innocence would be a violation of double jeopardy.[145] "Perhaps the most fundamental rule in the history of double jeopardy jurisprudence has been that [a] verdict of acquittal … could not be reviewed, on error or otherwise, without putting [a defendant] twice in jeopardy, and thereby violating the Constitution."[146]

A retrial is allowed for situations where there is a "manifest necessity" for a retrial. Practically, this means that the jury was deadlocked.[147] If, however, the case is dismissed due to insufficient evidence, double jeopardy applies, and the government may not re-try the defendant.[148] If the dismissal is procedural, such as for a lack of venue, double jeopardy does not apply.[149]

One key question for double jeopardy is when it attaches. The answer is that it attaches when the jury is sworn in.[150] Once it attaches, the government cannot retry someone who was acquitted. If there is a dismissal after the jury is sworn in, then there may be a double jeopardy issue. For a guilty plea, there is a split in the circuit courts. The Ninth Circuit follows the rule that attachment occurs when the court accepts the guilty plea.

In *U.S. v. Patterson*, 381 F.3d 859 (9th Cir. 2004), the defendant pleaded guilty to growing marijuana plants, and the issue at sentencing was how many plants he had grown. The maximum jail time he could have received was five years. Then, due to a decision of the Supreme Court that was issued while Patterson's case was pending, it was determined that a jury must decide how many marijuana plants Patterson had grown. The court, then, vacated Patterson's plea and scheduled a trial. At trial, he was found guilty and sentenced to 188 months (15 years and 8 months) in prison. The Ninth Circuit agreed that Patterson's Fifth Amendment rights were violated

---

[145] *Kepner v. United States*, 195 U.S. 100 (1904).

[146] *United States v. Scott*, 437 U.S. 82, 90 (1978) (citations omitted).

[147] *United States v. Razmilovic*, 507 F.3d 130 (2d Cir. 2007).

[148] *United States v. Johnson*, 963 F.3d 847 (9th Cir. 2020).

[149] *United States v. Moran-Garcia*, 966 F.3d 966 (9th Cir. 2020).

[150] *Crist v. Bretz*, 437 U.S. 28 (1978).

since he had been subject to a second prosecution for the same offense after conviction. The court reinstated the five-year sentence.

Two Punishments for the Same Crime

The Fifth Amendment bars the imposition of two sentences for the same crime. "When a defendant has violated two different criminal statutes, the double jeopardy prohibition is implicated when both statutes prohibit the same offense or when one offense is a lesser included offense of the other."[151] In *United States v. Davenport*, the defendant was convicted of receipt of child pornography and convicted of possession of child pornography. The Court held that Davenport's constitutional rights were violated since the two criminal statutes prohibited the same offense, stating, "It is impossible to 'receive' something without, at least at the very instant of 'receipt,' also 'possessing' it." In *Davenport*, the Court wrote, "because the prohibition against double jeopardy is a cornerstone of our system of constitutional criminal procedure, this error threatens the fairness, integrity, and public reputation of our judicial proceedings."

Sentence Enhancements and Strikes for Prior Convictions

Sentence enhancements usually do not implicate double jeopardy concerns.[152] "Sentencing enhancements are separate from the offense and related conduct, which is why a defendant can receive an enhancement as to one offense based on particular conduct and then be prosecuted separately based on that same conduct."[153]

Similarly, using prior convictions as enhancements does not violate the Fifth Amendment:

> But although the three-strikes statute might seem to violate this principle, the Supreme Court has long since determined that recidivist statutes do not violate double jeopardy because the enhanced punishment imposed for the later offense is not to be

---

[151] *United States v. Davenport*, 519 F.3d 940 (9th Cir. 2008).

[152] *Witte v. United States*, 515 U.S. 389 (1995).

[153] *United States v. Moore*, 670 F.3d 222 (2d Cir. 2012).

viewed as either a new jeopardy or additional penalty for the earlier crimes, but instead as a stiffened penalty for the latest crime, which is considered to be an aggravated offense because [it is] a repetitive one.[154]

Do Civil Penalties Count for Double Jeopardy Purposes?

At times, it is not clear if a defendant was criminally punished. If yes, then there cannot be a second punishment, due to double jeopardy. If a person was not criminally punished, then he or she would be subject to criminal punishment. This confusion typically occurs in the context of a person who receives a civil penalty that is similar to a criminal penalty. The Supreme Court has adopted the following seven-part test to determine whether a sanction/civil penalty is penal in nature, so as to prevent a second criminal action:

(1) Whether it involves an affirmative disability or restraint;

(2) Whether it has historically been regarded as a punishment;

(3) Whether it comes into play only on a finding of scienter;

(4) Whether its operation will promote the traditional aims of punishment—retribution and deterrence;

(5) Whether the behavior to which it applies is already a crime;

(6) Whether an alternative purpose to which it may rationally be connected is assignable for it; and

(7) Whether it appears excessive in relation to the alternative purpose assigned.[155]

Double Jeopardy in Another Jurisdiction

Finally, double jeopardy does not prevent another jurisdiction from pursuing criminal charges. This means that two states may charge someone with the same crimes, or that both the state and federal government may charge someone with the same crimes.[156] This is how the federal government was able to press charges against Derek

---

[154] *United States v. Kaluna*, 192 F.3d 1188 (9th Cir. 1999).

[155] *Kennedy v. Mendoza-Martinez*, 372 U.S. 144, 168-169 (1963); *Hudson v. United States*, 522 U.S. 93 (1997).

[156] *Heath v. Alabama*, 474 U.S. 82 (1985).

Chauvin after he was convicted in the Minnesota state court. Since the federal government is a different jurisdiction than the state court, the federal charges against Derek Chauvin did not violate his constitutional right to be protected against double jeopardy.

E. Sixth Amendment

Text of Sixth Amendment

The Sixth Amendment provides that:

> In all criminal prosecutions, the accused shall enjoy the right to a speedy and public trial, by an impartial jury of the State and district wherein the crime shall have been committed, which district shall have been previously ascertained by law, and to be informed of the nature and cause of the accusation; to be confronted with the witnesses against him; to have compulsory process for obtaining witnesses in his favor, and to have the Assistance of Counsel for his defense.

The Sixth Amendment provides many significant constitutional rights. It includes the right to a speedy trial, the right to an impartial jury, the right to be tried in the State and district where the crime was committed, the right to be informed of the charges, the right to confront witnesses, the right to present witnesses, and the right to an attorney. The right to an attorney means the right to an *effective* attorney, also known as effective assistance of counsel. We will discuss these rights below.

Speedy Trial

The beginning of the Sixth Amendment lists a right to a speedy trial. The purpose of the right to a speedy trial is "to minimize the possibility of lengthy incarceration prior to trial, to reduce the lesser, but nevertheless substantial, impairment of liberty imposed on an accused while released on bail, and to shorten the disruption of life caused by arrest and the presence of unresolved criminal charges."[157]

The right to a speedy trial begins when there is "either a formal indictment or information or else the actual restraints imposed by arrest and holding to answer a criminal charge that engage the particular protections of the speedy trial provision of the Sixth Amendment."[158]

There are four factors that the court will consider when determining if the constitutional right to a speedy trial was violated: (1) the length of the delay, (2) the reasons for the delay, (3) the accused's assertion of the right to a speedy trial, and (4) the prejudice caused by the delay. There is no single factor that is necessary or sufficient to establish a violation of this constitutional right.[159]

In *McNeely v. Blanas*, 336 F.3d 822 (9th Cir. 2003), the defendant's right to a speedy trial was violated when California did not try him for three years and could not adequately explain the delay. The Court held that "we reverse the decision of the district court and remand with directions to grant the petition for writ of habeas corpus. Because his Sixth Amendment right to a speedy trial has been violated, Petitioner shall be immediately released from custody with prejudice to re-prosecution of the criminal charges."

When the right to a speedy trial has been violated, the indictment must be dismissed and cannot be re-filed.[160]

Right To Confront Witnesses

The Confrontation Clause provides a right to "confront" witnesses who testify against a defendant. "The Confrontation Clause provides two types of protections for a criminal defendant: the right physically

---

[157] *United States v. MacDonald*, 456 U.S. 1, 8 (1982).

[158] *United States v. Marion*, 404 U.S. 307, 320 (1971).

[159] *Barker v. Wingo*, 407 U.S. 514, 530-33 (1972).

[160] *See Strunk v. United States*, 412 U.S. 434 (1973).

to face those who testify against him, and the right to conduct cross-examination."[161]

Face-to-Face Confrontation

The Supreme Court held that "the Confrontation Clause guarantees the defendant a face-to-face meeting with witnesses appearing before the trier of fact."[162] In *Coy v. Iowa*, the issue concerned a state statute that allowed children to testify from behind a screen or from an adjacent room. The defendant in that case was accused of sexually assaulting two 13-year-old girls. When the girls testified, they did so from behind a screen. One purpose of the statute was to prevent trauma to children. The statute was written for situations like what occurred in *Coy*, where underage victims would suffer from trauma if they had to face an alleged perpetrator of a crime against them.

Since the state statute prevented a defendant from a face-to-face confrontation with adverse witnesses, the Court held that "[i]t is difficult to imagine a more obvious or damaging violation of the defendant's right to a face-to-face encounter." The Court reasoned that face-to-face confrontation is essential for fairness and to ensure the integrity of the trial. "A witness 'may feel quite differently when he has to repeat his story looking at the man whom he will harm greatly by distorting or mistaking the facts. He can now understand what sort of human being that man is.'"

In *Coy*, the Court suggested that exceptions to the rule could exist but did not address any exceptions. Two years later, the Supreme Court upheld a statute that allowed for a child who was the alleged victim of sexual offenses to testify via closed circuit television.[163] For this to apply, the judge must determine "that testimony by the child victim in the courtroom will result in the child suffering serious emotional distress such that the child cannot reasonably communicate."

---

[161] *Coy v. Iowa*, 487 U.S. 1012, 1017 (1988).
[162] *Id.*
[163] *Maryland v. Craig*, 497 U.S. 836 (1990).

The Supreme Court later clarified that there is a "preference" for face-to-face confrontation, but there is no absolute right to face-to-face confrontation. "The central concern of the Confrontation Clause is to ensure the reliability of the evidence against a criminal defendant by subjecting it to rigorous testing in the context of an adversary proceeding before the trier of fact." Therefore, the Court identified two factors for when a witness may testify outside of the presence of the defendant: (1) when it is necessary to on public policy grounds, and (2) when there are procedures to make sure that the testimony is reliable.

In *Maryland v. Craig*, the Court applied these factors to the statute at issue in the case. The Court agreed that protecting alleged sexual offence victims from further trauma is an important public policy, and "the presence of these other elements of confrontation— oath, cross-examination, and observation of the witness' demeanor— adequately ensures that the testimony is both reliable and subject to rigorous adversarial testing in a manner functionally equivalent to that accorded live, in-person testimony." Crucially, the Court held that the courts must make case-specific inquiries into the child in each case. Will the specific child be traumatized by being in the presence of the defendant? The Court referred to this as a "case-specific finding of necessity."

Right to Cross-Examination

In *Crawford v. Washington*,[164] the trial court allowed the prosecution to introduce recorded video testimony of the defendant's wife. She apparently undermined the defendant's self-defense argument with her testimony. The prosecution chose to use the video instead of calling the defendant's wife as a witness because *spousal immunity* allows a spouse to refuse to testify against his or her spouse. The Supreme Court held that, because the defendant was not provided with an opportunity to cross-examine his wife, her testimony could not be used

---

[164] 541 U.S. 36 (2004).

in court. To use her testimony would be a violation of the defendant's Sixth Amendment right to cross-examine a witness.

The use of testimony from a preliminary hearing, or prior testimony that was recorded, is only allowed when (1) the witness is not currently available to testify and (2) the defendant was provided with an opportunity to cross-examine the witness when the testimony was given. A defendant need not actually have cross-examined the witness. What is needed is that the defendant had an *opportunity* to cross-examine the witness. In *Crawford*, the defendant was not afforded the opportunity to cross-examine his wife when her statements were recorded. Therefore, the Court held that the use of the defendant's wife's video-recorded testimony was a violation of the defendant's Sixth Amendment rights.

A significant limitation of this rule is that it applies only to testimonial evidence. While a precise definition of testimonial evidence remains unclear, "it applies at a minimum to prior testimony at a preliminary hearing, before a grand jury, or at a former trial; and to police interrogations."[165] In 2018, the Ninth Circuit agreed with other circuits that confessions of codefendants, which are usually not admissible, are admissible even though they are not subject to cross-examination, when the confession is non-testimonial.[166]

In one case, a federal court held that a statement made to an undercover informant was not testimonial, so the statement was allowed to be used at trial, even though the defendant did not have an opportunity to cross-examine the person who made the statement.[167] The Court reasoned that the statement was not testimonial in nature.

In another case, a petitioner filed a writ of habeas corpus, arguing that statements made to a doctor should not have been used in court because the defendant was not provided with an opportunity to

---

[165] *Id.*, 68.
[166] *Lucero v. Holland*, 902 F.3d 979 (9th Cir. 2018).
[167] *United States v. Saget*, 377 F.3d 223 (2d Cir. 2004).

cross-examine the maker of the statements.[168] The state court concluded that the statements were not testimonial "because they were made for purposes of diagnosis and treatment, rather than to inculpate" the defendant. The federal court affirmed, deferring to the state court because its decision was "not an unreasonable application of the legal principle established by Crawford." As the reader will recall, this is the standard that federal courts use, pursuant to the AEDPA.

Failure To Make a Good Faith Effort To Locate a Witness

The first prong of when prior testimony may be used is when the witness is not available to testify. The state must make a "good faith" effort to locate the witness. The use of prior testimony without making a good faith effort to locate a witness is a violation of a defendant's Sixth Amendment right to confront witnesses.[169] In *United States v. Rodriguez*,[170] the government used a witness's videotaped deposition rather than calling the person as a witness to testify. The Ninth Circuit held that since the government did not make a good faith effort to locate the witness, the defendant's Sixth Amendment right to confront witnesses was violated.

Limiting a Cross-Examination

A significant restriction of a cross-examination may violate the constitution. In *Ortiz v. Yates*,[171] the trial judge ruled that certain important questions could not be asked on cross-examination. The Ninth Circuit held that the restriction of the petitioner's right to cross-examine a witness violated the petitioner's constitutional rights. The court did note, however, that trial courts have wide latitude to impose *reasonable* limits on cross-examination, such as for "among other

---

[168] *Moses v. Payne*, 555 F.3d 742 (9th Cir. 2008).

[169] *Jackson v. Brown*, 513 F.3d 1057 (9th Cir. 2008). In this case, however, the court held that the violation did not have a "substantial and injurious effect or influence in determining the jury's verdict" and denied the petitioner's writ of habeas corpus.

[170] 880 F.3d 1151 (9th Cir. 2018).

[171] 704 F.3d 1026 (9th Cir. 2012).

things, harassment, prejudice, confusion of the issues, the witness' safety, or interrogation that is repetitive or only marginally relevant."

In another case concerning the limitation of a right to cross-examine a witness, the State's expert's report was based on inadmissible hearsay.[172] The trial court gave the petitioner a choice: have the hearsay admitted and then conduct a cross-examination of the State's expert, or skip the cross-examination. The Second Circuit held that the trial court offered the petitioner "a constitutionally-impermissible choice." The trial court should not have "required Howard to choose between his Sixth Amendment right to cross-examine Dr. Martin and his Sixth Amendment right to exclude the unreliable hearsay confession of a co-conspirator."

Is a 911 Call Subject to the Confrontation Clause?

Often, the State will seek to introduce a recording of a 911 phone call as evidence. May the State do so? Obviously, a defendant cannot cross-examine an audio/video recording. In *Davis v. Washington*, the Supreme Court addressed this issue.[173] The Court essentially answered that the use of a 911 recording is not a violation of the Confrontation Clause, but there may be some circumstances where it is.

The Court attempted to draw a line between testimony that is to prove what happened and testimony that is given to stop an emergency situation. The Court explained:

> Statements are nontestimonial when made in the course of police interrogation under circumstances objectively indicating that the primary purpose of the interrogation is to enable police assistance to meet an ongoing emergency. They are testimonial when the circumstances objectively indicate that there is no such ongoing emergency, and that the primary purpose of the interrogation is to establish or prove past events potentially relevant to later criminal prosecution.

---

[172] *Howard v. Walker*, 406 F.3d 114 (2d Cir. 2005) (note that this case is pre-*Crawford*).
[173] 547 U.S. 813 (2006).

The court placed a 911 call into the first category, that of "nontestimonial." Since the Confrontation Clause only applies to testimonial evidence, it does not apply to a 911 call.

Thus, "statements made during a 911 call for the purpose of facilitating police assistance" do not fall within the Confrontation Clause.[174] If, however, someone makes a 911 call after an emergency has concluded, the contents of the call may be considered testimonial, and the use of the audio/video recording will be a violation of the Sixth Amendment's Confrontation Clause.

Do Lab Reports Violate the Confrontation Clause?

Whether the State may use a lab report without producing the author of the report for cross-examination is a question that has not adequately been addressed by the Supreme Court. The Supreme Court has issued conflicting decisions, one with a clearer holding and one with a plurality decision, that are hard to square with each other. In a dissent to a denial of certiorari, Justice Gorsuch wrote, "This Court's most recent foray in this field, *Williams v. Illinois*, 567 U.S. 50 (2012), yielded no majority and its various opinions have sown confusion in courts across the country."[175] Interestingly enough, Justice Sotomayor joined the dissent.

The conflicting holdings and the lack of clear rule of law cause a major problem for petitioners in their writs of habeas corpus. As you will recall, the AEDPA (28 U.S. Code § 2254(d)) requires that the petitioner show that the state court's decision "resulted in a decision that was contrary to, or involved an unreasonable application of, clearly established Federal law, as determined by the Supreme Court of the United States." If the federal law is in flux, the federal court cannot determine that a state court's application of the law was unreasonable.

In *Washington v. Griffin*, the Second Circuit affirmed the denial of a writ of habeas corpus, in which the petitioner argued that

---

[174] *United States v. Fryberg*, 854 F. 3d 1126 (9th Cir. 2017)
[175] *Stuart v. Alabama*, 586 U.S. 202 (2018) (cert. denied).

the use of a DNA report violated his Sixth Amendment right to confront witnesses because he was not afforded an opportunity to cross-examine the author of the DNA report. The Court wrote, "A state court cannot be faulted for declining to apply a specific legal rule that has not been squarely established by [the Supreme] Court, nor even for incorrectly applying an established rule where reasonable jurists could disagree as to its application."[176]

In *Washington v. Griffin*, Chief Judge Katzmann authored a concurring opinion in which he suggests "an easier and more efficient route. For cases scheduled for trial, the prosecution could order that a defendant's DNA sample be collected and tested again and supervised by an analyst who is prepared and qualified to testify." He offers this time-consuming and costly suggestion as a practical solution, which suggests how big the problem is in Chief Judge Katzmann's eyes. What is clear is that the use of a lab report at trial, absent testimony of the author of the report, is potentially problematic. Sooner or later, the Supreme Court will have to weigh in on this issue, as argued by Justices Gorsuch and Sotomayor.

The Confrontation Clause Can Be Waived or Forfeited

A defendant can waive or forfeit the Sixth Amendment right to confront witnesses. Specifically, wrongful conduct, such as threats to the witness, violence, or murder, may result in a waiver of a Sixth Amendment right to confront witnesses.[177]

Effective Assistance of Counsel

The Sixth Amendment provides that "the accused shall … have the Assistance of Counsel for his defense." A petitioner is not only entitled to assistance of counsel but also to *effective* assistance of counsel.[178] In *Strickland v. Washington*, the Supreme Court articulated its famous two-part test to determine when a petitioner received ineffective

---

[176] 876 F.3d 395 (2d Cir. 2017).

[177] *United States v. Stewart*, 485 F.3d 666 (2d Cir. 2017).

[178] *McMann v. Richardson*, 397 U.S. 759, 771, fn. 14 (1970).

assistance of counsel.[179] First, the conduct of the attorney "fell below an objective standard of reasonableness." Second, "there is a reasonable probability that, but for counsel's unprofessional errors, the result of the proceeding would have been different. A reasonable probability is a probability sufficient to undermine confidence in the outcome."

The *Strickland* test "is rigorous, and the great majority of habeas petitions that allege constitutionally ineffective counsel founder on that standard."[180] In *Strickland*, the Court highlighted that "Judicial scrutiny of counsel's performance must be highly deferential." The AEDPA is also highly deferential to the state court's decision. The combination of these two deferential standards results in a situation where "[e]stablishing that a state court's application of Strickland was unreasonable under § 2254(d) is all the more difficult."[181] The Court has referred to this standard as "doubly deferential."[182] As well, "because the Strickland standard is a general standard, a state court has even more latitude to reasonably determine that a defendant has not satisfied that standard."[183]

Nonetheless, courts do grant writs of habeas corpus based on ineffective assistance of counsel. In *United States v. Nolan*,[184] there were significant problems with the lineup procedure that the police used, yet the petitioner's attorney failed to challenge the eyewitness identifications with a pre-trial motion. Then, at trial, the attorney failed "to call or even consult an expert to testify about the unreliability of the eyewitness identifications under the egregious circumstances presented in this case." The petitioner's attorney also "made no effort to preclude the Government from introducing a highly prejudicial Facebook photo of Nolan posing with what appears to be a handgun,

---

[179] *Strickland v. Washington*, 466 U.S. 668 (1984).

[180] *Lindstadt v. Keane*, 239 F.3d 191, 199 (2d Cir. 2001).

[181] *Harrington v. Richter*, 562 U.S. 86 (2011).

[182] *Cullen v. Pinholster*, 563 U.S. 170 (2011).

[183] *Knowles v. Mirzayance*, 556 U.S. 111 (2009).

[184] 956 F.3d 71 (2d Cir. 2020).

but which was actually a BB gun." The Court held that each of these omissions violated the petitioner's right to effective assistance of counsel.

In the following section, we will present some common scenarios where courts have granted writs based on ineffective assistance of counsel. Our presentation is intended to provide a detailed explanation about the different types of situations where parties sought and obtained a writ of habeas corpus. The reader should keep in mind that ineffective assistance of counsel claims are highly fact sensitive, and the rules of law must be applied to the specific facts of each case. What is presented below is intended as an overview and a starting point for ineffective assistance of counsel.

Failure To Investigate Mitigating Evidence

In *Andrus v. Texas*,[185] the petitioner was sentenced to death. He argued in his writ that he had received ineffective assistance of counsel for failure to investigate and present mitigating evidence at sentencing. Had counsel investigated the petitioner's background, counsel would have learned that petitioner's mother was addicted to drugs, worked as a prostitute, disappeared for weeks at a time, and brought home abusive boyfriends. Petitioner was sent to a juvenile detention facility at the age of 16, where he became "steeped in gang culture, dosed on high quantities of psychotropic drugs, and frequently relegated to extended stints of solitary confinement. The ordeal left an already traumatized Andrus all but suicidal." The decision notes the existence of other mitigating evidence, which was presented to the court in support of the petitioner's writ of habeas corpus.

The highest court in Texas decided that the petitioner received effective assistance of counsel and denied his state writ of habeas corpus. The Supreme Court disagreed, holding that the attorney's conduct fell below an objective standard of reasonableness:

---

[185] ____ .U.S 590 (2020).

Here, the habeas record reveals that Andrus' counsel fell short of his obligation in multiple ways: First, counsel performed almost no mitigation investigation, overlooking vast tranches of mitigating evidence. Second, due to counsel's failure to investigate compelling mitigating evidence, what little evidence counsel did present backfired by bolstering the State's aggravation case. Third, counsel failed adequately to investigate the State's aggravating evidence, thereby forgoing critical opportunities to rebut the case in aggravation. Taken together, those deficiencies effected an unconstitutional abnegation of prevailing professional norms.

The Supreme Court remanded the case back to the Texas court to determine if the petitioner was prejudiced by his counsel's deficient conduct. Prejudice is the second prong of the *Strickland* test, as mentioned earlier.

On May 19, 2021, the Texas Court of Criminal Appeals held that the petitioner was not prejudiced by his counsel's conduct and denied the writ of habeas corpus.[186] It is likely that Andrus will once again file a writ of habeas corpus in federal court, arguing that his Sixth Amendment rights were violated due to ineffective assistance of counsel.

In a similar case, the Supreme Court granted a petition for writ of habeas corpus, which was based on a failure to present mitigating evidence.[187] In that case, the mitigating evidence included the petitioner's "abusive childhood, his heroic military service and the trauma he suffered because of it, his long-term substance abuse, and his impaired mental health and mental capacity."

Recently, the Ninth Circuit granted a writ of habeas corpus for failure to investigate and present mitigating evidence at the penalty-phase of a trial. "Counsel's failure to investigate Noguera's background led to the failure to uncover an abundance of relevant and

---

[186] *Ex Parte Andrus*, 622 S.W.3d 892 (Tex. Crim. App. 2021).

[187] *Porter v. McCollum*, 558 U.S. 30 (2009).

87

compelling mitigating evidence. This failure undermines confidence in the outcome of the penalty phase."[188] The Ninth Circuit recently granted another writ of habeas corpus when an attorney "failed to request a mental health expert in advance of the sentencing hearing" and failed "to seek neurological or neuropsychological testing prior to sentencing."[189]

Use of Evidence Detrimental to the Defendant

Though difficult to believe, there are times when an attorney presents evidence that is *harmful* to his or her client. In *Buck v. Davis*,[190] the petitioner's attorney used an expert witness at sentencing who testified that the petitioner was likely to act violently in the future. The expert wrote in his report, "Race. Black: Increased probability." The expert also testified that race is a factor in predicting future violence. The expert's testimony made it more likely that the petitioner would receive the death penalty.[191]

The Supreme Court held this to be ineffective assistance of counsel because "[n]o competent defense attorney would introduce such evidence about his own client." Even worse, the expert argued that the petitioner was more likely to commit a violent act in the future because of his race. "Dr. Quijano's report said, in effect, that the color of Buck's skin made him more deserving of execution. It would be patently unconstitutional for a state to argue that a defendant is liable to be a future danger because of his race," yet the petitioner's own attorney made that argument!

The Court held that the attorney's conduct prejudiced the petitioner. Noting the speculative nature of determining whether someone is more likely to commit a violent act in the future, the Court pointed out that the expert's report showed "one thing would never change: the color of Buck's skin. Buck would always be black. And

---

[188] *Noguera v. Davis*, No. 17-99010 (9th Cir. July 20, 2021).

[189] *Jones v. Ryan*, 1 F.4th 1179 (9th Cir. 2021).

[190] 137 S. Ct. 759 (2017).

[191] We will discuss racial bias later in this chapter.

according to Dr. Quijano, that immutable characteristic carried with it an '[i]ncreased probability' of future violence. Here was hard statistical evidence—from an expert—to guide an otherwise speculative inquiry."

The Court continued, "The effect of this unusual confluence of factors was to provide support for making a decision on life or death on the basis of race."

Failure To Investigate Facts of the Case

In *Browning v. Baker*, Browning was convicted of murder and sentenced to death.[192] He was accused of robbing a jewelry store and murdering the owner of the store. The Ninth Circuit highlighted the lack of evidence to convict Browning and concluded that "[t]he upshot is that the prosecution presented a fundamentally weak case."

The court then turned to the ineffective assistance of counsel argument. One of the attorney's biggest failures was his failure to investigate the source of a bloody footprint at the scene of the crime. The attorney claimed that his failure to investigate was a trial strategy, saying that "if he attempted to determine the source of the shoeprints and discovered that the source was paramedics or responding officers, he would disprove his own theory that the prints were left by the assailant." The State court accepted this argument.

The Ninth Circuit, applying the reasonableness standard to evaluate AEDPA claims, held that the state court unreasonably applied the *Strickland* test. "Under *Strickland*, counsel's investigation must determine strategy, not the other way around." An attorney cannot fail to investigate on the basis that whatever he or she may find will undermine the attorney's theory or the trial. Rather, the *facts* must shape the trial strategy.

The court did acknowledge, however, that "when a decision not to investigate particular facts may be reasonable *when the attorney has reason to believe* doing so would reveal inculpatory evidence."

_____

[192] 875 F.3d 444 (9th Cir. 2017).

In *Weeden v. Johnson*, the court granted a petitioner's writ of habeas corpus, reversed her conviction, and ordered a new trial.[193] Weeden was 14 years old when she planned a robbery that resulted in the death of the victim. She was convicted of robbery and felony murder. Her attorney did not seek to have Weeden evaluated by a psychologist and did not retain an expert to testify about how "youth" would have affected Weeden's mental state. The Court held that "Weeden's counsel could not have reasonably concluded that obtaining a psychological examination would conflict with his trial strategy without first knowing what such an examination would reveal."

"The correct inquiry is not whether psychological evidence would have supported a preconceived trial strategy, but whether Weeden's counsel had a duty to investigate such evidence in order to form a trial strategy, considering 'all the circumstances.' *Strickland*, 466 U.S. at 691, 104 S. Ct. 2052. The answer is yes." In this case, Weeden's mental state was important since she was charged with felony murder, which requires "specific intent to commit the underlying felony."

The *Weeden* case provides a good opportunity to review the standard of review under the AEDPA. As we discussed at length earlier, the federal courts apply a deferential standard to a state court's decision in a writ of habeas corpus. But, if the state court decision does not address an issue, the federal court may apply its own review of the issue. In *Weeden*, the state court did not determine whether Weeden was prejudiced by her attorney's performance. The psychologist's report showed that Weeden was "slow to understand" what was happening and was "quite passive and vulnerable to being manipulated by others." This evidence would have shown that Weeden did not have the required mental state for the crime and would have undermined the witness's testimony about Weeden. Consequently, the Ninth Circuit applied its own review and held that there was a "reasonable

---

[193] 854 F.3d 1063 (9th Cir. 2017).

probability" that the jury would have reached a different conclusion had the jury been presented with the psychologist's testimony. The Court granted the writ.

In another case where the court granted a writ of habeas corpus based on counsel's failure to investigate the facts of the case, *Cannedy v. Adams*, a witness had information about the victim's potential motive to lie. The court held that "[c]ompetent counsel would not have failed to interview such a potentially important witness or to introduce the significant exculpatory evidence that she could have provided."[194] The failure to do so was prejudicial because:

> The prosecution's case rested on the jury's believing A.G.'s
> allegations, and its case was already weakened by
> inconsistencies in the government witnesses' testimony. Thus,
> had [the] evidence ... been admitted, it was reasonably likely
> that at least one juror would have ... concluded that a
> reasonable doubt existed as to whether A.G. fabricated her
> allegations.

The *Cannedy* case is a good illustration of how the *prejudice* prong works. To find prejudice, the court compared the weakness of the prosecution's evidence with the strength of the evidence that the attorney had failed to investigate. The court held that the allegations of ineffective assistance of counsel met the *Strickland* test "whether it is reasonably likely the result would have been different."

Failure To Interview Witness Before Allowing the Witness To Testify
The Ninth Circuit assumes "that it ordinarily falls below the *Strickland* level of required competence to put a witness on the stand without interviewing him. We look then to the question of prejudice."[195]

---

[194] *Cannedy v. Adams*, 706 F.3d 1148 (9th Cir. 2013).
[195] *Jackson v. Calderon*, 211 F.3d 1148 (9th Cir. 2000) (finding that no prejudice).

Failure To Object to Inflammatory Closing Argument

In *Zapata v. Vasquez*,[196] the prosecutor argued in closing arguments that the defendant shouted racist and ethnic epithets at the victim right before shooting the victim. The court highlighted two major problems with the prosecutor's claim. First, the prosecutor simply made it up. There was no evidence at trial about what was said to the victim prior to the shooting. Second, the claim was highly inflammatory.

Zapata was convicted of first-degree murder with numerous enhancements and was "sentenced to two consecutive terms of 25 years to life in prison." In his writ of habeas corpus, he argued that his conviction must be reversed due to prosecutorial misconduct and ineffective assistance of counsel. He argued that this attorney should have objected to the inflammatory and false comments made during the prosecution's closing argument. Due to procedural issues, the court did not consider the claim of prosecutorial misconduct but considered it in relation to the claim of ineffective assistance of counsel.

The California state court held that prosecutorial misconduct was clear, stating that "the fiction thus spun by the prosecutor was both inflammatory and wholly extraneous to any issue properly before the jury." The state court, however, held that Zapata's attorney may have had a "tactical reason" for not objecting to the closing argument and denied the writ.

The federal court held that the state's determination was unreasonable. Typically, a failure to object during opening or closing arguments is within an attorney's discretion, and a failure to object is not ineffective. However, in this case, "the remarks—fabricated from whole cloth, designed to inflame the passions of the jury and delivered in the waning moments of trial—unquestionably were 'egregious misstatements.'"

For prejudice, the federal court evaluated the evidence and concluded that the evidence to convict was weak. It was based on eyewitnesses who all had various grudges against Zapata. One witness

---

[196] 788 F.3d 1106 (9th Cir. 2015).

was Zapata's ex-girlfriend; one witness was upset at Zapata for beating up her boyfriend; etc.

The federal court granted the writ of habeas corpus, stating, "Defense counsel's failure to object to the prosecutor's inflammatory, fabricated and ethnically charged epithets, delivered in the moments before the jury was sent to deliberate Zapata's case, constituted ineffective assistance of counsel."

Failure To Object to Venue/Lack of Knowledge of the Law
In *Cornell v. Kirkpatrick*,[197] Cornell was charged with the rape of two women on two separate occasions. His trial was held in Ontario County, despite the fact that one of the women alleged that she had been raped in Monroe County. Cornell's attorney did not object to the trial on Ontario County, which was obviously the wrong venue (location) for a trial for one of the alleged rapes.

The prosecution argued that it had jurisdiction for both cases in Ontario County, based on an incorrect application of the law. Cornell's attorney did not research New York law, so he was not aware of the incorrect application of the law. In New York, a defendant must be tried in the county where the crime allegedly occurred. The limited exception to this rule, which was cited by the prosecutor, clearly did not apply to the facts of the case, and Cornell's attorney should have known that. Therefore, the attorney's performance was deficient.

The court then turned to the prejudice prong of the *Strickland* analysis. The court held that Cornell was prejudiced because, had his attorney argued that the prosecution failed to satisfy its burden of proof in showing that the alleged rape was committed in Ontario County, "the jury would have found by at least a preponderance of the evidence that Victim # 2's alleged rape happened in Monroe County," and the charge would have been dismissed.

The court held, "Cornell's counsel, for no strategic reason, did not raise a likely meritorious challenge to venue and thus allowed for

---

[197] 665 F.3d 369 (2d Cir. 2011).

the allegations of both victims to be tried simultaneously." The court, therefore, granted the writ of habeas corpus and reversed the conviction for one of the rapes.

Failure To Research the Law

In 2014, the Supreme Court noted, "An attorney's ignorance of a point of law that is fundamental to his case combined with his failure to perform basic research on that point is a quintessential example of unreasonable performance under *Strickland*."[198] The Court remanded the case to the lower court to determine whether the petitioner was prejudiced by the attorney's ignorance and failure to perform basic research.

Failure To Object to Erroneous Jury Instruction

In *Cox v. Donnelly*,[199] the judge gave an instruction to the jury that placed the burden on the defendant to prove his innocence, as opposed to placing the burden on the prosecution to show the defendant's guilt. The Supreme Court previously held that when intent is an issue, a jury instruction that says "the law presumes that a person intends the ordinary consequences of his voluntary acts" is unconstitutional.[200] The Supreme Court stated that this type of jury instruction "violates the Fourteenth Amendment's requirement that the State prove every element of a criminal offense beyond a reasonable doubt."

In *Cox*, the Court found that "we cannot characterize counsel's failure to object to any of the three unconstitutional intent instructions as 'reasonable.'" For prejudice, the Court noted that "the jury made two requests for supplemental instruction on intent," and the jury announced that it was deadlocked before eventually finding Cox to be guilty. The Court highlighted that the "chronology attests to the significance of the intent issue in the jury's deliberations, and

---

[198] *Hinton v. Alabama*, 571 U.S. 263 (2014).
[199] 387 F.3d 193 (2d Cir. 2004); 432 F.3d 388 (2d Cir. 2005).
[200] *Sandstrom v. Montana*, 442 U.S. 510 (1979).

establishes the magnitude of the error counsel made in failing to object to the erroneous charge."

In addressing whether the state court's determination was an unreasonable application of the law, the Court held, "Where counsel, for no strategic reason, repeatedly fails to object to a clearly unconstitutional charge on the key issue in a criminal case, the rejection of an ineffectiveness claim on that basis simply cannot be viewed as reasonable."

Failure To Investigate Possible Mental Illness

The Court has found ineffective assistance of counsel when "trial counsel failed to conduct any investigation at all into his client's psychiatric history and therefore neglected to pursue a potentially successful defense."[201] In that case, the attorney had actual knowledge of the petitioner's "extensive history of mental problems" yet failed to investigate the extent of the mental illness and failed to consider the effect of the mental illness on the trial strategy. For the prejudice prong, the Court noted that *malice* was an element of the crime, and had the attorney investigated and presented evidence of the petitioner's mental illness, a reasonable probability existed that the jury would have found the petitioner not guilty of *intentional* murder. The Court granted the petition for writ of habeas corpus.

In a similar case, the Court held that a "failure to arrange a psychiatric examination or utilize available psychiatric information also falls below acceptable performance standards." The attorney in that case did not interview witnesses and did not conduct an investigation into the facts of the case. The Court remanded the case for a consideration of whether the petitioner was prejudiced by his attorney's deficient performance.[202]

---

[201] *Seidel v. Merkle*, 146 F.3d 750 (9th Cir. 1998).
[202] *Turner v. Duncan*, 158 F.3d 449 (9th Cir. 1998).

Conflicts of Interest

"Where a constitutional right to counsel exists, our Sixth Amendment cases hold that there is a correlative right to representation that is free from conflicts of interest."[203] To show a conflict of interest, "a defendant who raised no objection at trial must demonstrate that an actual conflict of interest adversely affected his lawyer's performance."[204] The Supreme Court subsequently clarified that "'an actual conflict of interest' meant precisely a conflict that affected counsel's performance—as opposed to a mere theoretical division of loyalties."[205] Similarly, in a footnote in another case, the court wrote, "An 'actual conflict,' for Sixth Amendment purposes, is a conflict of interest that adversely affects counsel's performance." The key question "is what the advocate [found] himself compelled to refrain from doing because of the conflict."[206]

When there is an actual conflict of interest that adversely affects an attorney's performance, the petitioner is not required to show prejudice. The Court has "simply presumed such effect, where assistance of counsel has been denied entirely or during a critical stage of the proceeding. When that has occurred, the likelihood that the verdict is unreliable is so high that a case-by-case inquiry is unnecessary."[207] Ineffective assistance of counsel, due to a conflict of interest, is an exception to the *Strickland* rule, which requires a showing of prejudice. If an actual conflict of interest is established, a petitioner need not show prejudice, which is presumed.

One example of a situation where there is a conflict of interest that adversely affects an attorney's performance is when an attorney represents co-defendants and fails to take a certain action on behalf of one defendant on the basis that the action will harm the other defendant. In *Mickens v. Taylor*, the Court wrote that it has "stressed

---

[203] *Wood v. Georgia*, 450 U.S. 261 (1981).

[204] *Cuyler v. Sullivan*, 446 U.S. 335 (1980).

[205] *Mickens v. Taylor*, 535 U.S. 162 (2002).

[206] *Lockhart v. Terhune*, 250 F.3d 1223 (9th Cir. 2001).

[207] *Mickens v. Taylor*, 535 U.S. 162 (2002).

the high probability of prejudice arising from multiple concurrent representation." Nonetheless, a petitioner must show that an actual conflict of interest existed.

In *Lockhart v. Terhune*, the Ninth Circuit granted a petitioner's writ of habeas corpus. The petitioner was charged with the murder of two people, and the prosecutor introduced evidence that the petitioner had previously murdered a third person (though the petitioner was not charged with this murder). "The prosecution offered evidence of Lockhart's alleged involvement in the Cooper killing in order to establish Lockhart's identity as the perpetrator in the Lane and Jamerson shooting."

Petitioner's counsel represented someone else who was connected to the first murder. The attorney did not argue that the petitioner was innocent of committing the first murder since to do so would implicate the attorney's other client. The Court wrote that the attorney, named Hove, "was unable to exploit this defense fully. We can discern no tactical justification for Hove's decisions and, therefore, conclude that he was likely motivated by a desire to protect his other client." Though it is possible to waive a conflict of interest, the Court held "that Lockhart's waiver of his attorney's conflict of interest was not knowing and intelligent." For these reasons, the Court granted the writ of habeas corpus and ordered that the petitioner either be released or for the state to hold a new trial.

Another example of a possible conflict of interest occurred in *Alberni v. McDaniel*.[208] In that case, the petitioner's attorney failed to impeach a witness who was a former client of the attorney. The court listed a litany of items that the attorney did not ask about:

> Mr. Buchanan proceeded to cross-examine Mr. Flamm. He did not impeach Mr. Flamm with his prior felony conviction. He did not impeach Mr. Flamm based on the fact that he violated his probation when he accepted drugs from Mr. Alberni. He did not impeach Mr. Flamm with the inconsistencies in his

---

[208] 458 F.3d 860 (9th Cir. 2006).

testimony. He did not impeach Mr. Flamm by pointing out the inconsistencies between his and Mr. Alberni's testimony. Although he did ask him whether he had heard Mr. Alberni had called him a rat, he did not press Mr. Flamm on whether he was angered by that. He did not question Mr. Flamm regarding who started the altercation. He did not press Mr. Flamm when he contended he did not remember Mr. McElroy being present. He did not ask Mr. Flamm about Mr. Alberni's claim that he hit him with his hand, not with a gun.

In all fairness to the attorney in *Alberni v. McDaniel*, the attorney raised the conflict-of-interest issue and was told by the court, "I hereby absolve you of any possible conflict of interest and the issue that is before the Court." The cross-examination was brief; it took up only three pages of the transcript. The Ninth Circuit remanded the matter for a hearing to determine whether there was a "link between deficient performance and the conflict of interest." The Court wanted to know if there were "legitimate tactical reasons for Mr. Buchanan's decision not to impeach Mr. Flamm on these matters. We will not speculate about his cross-examination strategy."

Outside of issues involving joint representation, it is unclear if the court can presume prejudice in conflict-of-interest cases. In *Mickens*, the Court highlighted "the high probability of prejudice arising from multiple concurrent representation, and the difficulty of proving that prejudice … Not all attorney conflicts present comparable difficulties." Based on this, subsequent courts have been unwilling to find a conflict of interest in other situations. We now turn to two of those situations.

Conflict Due to Romantic Considerations—In *Earp v. Ornoski*,[209] the petitioner's attorney entered into a relationship with the petitioner. The Court held that the petitioner must show prejudice from the potential conflict, and the petitioner did not do so. The exception to

---

[209] 431 F.3d 1158 (9th Cir. 2005).

the *Strickland* rule does not apply "to conflicts stemming from intimate relations with clients."

The Ninth Circuit also relied on the standard of review under the AEDPA. The court deferred to the state court's determination, which was not unreasonable. The court wrote the following:

> Although we would perhaps reach a different conclusion if addressing this claim on direct review, the Supreme Court has not spoken to this issue and has expressly limited its constitutional conflicts jurisprudence. Accordingly, we hold that the state court's determination ... was neither contrary to, nor an unreasonable application of, established federal law.

This case serves as a good reminder of how the AEDPA changed the standards for writs of habeas corpus, despite President Clinton's claim to the contrary.

Though the court denied the conflict-of-interest claim, the court remanded the case for a hearing about ineffective assistance of counsel for failure to present mitigating evidence, and for prosecutorial misconduct. Upon remand, the district court again denied the petitioner's writ, which then reached the Ninth Circuit for the second time. The Ninth Circuit again remanded the case for another evidentiary hearing about the prosecutorial misconduct claim.[210]

In the district court for a third time, the court denied the writ, and the claim reached the Ninth Circuit for the third time. This time, however, the Ninth Circuit affirmed the denial of the petitioner's writ and allowed the petitioner's death sentence to stand.[211] Mr. Earp filed his writ in 2001, and it was ultimately denied in 2018. He filed a *writ of certiorari* for the United States Supreme Court to agree to hear the case. The writ of certiorari was denied in the end of 2018.

Monetary Conflict—In one case, the court agreed to allow a last-minute substitution of attorney when the new attorneys agreed to

---

[210] *Earp v. Cullen*, 623 F.3d 1065 (9th Cir. 2010).
[211] *Earp v. Davis*, 881 F.3d 1135 (9th Cir. 2018).

be ready by the trial date.[212] On the morning of the trial date, the attorneys filed a motion for a continuance of the trial. The court told the attorneys that they could either try the case that day or that the court would grant the continuance and the attorneys would pay $3,600 for the witness and jury fees that would be incurred due to the delay. The attorneys chose the trial, even though the attorneys were not fully prepared. The attorneys also expressed concern that the payment would be considered a "sanction," and they would have to report the sanction to the California bar.

One issue in the case is whether the attorneys' choice of holding the trial without being fully prepared, in order to avoid being sanctioned and having to report that sanction to the California bar, was a conflict of interest. If yes, then the petitioner does not have to show *actual prejudice*, which is presumed. If no, then the petitioner must show that she was prejudiced by the attorneys' decision.

The Court issued a confusing decision. The Court assumed, without deciding, that prejudice should be presumed to pecuniary conflicts of interest yet decided that the presumption should not apply to this case. The Court reasoned that a presumption of prejudice applies when it is difficult to determine if a petitioner was prejudiced and there is a substantial likelihood of prejudice. In this case, the petitioner simply alleged that her attorneys were unprepared but did not allege that the result would have been different had the attorneys prepared for trial. On this basis, the Court denied the writ of habeas corpus.

The concurring opinion agreed with the result but accused the Court of creating "a new rule." If there was an actual conflict, then prejudice is presumed. The concurring opinion highlighted that the Court held that an actual conflict existed but did not presume prejudice. In the concurring opinion, the judge "would hold that there was no 'actual conflict' that adversely affected counsel's performance, and thus Sullivan's presumed prejudice rule did not apply."

---

[212] *United States v. Walter-Eze*, 869 F.3d 891 (9th Cir. 2017).

Conflict of Interest Due to an Attorney's Racism

Ezzard Ellis was convicted of murder with a special circumstance, attempted murder, and robbery and was sentenced to life without the possibility of parole. In 2003, seven years after his conviction became final, Ellis received from an article from a friend, in which attorney Donald Ames had made numerous racist comments. The article quoted Ames' daughters, who described their father's "frequent use of deprecating remarks and racial slurs about his clients."

Ames had represented Ellis in Ellis' trial. Ellis obtained declarations from Ames' daughters and from numerous other people who heard Ames use racial epithets to describe clients, court staff, and other attorneys. Ellis argued that he had been deprived of effective assistance of counsel since his attorney was racist.

Initially, the Court denied the writ of habeas corpus.[213] The Court reasoned that Ellis did not show either a deficient performance or prejudice from the racism. The Court held, "When defense counsel does not express his racist views to his client, no conflict will be presumed, and the defendant must show both deficient performance and prejudice to establish a Sixth Amendment violation."

In 2020, after Ellis petitioned for a rehearing in banc, the government changed its position and agreed with Ellis.[214] The Court then granted the writ of habeas corpus with the following instructions: "On remand, the district court is directed to enter an order granting a conditional writ of habeas corpus, releasing Ellis from custody unless the State of California retries him within a reasonable period of time."

The Court did not explain its rationale, and three judges signed a concurring opinion to explain the rationale of the case. Remember the standard of review that federal courts apply to state court decisions? The concurring opinion noted that the state court had applied the wrong legal standard, which allowed the federal court to

---

[213] *Ellis v. Harrison*, 891 F.3d 1160 (9th Cir. 2018).
[214] *Ellis v. Harrison*, 947 F.3d 555 (9th Cir. 2020).

review the case *de novo*, which means "anew." On a *de novo* review, the court does not have to be deferential to the state court decision.

The Ninth Circuit presumed prejudice to Ellis. "A trial is fundamentally unfair if defense counsel harbors extreme and deep-rooted ill will toward the defendant on account of his race." The Court noted:

> Counsel's performance is the sum of countless discretionary actions—and inactions—on behalf of a client.... When defense counsel makes these discretionary decisions in disregard of the client's interests on account of counsel's racism, the cumulative effect will be to impair the defense, but there is no way to pinpoint how it does so.

The concurring opinion limited its decision to situations where "a lawyer's racial bias against racial minorities is so extreme and deep-rooted that it would be impossible for him to fairly represent a non-white defendant." In this case, the concurring opinion stated that "[t]he overwhelming evidence of his virulent racism is reliable, coming from his family and colleagues. That Ames felt free to express his racial hatred in the office and at the courthouse indicates [that] he did not know or care that his views were unprofessional as well as repugnant." The court granted the writ of habeas corpus.

This case illustrates the importance of being persistent in filing a writ of habeas corpus and the value of patience. The petitioner filed his writ in state court in 2003 and filed his federal writ in 2005. After numerous remands and evidentiary hearings, the writ was granted in 2020.

The case also illustrates the importance of considering new arguments that were not raised in previous cases and for which no case law exists to support the claim. The petitioner argued that he received ineffective assistance of counsel due to conflict of interest. The conflict of interest occurred because the petitioner's attorney was a racist. Prior to this case, there was no case that held that a racist attorney created a conflict of interest that warranted a new trial. Ellis, the petitioner, created precedent for other incarcerated individuals.

While the court in *Ellis* granted the writ of habeas corpus, it was the concurring decision that provided the rationale. Although the concurring decision is not binding precedent on future cases, it should be cited to in depth in relevant cases, and a future petitioner may urge the court to accept the rationale in the concurring opinion as the rule of law.

Ineffective Assistance During Plea Negotiations
A defendant is entitled to effective assistance of counsel during plea negotiations.[215] If an attorney unreasonably advises a defendant to reject a plea offer, a petitioner may argue that he or she received ineffective assistance of counsel.

In *Lafler v. Cooper*, the prosecution offered a plea deal of 51–85 months in exchange for a guilty plea. The defendant's attorney advised him to reject to deal because, in the attorney's opinion, the prosecution would not be able to prove its case. The defendant was found guilty and sentenced to a minimum 185–360--month sentence.

The Supreme Court looked to the *Strickland* factors that we have addressed extensively in this section. First, "all parties agree the performance of respondent's counsel was deficient when he advised respondent to reject the plea offer on the grounds he could not be convicted at trial." The prejudice prong was the more complicated factor. The Court held that there is a "reasonable probability" that the petitioner would have accepted the plea and that the conviction and/or sentence "would have been less severe."

After addressing the *Strickland* factors, the Court turned to fashioning a remedy for the ineffective assistance of counsel. The Court essentially held that the appropriate remedy would be for the prosecution to re-offer the plea deal.

In *Hill v. Lockhart*, an earlier Supreme Court case, the Supreme Court addressed the reverse scenario when a defendant pleaded guilty due to ineffective assistance of counsel. In that case,

---

[215] *See Hill v. Lockhart*, 474 U.S. 52 (1985); *Lafler v. Cooper*, 566 U.S. 156 (2012).

Hill pleaded guilty to first-degree murder and theft. In his petition for writ of habeas corpus, Hill argued that his attorney had failed to inform him that, as a second offender, he would have to serve half of his sentence before he could be eligible for parole. Hill alleged that his attorney had told him that he'd be eligible for parole after completing one third of his sentence.

The Court applied the *Strickland* test and found that Hill had failed to allege prejudice since Hill "did not allege in his habeas petition that, had counsel correctly informed him about his parole eligibility date, he would have pleaded not guilty and insisted on going to trial."

In *Missouri v. Frye*, the petitioner was arrested for driving without a license, for the fourth time.[216] Because the petitioner was arrested for the fourth time for the same infraction, Missouri law provides that the petitioner could have been charged with a felony and could have been sentenced to up to four years in prison. The prosecutor offered to reduce the charge to a misdemeanor and to a sentence of 90 days in prison in exchange for a guilty plea. Mr. Frye's attorney, however, never informed him of the offer, which lapsed.

The Court applied the *Strickland* test and remanded to determine if the petitioner was prejudiced. Even though the petitioner alleged that he would have accepted the offer had he been told about it, Missouri has a quirk in its law that allows the prosecution to cancel plea offers and the court to reject plea offers. Since Frye was arrested *for a fifth time* for driving without a license while this case was pending, it is possible that the prosecutor would have withdrawn the plea or that the court would have rejected the plea.

In response to the decision in *Frye*, some courts hold a *Frye* hearing. In this hearing, the court ensures that a defendant has full knowledge of a plea offer and that the defendant knowingly and willingly rejects the plea offer.[217] "In a *Frye* hearing, the court strives

---

[216] 566 U.S. 134 (2012).

[217] *See, e.g., United States v. Albarran*, 943 F.3d 106 (2d Cir. 2019).

to ensure that a full and accurate communication on the subject has occurred."

The Attorney Told the Defendant the Wrong Maximum Sentence

Relating to the previous section about plea bargains, what happens if a defendant rejects a plea offer when the defendant was misinformed about the maximum sentence that he could receive at trial?

In *United States v. Gordon*, the petitioner's counsel told him that his sentence would be 120 months if convicted and 92–115 months if the petitioner accepted the plea deal, though the attorney also mentioned that he believed the sentence would come down to 84 months.[218] The petitioner rejected the deal. When the petitioner's attorney received the pre-sentencing report and saw that the sentencing range was 262–327 months, the attorney informed the court that he had misinformed the petitioner about the sentence range. The attorney asked to be relieved, and another attorney was appointed to argue ineffective assistance of counsel. The court denied the claim and sentenced the petitioner to 210 months in prison.

Since the claim originated in federal court, the petitioner filed a 28 U.S.C. § 2255 motion (the federal equivalent of a writ of habeas corpus), arguing that his Sixth Amendment rights were violated. The district court agreed and granted the writ, and the Second Circuit Court of Appeals affirmed the district court's decision.

Both courts applied the *Strickland* test. First, "[b]y grossly underestimating Gordon's sentencing exposure in a letter to his client, Dedes breached his duty as a defense lawyer in a criminal case 'to advise his client fully on whether a particular plea to a charge appears desirable.'"

To establish prejudice, the petitioner argued that he would have accepted the plea deal had he been aware of the correct maximum sentence that he faced. The court noted that objective evidence was required because a "self-serving" statement is insufficient to establish

---

[218] 156 F.3d 376 (2d Cir. 1998).

a reasonable probability that a petitioner would have accepted a plea deal.

Here, the court found that a large disparity between a plea offer and an actual sentence is considered objective evidence that a petitioner would have accepted a plea had the petitioner been adequately represented. The petitioner's writ of habeas corpus was granted, though the court granted a new trial (and opportunity to renegotiate a plea) instead of reinstating the previous plea deal.[219]

Failure To Advise About Adverse Immigration Consequences

We have been discussing effective assistance of counsel and have addressed ineffective assistance of counsel during plea negotiations. What happens if an attorney tells a noncitizen resident of the United States that a plea will not result in a deportation, and this advice is incorrect? Under U.S. immigration law, a noncitizen who resides in the United States will be deported upon a conviction for a felony.[220]

In *Lee v. United States*,[221] the petitioner had been living in the United States for 35 years, since he was 13 years old. He was charged with the possession of drugs with intent to distribute, and he asked his attorney numerous times whether a plea deal would have immigration consequences. His attorney answered that he would not be subject to deportation. Relying on his attorney's advice, the petitioner pleaded guilty and was sentenced to one year and one day in jail.

A possible reason that this case made its way to the Supreme Court is because the petitioner's defense was weak. The government argued that the petitioner was not *prejudiced* by his attorney's mistake. The government further argued that the petitioner would have been deported even had he gone to trial since the petitioner would have unquestionably been found guilty at trial. This argument presented an

---

[219] There were some potential issues with the first plea offer in that it was not in writing and may have been intended to be a minimum.

[220] The specifics of when this applies and when it does not apply fall outside the scope of the subject of this book.

[221] 137 S. Ct. 1958 (2017).

interesting question for the Supreme Court: If a party will be found guilty anyway, did the party receive ineffective assistance of counsel by agreeing to plead guilty?

The Supreme Court rejected the government's argument. Relying on *Hill v. Lockhart*, the Court held that the courts should focus on the *decision-making*, not on the outcome. Here, the petitioner received ineffective assistance of counsel in his decision-making, which prejudiced him by causing him to make a decision (plead guilty) that he otherwise would not have made. Therefore, the petitioner received ineffective assistance of counsel.

The Supreme Court voiced its concern over accepting "*post hoc* assertions from a defendant about how he would have pleaded but for his attorney's deficiencies." In this case, the Court noted the significant amount of evidence showing that the attorney's advice about the deportation consequences was the main reason that the petitioner had agreed to plead guilty.

As to the fact that he would likely have been found guilty, the court said, "But for his attorney's incompetence, Lee would have known that accepting the plea agreement would *certainly* lead to deportation. Going to trial? *Almost* certainly." The Court noted that, had the petitioner been found guilty at trial, he would have received, perhaps, another year to his sentence. When faced with a balancing of one year in prison with a guaranteed deportation against the *possibility* of two years in prison with a deportation, the petitioner would have chosen the latter had he received effective assistance of counsel. The Supreme Court granted the writ of habeas corpus.

A few years before the *Lee* case, the Supreme Court held that an attorney must advise his or her client about any deportation risks.[222] "The weight of prevailing professional norms supports the view that counsel must advise her client regarding the risk of deportation." If the immigration law is clear about a deportation, then the attorney must inform the client. If the "deportation consequences of a particular plea

---

[222] *See Padilla v. Kentucky*, 559 U.S. 356 (2010).

are unclear or uncertain," the "attorney need do no more than advise a noncitizen client that pending criminal charges may carry a risk of adverse immigration consequences."

In 2019, the Second Circuit applied these cases to a situation where a defendant asked his attorney about the immigration consequences to entering a guilty plea and was told by his attorney that he would not be deported.[223] The court granted the petition and vacated the plea. The court was bothered by "the Government's troubling changing positions in this matter" and quoted "then-Attorney General Robert F. Kennedy's cautioning words: 'It is, after all, not the Department of Prosecution but the Department of Justice.... [T]he interest of the Government ... is not that it shall win a case, but that justice shall be done.'"[224]

Failure To File a Notice of Appeal

Typically, there is a relatively short deadline in which to file a notice of appeal. A notice of appeal is a simple document that states that the defendant will appeal the guilty verdict (or plea of guilt) and/or sentence. If a notice of appeal is not filed within the time limit, then the defendant forfeits his or her right to appeal.

In *Roe v. Flores-Ortega*,[225] the Supreme Court held that the *Strickland* test applies to claims that an attorney was ineffective for failing to file a notice of appeal. First, the court analyzed the possible scenarios: (1) the attorney was instructed to file a notice of appeal but did not do so; (2) the attorney was told not to file a notice of appeal; (3) the defendant was not clear about whether to file a notice of appeal.

---

[223] *Doe v. United States*, 915 F.3d 905 (2d Cir. 2019). Since the petitioner had been released from prison and could no longer bring a writ of habeas corpus, he filed a writ of coram nobis, one of the remedies that are available to someone who is no longer in custody but seeks to challenge a conviction.

[224] In a similar case, the Second Circuit reached the same conclusion. *See Kovacs v. United States*, 744 F.3d 44 (2d Cir. 2014).

[225] 528 U.S. 470 (2000).

The first two situations are easy to address. A failure to file a notice of appeal when instructed to do falls below an objective standard of reasonableness. "Counsel's failure to do so cannot be considered a strategic decision; filing a notice of appeal is a purely ministerial task, and the failure to file reflects inattention to the defendant's wishes." If an attorney is affirmatively told not to file a notice of appeal, however, then the attorney acts reasonably by not filing a notice of appeal.

The Court looked to when an attorney should consult with his or her client about a possible appeal and held that "counsel has a constitutionally imposed duty to consult with the defendant about an appeal when there is reason to think either (1) that a rational defendant would want to appeal (for example, because there are nonfrivolous grounds for appeal), or (2) that this particular defendant reasonably demonstrated to counsel that he was interested in appealing."

As noted above, there are limited circumstances where the court presumes that prejudice occurred. In this case, since the petitioner was deprived of an appeal and, therefore, forfeited an important judicial proceeding, there is a presumption that the petitioner was prejudiced. "Put simply, we cannot accord any 'presumption of reliability' to judicial proceedings that never took place." Practically, this means that even if a defendant cannot show that he or she possesses meritorious arguments on appeal, the very fact that the defendant was denied a right to appeal means that the defendant was prejudiced.

The court stated a concise summary of the prejudice requirement as follows:

> [A] showing of actual prejudice (i.e., that, but for counsel's errors, the defendant might have prevailed) when the proceeding in question was presumptively reliable, but presuming prejudice with no further showing from the defendant of the merits of his underlying claims when the violation of the right to counsel rendered the proceeding presumptively unreliable or entirely nonexistent.

The Supreme Court remanded the case for a hearing about whether the attorney held discussions with the petitioner about an appeal and what conclusions were reached during those discussions.

In *Campusano v. United States*,[226] the Second Circuit extended the holding in *Roe* one step further. Then Circuit Judge Sotomayor, who was a judge on the Second Circuit Court of Appeals before she was elevated to the Supreme Court, wrote the decision (the fact that she wrote this decision will turn out to be significant). As part of a plea agreement, the defendant *waived* his right to appeal. In his petition, Campusano alleged that he requested from his attorney to file a notice of appeal, and his attorney did not do so.

Since the prejudice to the petitioner is presumed, as determined in *Flores-Ortega*, the court granted the writ of habeas corpus. Even if the petitioner had waived his right to appeal, there are situations where the waiver could be overturned. As well, even if the attorney believed that the appeal was waived, the attorney could have filed an *Anders* brief on appeal.[227]

The Court wrote that "applying the *Flores-Ortega* presumption to post-waiver situations will bestow on most defendants nothing more than an opportunity to lose.... But rare as they might be, such cases are not inconceivable, and we do not cut corners when Sixth Amendment rights are at stake." Since Campusano was deprived of his right to appeal, he was entitled to habeas relief.

Fast-forward 13 years, and the Supreme Court heard oral arguments on this very issue.[228] The Justice who delivered the opinion of the Court was none other than Justice Sotomayor, who authored the opinion in *Campusano*. In *Garza v. Idaho*, the petitioner had pleaded guilty and waived his rights to appeal. The petitioner told his attorney to file a notice of appeal, and the attorney did not do so. Instead, the

---

[226] 442 F.3d 770 (2d Cir. 2006).

[227] An *Anders* brief is an appellate brief that is filed when an attorney believes that all potential arguments are frivolous. In the *Anders* brief, the attorney requests that the court examine the record and determine if any issues exist.

[228] *Garza v. Idaho*, 586 U.S. ___, 139 S. Ct. 738 (2019).

attorney told the petitioner that "an appeal was problematic because he waived his right to appeal."

The Supreme Court does not agree to accept many cases. One situation where the Supreme Court may agree to hear a case is when there is a split in the circuit courts about the law. In *Garza*, the Court noted that eight circuit courts held that there is ineffective assistance of counsel when an attorney fails to file a notice of appeal when the appeal was waived, and two courts held that, in such a situation, the assistance of counsel was effective. One of the eight cases that the court cited to was *Campusano*.

In *Garza*, the precise issue was whether the courts should apply a presumption of prejudice when a defendant waives an appeal and the attorney does not follow the client's instructions to file a notice of appeal, or whether the petitioner must establish prejudice, which is the general rule that was established in *Strickland*.

The Court held that there is a presumption of prejudice, reasoning "that even the broadest appeal waiver does not deprive a defendant of all appellate claims. Accordingly, where, as here, an attorney performed deficiently in failing to file a notice of appeal despite the defendant's express instructions, prejudice is presumed."

The government argued that the petitioner did not have a right to appeal since the right to appeal had been waived. The court found this argument to be incorrect, stating that "Garza did retain a right to his appeal; he simply had fewer possible claims than some other appellants."

The Right to Effective Assistance of Counsel on Appeal
There is a right to effective assistance of counsel on appeal.[229] In Michigan, a law was passed that required a defendant who had pleaded guilty or nolo contendere to apply for permission from the court to file an appeal. Since an automatic right to appeal no longer existed for someone who pleaded guilty, Michigan stopped providing attorneys to

---

[229] *See Halbert v. Michigan*, 545 U.S. 605 (2005).

represent indigent people who pleaded guilty and who wanted to appeal.

The Supreme Court held that the defendant was entitled to an attorney for the appeal. Since there is a right to counsel on appeal, it follows that there is a right to *effective* counsel on appeal.[230]

Ineffective Assistance Based on Failure To Suppress Evidence (Fourth Amendment)

In an earlier section, we discussed whether a writ of habeas corpus may be premised on a Fourth Amendment violation. The Supreme Court concluded that the answer to this question is no.

In *Kimmelman v. Morrison*,[231] the issue before the Supreme Court was whether a petitioner may claim that she received ineffective assistance of counsel due to her attorney's failure to move to suppress evidence that was seized in violation of the Fourth Amendment. In that case, the police entered the petitioner's home without permission and without a search warrant and seized evidence. At trial, the petitioner's attorney waited too long to try to suppress the evidence, so the court denied the attempt to suppress the evidence.

The Supreme Court agreed that ineffective assistance of counsel (Sixth Amendment) may be premised on a failure of counsel to seek to suppress evidence (Fourth Amendment). The Court reasoned that "[a]lthough a meritorious Fourth Amendment issue is necessary to the success of a Sixth Amendment claim like respondent's, a good Fourth Amendment claim alone will not earn a prisoner federal habeas relief. Only those habeas petitioners who can prove under *Strickland* that they have been denied a fair trial by the gross incompetence of their attorneys will be granted the writ and will be entitled to retrial without the challenged evidence." Thus, for an ineffective assistance of counsel claim based on a failure to suppress evidence, the petitioner

---

[230] *See Lafler v. Cooper*, 566 U.S. 156 (2012). *See also Evitts v. Lucey*, 469 U.S. 387 (1985).
[231] 477 U.S. 365 (1986).

will have to show a successful Fourth Amendment argument together with a successful Sixth Amendment argument—including prejudice.

The Right to Self-Representation

The Sixth Amendment provides a constitutional right to self-representation.[232] This right is not explicit in the Sixth Amendment; rather, it emerges from the fact that the Sixth Amendment provides its protections "directly to the accused; for it is he who suffers the consequences if the defense fails." Therefore, "the right to defend is given directly to the accused."

If a defendant abuses his right of self-representation, through serious misconduct or a failure to follow the court's rules, the court may refuse to let a defendant defend himself. In *United States v. Engel*, one of the cases concerning the 2014 standoff between the Bundy family and the government, the defendant represented himself and asked a question that he knew would not be allowed by the court. The court then ordered an attorney to represent the defendant and refused to let the defendant continue to represent himself. The appointed attorney objected, telling the court that the defendant "had 'done a fairly remarkable job' representing himself thus far and that a less drastic sanction was appropriate, [but] the district court disagreed."

The defendant was found guilty of Obstruction of the Due Administration of Justice, and Interstate Travel in Aid of Extortion. He was sentenced to 168 months in prison and fined almost $1,700,000.

On appeal, the Court of Appeals found that the defendant's constitutional rights were violated. The Court noted:

> Engel was not defiant and did not engage in blatantly outrageous conduct, such as threatening a juror or taunting the district judge. To the contrary, Engel merely asked a question prejudicial to the government. When the government objected, Engel remained calm and ultimately acquiesced in the court's

---

[232] *See Faretta v. California*, 422 U.S. 806 (1975).

decision to revoke his right to self-representation. He was never removed from the courtroom, nor did he need to be removed.

Furthermore, the Court noted that a single violation of a court order is not a good reason to terminate a defendant's right of self-representation. The Court also noted:

> We are sympathetic to the situation the district court faced. The risk of declaring a mistrial after twenty-one days of trial in a high-profile case with six co-defendants is a risk that ought to be avoided. But the Sixth Amendment guarantees a defendant's right to represent himself. And that right can be revoked only when the defendant exhibits clearly defiant or obstructionist misconduct. Engel's conduct here falls far short of that standard.

Therefore, the Court granted the writ of habeas corpus and vacated the judgment of guilt and the sentence.

In a remarkable development, the government then agreed to dismiss the charges,[233] stating:

> The government has reviewed and evaluated the evidence relating to defendant Engel against the backdrop of the passage of time and changed circumstances since his 2017 trial and has determined that dismissal is warranted in the interests of furthering the ends of justice.

In *United States v. Engel*, the defendant was sentenced to 168 months in prison. By filing his writ of habeas corpus, his original sentence was vacated, and the charges were dismissed. Instead of receiving 168 months in prison, the defendant received zero months in prison! This case illustrates the powerful potential of a writ of habeas corpus to protect against unlawful imprisonment.

---

[233] *United States v. Engel*, No. 2: 16-cr-00046-GMN-NJK-15 (D. Nev. Sept. 8, 2020).

The Right to a Unanimous Jury Verdict

The Sixth Amendment provides a right to a jury trial. For hundreds of years, going all the way back to 14th-century England, unanimous jury verdicts were required in order to find a defendant guilty. Louisiana and Oregon, however, allowed for convictions when up to two of the 12 jurors disagreed with the guilty verdict. In *Ramos v. Louisiana*,[234] Ramos was convicted by a vote of 10–2 and was sentenced to life in prison without parole. He challenged his conviction, arguing that the Sixth Amendment required a unanimous jury verdict.

In the decision, the Supreme Court noted the significant racially motivated reasons for passing those laws in Louisiana and Oregon, which were passed in 1898 and in the 1930s, respectively. The Supreme Court held that the phrase "trial by an impartial jury," which is found in the Sixth Amendment, means a trial with a unanimous verdict, stating that "[i]f the term 'trial by an impartial jury' carried any meaning at all, it surely included a requirement as long and widely accepted as unanimity."

The Court concluded with the following particularly compelling summary:

> On what ground would anyone have us leave Mr. Ramos in prison for the rest of his life? Not a single Member of this Court is prepared to say Louisiana secured his conviction constitutionally under the Sixth Amendment. No one before us suggests that the error was harmless. Louisiana does not claim precedent commands an affirmance. In the end, the best anyone can seem to muster against Mr. Ramos is that, if we dared to admit in his case what we all know to be true about the Sixth Amendment, we might have to say the same in some others. But where is the justice in that? Every judge must learn to live with the fact he or she will make some mistakes; it comes with the territory. But it is something else entirely to perpetuate

---

[234] 590 U.S. ___, 140 S. Ct. 1390 (2020).

something we all know to be wrong only because we fear the consequences of being right.

After the *Ramos* decision, the next question was whether the *Ramos* rule is retroactive. Could every person convicted by less than a unanimous verdict argue that his or her Sixth Amendment right to a unanimous verdict had been violated? Could those people seek to overturn their convictions through a writ of habeas corpus?

In *Edwards v. Vannoy*,[235] the petitioner was convicted by less than a unanimous jury of robbery, kidnapping, and rape and was sentenced to life in prison without parole. While his writ of habeas corpus was pending, the Supreme Court decided *Ramos*. Had Edwards' appeal been pending, the *Ramos* rule would have applied to him. Since Edwards did not have an appeal pending, the question was whether the *Ramos* decision applied to a pending writ of habeas corpus.

The Court held that the *Ramos* case did not apply to a pending writ of habeas corpus. The Court looked to the regular rules of retroactivity. A new constitutional rule may be applied retroactively if it is a "watershed" rule.[236] In *Edwards*, the Court noted that it "has *never* found that any new procedural rule actually satisfies that purported exception."

While the Court was motivated by the finality of proceedings, which explains the difference between applying a new rule to a case on appeal and not applying a new rule to a case on a writ of habeas corpus unless it is a "watershed" rule, one can ask, as the Court wrote in *Ramos*, "where is the justice in that?"

The Right to a Jury Verdict For ALL Factual Determinations

In *Cunningham v. California*,[237] Cunningham was to be sentenced to the mid-range sentence, unless the judge determined that there were

---

[235] ___ U.S. ___, 141 S. Ct. 1547 (2021).
[236] *Teague v. Lane*, 489 U.S. 288, 311 (1989) (plurality opinion).
[237] 549 U.S. 270 (2007).

"circumstances in aggravation." If such circumstances existed, then the judge could sentence Cunningham to the upper term sentence. The judge found that there were circumstances in aggravation and sentenced Cunningham to 16 years (upper term) instead of 12 years (middle term). Cunningham challenged his sentence, arguing that he had a right to have a jury determine the facts of the case. Cunningham argued that when a judge decides if circumstances in aggravation exist, the judge usurps the fact-finding role of the jury. Furthermore, the facts need to be found based on a "preponderance of evidence," not based on beyond a reasonable doubt.

The Supreme Court easily struck down the California law. "This Court has repeatedly held that, under the Sixth Amendment, any fact that exposes a defendant to a greater potential sentence must be found by a jury, not a judge, and established beyond a reasonable doubt, not merely by a preponderance of the evidence."

In a related case, the Supreme Court addressed whether a judge could increase a *minimum* of a sentence without a jury determination. In *United States v. Haymond*,[238] Haymond had been sentenced to 38 months in prison. The judge then found that Haymond had violated the conditions of his supervised release. Normally, Haymond could have been sentenced to the maximum of his original sentence.

A law, however, required the judge to add five years to the original sentence. Therefore, instead of there being no minimum sentence, there was at least a five-year minimum sentence. At sentencing, the judge went out of his way to comment that he did not think it was legal to sentence Haymond without a jury determining the facts, but the judge said that he was required to impose the sentence by law.

The Supreme Court held that Haymond's Sixth Amendment rights were violated, stating, "So just like the facts the judge found at the defendant's sentencing hearing in *Alleyne*, the facts the judge

---

[238] 588 U.S. ___, 139 S. Ct. 2369 (2019).

found here increased 'the legally prescribed range of allowable sentences' in violation of the Fifth and Sixth Amendments."

The opening of the decision is noteworthy and should be cited in any case that concerns issues with a jury trial. "Only a jury, acting on proof beyond a reasonable doubt, may take a person's liberty. That promise stands as one of the Constitution's most vital protections against arbitrary government."

F. Eighth Amendment

Text of Eighth Amendment

The Eighth Amendment provides that "Excessive bail shall not be required, nor excessive fines imposed, nor cruel and unusual punishments inflicted."

Cruel and Unusual Punishment—A Brief History

The Eighth Amendment is premised on the Virginia Declaration of Rights of 1776, which itself is premised on the English Bill of Rights of 1689. While the English law was intended to prevent judges from imposing unlawful sentences, "the principal concern of the American Framers appears to have been with the legislative definition of crimes and punishments."[239] Therefore, the Eighth Amendment applies to criminal punishments.[240]

Cruel and Unusual Punishment—Proportionality and Three Strikes

There may be a tendency to think that the Eighth Amendment protects against *all* disproportionate sentencing. The Supreme Court, however, has mostly rejected this approach. The Court noted that legislatures always believe that the penalties they enact are proportionate to the crime. There is no way for the Supreme Court (or any court) to

---

[239] *Ingraham v. Wright*, 430 U.S. 651, 665 (1977).
[240] *Id.*, 666.

evaluate whether a penalty is disproportionate unless the court imposes its own subjective values and overrides the legislature.[241]

In *Harmelin v. Michigan*, Justice Kennedy wrote a concurring opinion in which he wrote that the Eighth Amendment "forbids only extreme sentences that are 'grossly disproportionate' to the crime." There was no majority opinion in that case, and Justice Kennedy's concurring opinion became the accepted holding in *Harmelin*. For example, the Ninth Circuit "follows the narrow proportionality rule established by Justice Kennedy's concurrence in *Harmelin*."[242] A few years later, the Supreme Court adopted Justice Kennedy's analysis.[243]

The rule, then, is that the term "cruel and unusual punishment" applies narrowly to situations where a defendant receives an extreme sentence that is grossly disproportionate to the crime. This would mean that if a person is sentenced to life in prison for stealing a small amount, the punishment may violate the Eighth Amendment. A disproportionate sentence is one that is extreme relative to the law that was violated. What if someone was sentenced to 25 years to life in prison for stealing $1,200 worth of golf clubs? Is that an extreme sentence that is grossly disproportionate to the crime?

In 2003, the Supreme Court addressed this question in the context of California's three-strike law.[244] Pursuant to the law, a defendant who is convicted of a felony and has previous convictions for serious felonies is sentenced to 25 years to life in prison. Does such a sentence violate a defendant's constitutional right to not receive a cruel and unusual punishment?

The Court held that the penalty was not a violation of the Eighth Amendment's bar against cruel and unusual punishment. The Court reasoned that, "[w]hen the California Legislature enacted the three strikes law, it made a judgment that protecting the public safety

---

[241] *Harmelin v. Michigan*, 501 U.S. 957 (1991).

[242] *United States v. Harris*, 154 F.3d 1082 (9th Cir. 1998).

[243] *See Ewing v. California*, 538 U.S. 11 (2003).

[244] *Id.*

requires incapacitating criminals who have already been convicted of at least one serious or violent crime. Nothing in the Eighth Amendment prohibits California from making that choice."

The precise issue was not whether being sentenced to life in prison for stealing $1,200 worth of merchandise is cruel and unusual. The Court, instead, noted that "[t]he gravity of his offense was not merely 'shoplifting three golf clubs.' Rather, Ewing was convicted of felony grand theft for stealing nearly $1,200 worth of merchandise after previously having been convicted of at least two 'violent' or 'serious' felonies."

The Court concluded, "Ewing's sentence of 25 years to life in prison, imposed for the offense of felony grand theft under the three strikes law, is not grossly disproportionate and therefore does not violate the Eighth Amendment's prohibition on cruel and unusual punishments."

When DOES the Eighth Amendment Apply?

If the Eighth Amendment does not apply to a situation like the one in *Ewing*, it is fair to ask when *does* the Eighth Amendment apply? Below, we will discuss when a writ of habeas corpus may be premised on a violation of the Eighth Amendment's protection against cruel and unusual punishment.

The "Extraordinary Case" Where the Penalty Is Grossly Disproportionate to the Crime
First, there are a limited number of cases where a penalty is grossly disproportionate to the crime. The Supreme Court has noted that this only applies in the "extraordinary case."[245]

---

[245] *Lockyer v. Andrade*, 538 U.S. 63 (2003). In this case, a defendant stole $150 worth of video tapes. He was charged with a felony since petty theft with a prior conviction is considered a felony in California (technically, it is considered a "wobbler," which means that the prosecutor has discretion to charge the defendant with either a misdemeanor or a felony). The defendant was sentenced to 25 years to life as a third strike. The Supreme Court held that there was no violation of the petitioner's constitutional rights.

One example occurred in *Gonzalez v. Duncan*.[246] In that case, the petitioner did not update his sex offender registration within five days of his birthday, as he was required by law to do. Because the case was a "three-strike" case, the petitioner was sentenced to 28 years to life in prison. The Ninth Circuit held that the sentence was grossly disproportionate to the crime, reasoning that a failure to register "is only tangentially related to the state's interest in ensuring that sex offenders are available for police surveillance," since the registration is a "back-up measure" to make sure that the police have the correct contact information. Regarding the sentence, a failure to register may result in a sentence of between 16 months and 3 years. The 28 years to life sentence was 21 times the minimum sentence and 9 times the maximum sentence.

The court also compared the sentence with the sentence for other crimes, with other states' sex offender registration requirements, and with other states' penalties for not registering in a timely manner. Based on all the comparisons, the court found that a sentence of 28 years to life "is at the margin of what the states have deemed an appropriate penalty for violation of sex offender registration laws [which] supports our finding that Gonzalez's sentence is unusual."

Yet, in a similar case a few years later, the Ninth Circuit faced a similar fact pattern but held that a sentence of 26 years to life was not cruel or unusual.[247] In that case, the petitioner was charged with failing to update his sex offender registration after a *change of address*. In contrast, in *Gonzalez*, the petitioner had updated his address when he moved but did not file an annual registration within five days of his birthday.

The Ninth Circuit held that the distinction between these two failures to file is important. A failure to file a change of address means that the authorities will not be able to locate the sex offender. Therefore, "a conviction for failure to register after an address change

---

[246] 551 F.3d 875 (9th Cir. 2008).
[247] *Crosby v. Schwartz*, 678 F.3d 784 (9th Cir. 2012).

is directly related to the state's interest in ensuring that it knows the whereabouts of its sex offenders."

A failure to file an annual registration, on the other hand, is "a purely regulatory offense," intended as "a mere backup measure to ensure the authorities have accurate information." Therefore, a "failure to comply with the annual registration requirement is a technical violation that by itself poses no danger to society." On this basis, the Ninth Circuit affirmed the denial of the writ of habeas corpus, and the petitioner's sentence of 26 years to life was upheld.

Life Without Parole Sentences for Minors

Kuntrell Jackson was 14 years old when he went with some friends to rob a video store. At some point, he learned that one of his friends was carrying a gun, and he decided to stay outside. He then went into the video store and, moments later, saw his friend shoot and kill the clerk.

Evan Miller was 14 years old when he and a friend committed murder. Miller "had by then been in and out of foster care because his mother suffered from alcoholism and drug addiction and his stepfather abused him. Miller, too, regularly used drugs and alcohol; and he had attempted suicide four times, the first when he was six years old."[248]

Each of the teenagers received a mandatory sentence of life in prison without parole. However, in 2010, in *Graham v. Florida*, the Supreme Court held that a juvenile could not be sentenced to life in prison without parole when the juvenile commits a nonhomicide crime.[249] *Graham* was predicated on the fact that the characteristics of youth should be considered when sentencing a juvenile. In *Miller*, the question concerned a mandatory sentence of life in prison without parole.

If *Graham* stands for the principle that youthful factors should be considered when sentencing a juvenile, then a mandatory sentence of life in prison would serve to ignore any potentially relevant factors of youth. In *Miller*, the court stated, "But the mandatory penalty

---

[248] *Miller v. Alabama*, 567 U.S. 460 (2012).
[249] *Graham v. Florida*, 560 U.S. 48 (2010).

schemes at issue here prevent the sentencer from taking account of these central considerations. By removing youth from the balance—by subjecting a juvenile to the same life-without-parole sentence applicable to an adult—these laws prohibit a sentencing authority from assessing whether the law's harshest term of imprisonment proportionately punishes a juvenile offender."

The court summarized its decision as follows:

Mandatory life without parole for a juvenile precludes consideration of his chronological age and its hallmark features—among them, immaturity, impetuosity, and failure to appreciate risks and consequences. It prevents taking into account the family and home environment that surrounds him—and from which he cannot usually extricate himself—no matter how brutal or dysfunctional. It neglects the circumstances of the homicide offense, including the extent of his participation in the conduct and the way familial and peer pressures may have affected him. Indeed, it ignores that he might have been charged and convicted of a lesser offense if not for incompetencies associated with youth—for example, his inability to deal with police officers or prosecutors (including on a plea agreement) or his incapacity to assist his own attorneys.

To be clear, the Court in *Miller* did not say that it was unconstitutional to sentence a juvenile to life in prison without parole. Rather, the Court held that a *mandatory* sentence was unconstitutional.

In 2021, the Supreme Court addressed the next aspect of this line of case.[250] Brett Jones was 15 years old when he killed his grandfather. He was initially sentenced to mandatory life in prison without parole. Due to *Miller*, his sentence was vacated. At the resentencing, the judge acknowledged the discretion in sentencing and then again sentenced Jones to life in prison without parole. The judge did not state on the record what factors led him to sentence Jones to

---

[250] *Jones v. Mississippi*, 593 U.S. ___, 141 S. Ct. 1307 (2021).

life in prison without parole, and he did not make any written findings of fact.

The Supreme Court held that as long as the judge acknowledged the discretion involved when sentencing a juvenile to life in prison without parole, then there is not a violation of the Eighth Amendment. In *Jones*, the Supreme Court held that "the Court's precedents require a discretionary sentencing procedure in a case of this kind. The resentencing in Jones's case complied with those precedents because the sentence was not mandatory and the trial judge had discretion to impose a lesser punishment in light of Jones's youth."

Regarding the claim that Jones rehabilitated himself and should not have to spend the rest of his life in prison for a crime that he committed when he was 15 years old, the Court suggested that Jones "present those arguments to the state officials authorized to act on them, such as the state legislature, state courts, or Governor. Those state avenues for sentencing relief remain open to Jones, and they will remain open to him for years to come."

To conclude the decision with the sympathetic recognition that Jones may have rehabilitated himself is an odd twist for the Court. In the penultimate paragraph, the Court suggested numerous ways for a state to ensure that juveniles are not sentenced to life without parole. This too is odd.

Reading between the lines, one wonders if the Supreme Court is attempting to pressure the states to change their laws. Until that happens, despite claiming that its "holding today is far from the last word on whether Jones will receive relief from his sentence," the Supreme Court's holding is the last word for Jones, who was sentenced to life in prison without parole for a crime that he committed at the age of 15.

Disproportionality in Death Penalty Cases
We previously established that courts avoid second-guessing legislative decisions about punishment. Only on the rare occasion will

124

a court hold that a punishment is cruel and unusual, such as a punishment of life in prison for the failure to file an annual sex offender registration. Yet, a punishment of life in prison for the failure of a sex offender to file a change of address is not a cruel and unusual punishment.

For death penalty cases, the Court takes a stricter view. Over the years, the Court has restricted the use of the death penalty in a variety of circumstances. A punishment of death for rape is an unconstitutional violation of the Eighth Amendment.[251] A punishment of death is unconstitutional "where a defendant did not take life, attempt to take it, or intend to take life." [252]

In the years following its focus on what types of crimes may be subject to the death penalty, the Court focused on which individuals could receive the death penalty. Someone who is mentally retarded cannot be executed.[253] In *Atkins v. Virginia*, the petitioner had an IQ of 59. The Court highlighted "that today our society views mentally retarded offenders as categorically less culpable than the average criminal."

Not long after *Atkins* was decided, the Supreme Court turned to the question about whether the death penalty for a juvenile is a cruel and unusual punishment in *Roper v. Simmons*.[254] The Court held that someone who commits a crime when he or she is under the age of 18 cannot be sentenced to death. Noting that the age of 18 is somewhat arbitrary, the Court reasoned that "[t]he age of 18 is the point where society draws the line for many purposes between childhood and adulthood. It is, we conclude, the age at which the line for death eligibility ought to rest."

---

[251] *See Coker v. Georgia*, 433 U.S. 584 (1977).
[252] *See Edmund v. Florida*, 458 U.S. 782 (1982).
[253] *Atkins v. Virginia*, 536 U.S. 304 (2002).
[254] *Roper v. Simmons*, 543 U.S. 551 (2005).

***The Future of the Eighth Amendment (1): Should the Death Penalty
Be Considered Disproportionate for Anyone Under the Age of 25?***

One of the driving forces of the Supreme Court's death-penalty
jurisprudence is that "the words of the [Eighth] Amendment are not
precise, and that their scope is not static. The Amendment must draw
its meaning from the *evolving standards of decency that mark the
progress of a maturing society* [emphasis added]."[255]

In the years since *Roper*, much research has shown that
teenagers do not fully mature until around the age of 25.[256] Dr.
Laurence Steinberg, a distinguished psychology professor and one of
the world's leading experts on adolescence, has written many scientific
articles and has provided expert testimony about adolescent brain
development at several criminal trials. In one of his publications, he
wrote:

> [R]isk-taking increases between childhood and adolescence as
> a result of changes around the time of puberty in what I refer to
> as the brain's socio-emotional system that lead to increased
> reward-seeking, especially in the presence of peers. Risk-
> taking declines between adolescence and adulthood because of
> changes in what I refer to as the brain's cognitive control
> system—changes which improve individuals' capacity for self-
> regulation, which occur gradually and over the course of
> adolescence and young adulthood. The differing timetables of

---

[255] *Trop v. Dulles*, 356 U.S. 86, 100-01 (1958) (plurality opinion).

[256] *See* Christopher Ramos, "*Adolescent Brain Development, Mental Illness and the
University-Student Relationship*," 24 S Cal Rev L & Soc Just 343 (2015). Another
study found that "The 'immaturity gap' represents the cleavage between adolescents'
intellectual maturity—which reaches near-adult levels by age 16—and psychosocial
maturity of judgment, which may not emerge fully for another decade. This
disjunction in decision-making ability provides the basis for finding youths' criminal
responsibility diminished." Barry C. Feld, B.J. Casey & Yasmin Hurd, "Adolescent
Competence and Culpability: Implications of Neuroscience for Juvenile Justice
Administration, A Primer on Criminal Law and Neuroscience," Stephen J. Morse &
Adina L. Roskies eds., (2013).

these changes—the increase in reward-seeking, which occurs early and is relatively abrupt, and the increase in self-regulatory competence, which occurs gradually and is not complete until the mid-20s, makes mid-adolescence a time of heightened vulnerability to risky and reckless behavior.[257]

Some aspects of the *Roper* decision could be applied to individuals who are above the age of 18. In *Roper*, the Court highlighted that "[i]t is difficult even for expert psychologists to differentiate between the juvenile offender whose crime reflects unfortunate yet transient immaturity, and the rare juvenile offender whose crime reflects irreparable corruption." The new science shows that this applies in the same way to people in their early-to-mid-20s.

Just as *Roper* concluded that the retribution and deterrence justifications for the death penalty do not apply to someone under the age of 18, this could easily be extended to someone in his early-to-mid-20s.

- *Roper*: "Retribution is not proportional if the law's most severe penalty is imposed on one whose culpability or blameworthiness is diminished, to a substantial degree, by reason of youth and immaturity."
- *Roper*: "[T]he same characteristics that render juveniles less culpable than adults suggest as well that juveniles will be less susceptible to deterrence."

Due to the "evolving standards of decency that mark the progress of a maturing society," one wonders if the Supreme Court will bar the execution of those who committed crimes under the age of 25. A defendant or petitioner in his or her early 20s who is facing the death penalty, or who has already been sentenced to death, should consider arguing whether the death penalty for someone that age is unconstitutional, as an extension of *Roper*.

---

[257] Dr. Laurence Steinberg, "*A Social Neuroscience Perspective on Adolescent Risk-Taking*," 28 Developmental Review 76, 83 (2008).

The Future of the Eighth Amendment (2): Is the Death Penalty Always Disproportionate to the Crime?

As we mentioned, the Eighth Amendment "must draw its meaning from the evolving standards of decency that mark the progress of a maturing society." In 1977, Justice Brennan authored a dissenting opinion in *Gregg v. Georgia*.[258] He argued that the death penalty itself is a cruel and unusual punishment. Focusing on the "evolving standards," Justice Brennan argued that "'moral concepts' require us to hold that the law has progressed to the point where we should declare that the punishment of death, like punishments on the rack, the screw, and the wheel, is no longer morally tolerable in our civilized society."

A more recent Supreme Court holding has all but made it impossible for the death penalty to be declared unconstitutional.[259] However, it is noteworthy that the Court did not refer to the "evolving standards of decency that mark the progress of a maturing society" in its decision.

As a critique, there is no doubt that the death penalty was available since the founding of the United States of America. The question, however, is how to take into account the "evolving standards of decency." In writing, "But it does mean that the judiciary bears no license to end a debate reserved for the people and their representatives," the Court abandoned the notion of "evolving standards of decency."

One expects this to be an issue that comes before the Court in the future. Should that occur, it is worthwhile to keep Justice Brennan's argument in the back of our minds. Perhaps, one day, the

---

[258] 428 U.S. 153 (1976) (Brennan, J., dissenting).
[259] *See Bucklew v. Precythe*, 587 U.S. ___, 139 S. Ct. 1112 (2019) (noting, "The Constitution allows capital punishment ... Nor did the later addition of the Eighth Amendment outlaw the practice. On the contrary—the Fifth Amendment, added to the Constitution at the same time as the Eighth, expressly contemplates that a defendant may be tried for a 'capital' crime and 'deprived of life' as a penalty, so long as proper procedures are followed.").

"evolving standards" will be reintroduced and will be such that the death penalty itself will be declared unconstitutional.

The Future of the Eighth Amendment (3): Is a Significant Delay Between Sentencing and Execution Considered a Cruel and Unusual Punishment?

When Richard Gerald Jordan was 30 years old, he was sentenced to death. A staggering 42 years later, his petition for certiorari reached the Supreme Court. Jordan argued that such a long delay in carrying out his execution was a cruel and unusual punishment. Though the Supreme Court did not agree to hear the case, Justice Breyer presented a compelling argument in dissent.[260]

Justice Breyer argued that a long delay before execution means that a prisoner will have to spend many, many years in the terrible conditions of death row. "In my view, the conditions in which Jordan appears to have been confined over the past four decades reinforce the Eighth Amendment concern raised in his petition."

In the United States, the death row prisoner waits on average 19 years before being executed. Though the petition for certiorari was denied, this is an issue to look out for.

G. Due Process (Fifth and Fourteenth Amendments)

Text of the Fifth and Fourteenth Amendments

The Fifth Amendment was quoted in full earlier in the section about the Fifth Amendment. There, we did not focus on the last line of the Fifth Amendment: "nor be deprived of life, liberty, or property, without due process of law." The Fifth Amendment applies to the *federal* government. Due process requirements were later applied to *state* governments via the Fourteenth Amendment, which was passed in 1868. The Fourteenth Amendment states that "nor shall any State

---

[260] *Jordan v. Mississippi*, 138 S. Ct. 2567 (2018).

deprive any person of life, liberty, or property, without due process of law."

Due process essentially means a fair process. A person cannot be incarcerated if the process that led to the incarceration is not fair. In the following sections, we will address some of the more common scenarios where a petitioner's due process rights are violated.

Prosecutorial Misconduct—Using Arguments To Inflame the Passion of the Jury

In the closing argument in *Darden v. Wright*, the prosecutor referred to the defendant as an "animal."[261] The prosecutor made many other outrageous comments, such as, "I wish [Mr. Turman] had had a shotgun in his hand when he walked in the back door and blown his [Darden's] face off. I wish that I could see him sitting here with no face, blown away by a shotgun." Nevertheless, the Court held that the prosecutor's statements "did not deprive petitioner of a fair trial."

The standard that the Court looks to "is whether the prosecutors' comments so infected the trial with unfairness as to make the resulting conviction a denial of due process." In *Darden*, the Court focused on the fact that the prosecution did not misstate the evidence, and the judge told the jury that "their decision was to be made on the basis of the evidence alone, and that the arguments of counsel were not evidence." The Court also noted that the evidence against the petitioner was very strong, which would have "reduced the likelihood that the jury's decision was influenced by [the] argument." Finally, the Court noted that the petitioner's attorney, due to a unique procedural rule, made a convincing rebuttal argument after the prosecution's inflammatory arguments.

In *Rowland v. Chapman*, the prosecutor told the jury that if he was on the jury, he would vote to convict the defendant.[262] The Ninth Circuit held that there was no due process violation, because "the

---

[261] 477 U.S. 168 (1986).
[262] 876 F.3d 1174 (9th Cir. 2017).

prosecutor's improper remarks expressing his personal opinion about the appropriateness of the death penalty for Rowland did not undermine the fundamental fairness of the trial."

A good summary of the law concerning a prosecutor's improper statements is found in *Barnett v. Roper*:

> Improper remarks by the prosecutor can violate the Fourteenth Amendment if they "so infected the trial with unfairness as to make the resulting conviction a denial of due process." "The court should only grant habeas corpus relief if the state's 'closing argument was so inflammatory and so outrageous that any reasonable trial judge would have *sua sponte* declared a mistrial.'" Relief will be granted only upon a showing of a reasonable probability that the outcome would have been different but for the improper statement.[263]

Prosecutorial Misconduct—Misstating the Law

What happens if the prosecutor misstates the law? Would that be enough to grant a writ of habeas corpus? Theoretically, the answer is yes. Practically, in a case where the prosecutor told the jury that the defendant did not have a presumption of innocence, the court still denied the writ.

In *Ford v. Peery*, a 2021 case from the Ninth Circuit, the prosecutor told the jury:

> *This idea of this presumption of innocence is over.* Mr. Ford had a fair trial. We were here for three weeks where … he gets to cross-examine witnesses; also an opportunity to present information through his lawyer. He had a fair trial. This system is not perfect, but he had a fair opportunity and a fair trial. *He's not presumed innocent anymore.*[264]

---

[263] 541 F.3d 804 (8th Cir. 2008) (citing *Donnelly v. DeChristoforo*, 416 U.S. 637, 643 (1974); *Weaver v. Bowersox*, 438 F.3d 832, 840 (8th Cir. 2006); *Shurn v. Delo*, 177 F.3d 662, 667 (8th Cir. 1999)).
[264] 999 F.3d 1214 (9th Cir. 2021).

The prosecutor obviously misstated the law. Everyone knows that a defendant is presumed innocent. Of all errors to make, this was a big one. The presumption of innocence lies at the heart of criminal jurisprudence. It is a "basic component of a fair trial under our system of criminal justice."[265] The court then analyzed whether the petitioner was prejudiced, meaning whether the misstatement of the law affected the outcome of the case.

Despite the significant misstatement of the law, the court denied the writ. The court reasoned that if it was presented the case on a *de novo* review (remember that the AEDPA requires the federal courts to defer to the state court decision, and the federal court will grant a writ of habeas corpus only when the state decision was an unreasonable application of the law), "we would conclude that there was a reasonable probability of a different outcome absent the prosecutor's misstatement of the law." However, because the state court conclusion was not unreasonable, the writ was denied.

In a different 2021 case, the court reversed a conviction due to misstatements of the law. In *United States v. Velazquez*,[266] the prosecutor "trivialized" the "reasonable doubt standard." The prosecutor "compared the reasonable doubt standard to making decisions like going for a drive or eating a meal—with the confidence that things will not go awry." In doing so, the prosecutor lowered the bar for what is considered "reasonable doubt" and made it easier to obtain a conviction.

Prosecutorial Misconduct—Not Correcting False Testimony

A defendant's due process rights are clearly violated when a prosecutor uses false evidence to obtain a conviction. What happens when a witness for the prosecution falsely answers a question during cross-examination? Does the prosecutor have a duty to correct the false testimony?

---

[265] *Estelle v. Williams*, 425 U.S. 501 (1976).
[266] No. 19-50099 (9th Cir 2021).

In *Napue v. Illinois*, a state witness testified that he was not promised leniency in exchange for his testimony. This was a lie. The Court held, "[t]he principle that a State may not knowingly use false evidence, including false testimony, to obtain a tainted conviction, *implicit in any concept of ordered liberty*, does not cease to apply merely because the false testimony goes only to the credibility of the witness."[267]

A few years later, the Supreme Court held that "[a] new trial is required if the false testimony could ... in any reasonable likelihood have affected the judgment of the jury."[268]

In *Dow v. Virga*, the state prosecutor elicited false testimony, did not correct the testimony, and then argued in closing arguments that the false testimony supported a finding of guilt.[269] Focusing on whether the false evidence could have affected the judgment, the Court held, "[t]he evidence against Dow was weak and the prosecutor's arguments undoubtedly had an effect on the jury's decision. Thus, Dow was deprived of his constitutional right to due process of law." The Court granted the writ of habeas corpus.

Prosecutorial Misconduct—Failure To Disclose Exculpatory Evidence (Brady *Violation)*

In the previous section, we cited the *Napue* and *Giglio* decisions. These two cases are often cited along with a third case, *Brady v. Maryland.*[270] *Brady* has been cited to approximately 45,000 times!

In *Brady*, the Court held "that the suppression by the prosecution of evidence favorable to an accused upon request violates due process where the evidence is material either to guilt or to punishment, irrespective of the good faith or bad faith of the prosecution." Through decades of Supreme Court decisions, the *Brady*

---

[267] 360 U.S. 264 (1959) [emphasis added].

[268] *Giglio v. United States*, 405 U.S. 150 (1972).

[269] 729 F.3d 1041 (9th Cir. 2013).

[270] 373 U.S. 83 (1963).

rule was extended to two important situations: (1) the prosecution must turn over impeachment evidence and (2) the prosecution must turn over evidence even if it was not requested by the defendants.[271]

The standard that the court looks to "is not whether the defendant would more likely than not have received a different verdict with the evidence, but whether in its absence he received a fair trial, understood as a trial resulting in a verdict worthy of confidence."[272] The prosecution must "disclose known, favorable evidence rising to a material level of importance."

There are three elements of a *Brady* claim: (1) the exculpatory or impeachment evidence must be favorable to the defendant; (2) the government did not produce the evidence to the defendant; (3) the defendant was prejudiced.[273]

- A Brady violation exists even if the government inadvertently fails to produce the evidence.
- The prosecutor must turn over information known to other government agencies.[274]

The legal databases are full of decisions where a writ of habeas corpus was granted, and a verdict of guilt was vacated, due to the government's violation of the *Brady* rule. We present a few of these decisions below.

Smith v. Cain[275]

Smith was convicted of five counts of first-degree murder. There was no evidence connecting him to the murder; his conviction was based on a single eyewitness. In court, the witness testified that "he had been face to face with Smith during the initial moments of the robbery." After his conviction, Smith succeeded in obtaining the police files and

---

[271] *Kyles v. Whitley*, 514 U.S. 419 (1995).

[272] *Id.*, 434.

[273] *See Strickler v. Greene*, 527 U.S. 263 (1999).

[274] *See Youngblood v. West Virginia*, 547 U.S. 867 (2006). *See also United States v. Cano*, 934 F.3d 1002 (9th Cir. 2019).

[275] 565 U.S. 72 (2012).

found numerous notes in which an officer wrote down that the witness was not able to identify any of the perpetrators. These notes were not turned over to Smith.

While highlighting "that evidence impeaching an eyewitness may not be material if the State's other evidence is strong enough to sustain confidence in the verdict," the Court noted that there was no other evidence to support Smith's conviction. The *only* evidence was the testimony of the eyewitness, and the prosecution failed to turn over the relevant police files to the defendant. Therefore, the Court vacated the conviction.

Milke v. Ryan[276]

This case involves the tragic murder of a four-year-old boy and the imprisonment of the boy's mother for the crime. Debra Milke was convicted of the murder in 1990 and spent more than 20 years on death row. There was no direct evidence linking her to the crime. The only evidence of her guilt was provided by the detective who interviewed Debra. He claimed that he gave her a *Miranda* warning, and she confessed. She denied both of these claims.

The Court summed up this case as follows: "The judge and jury believed Saldate [the detective, A.S.], but they didn't know about Saldate's long history of lying under oath and other misconduct. The state knew about this misconduct but didn't disclose it, despite the requirements of *Brady* and *Giglio*."

The prosecution's Brady violation was egregious. The detective had a history of lying, and the prosecution never told the defense about the detective's history. In numerous cases, the detective lied in court or violated suspects' *Miranda* rights. The detective's personnel file contained instances of the detective lying to his superiors. "[T]he report showed that Saldate had suffered a five-day suspension for accepting sexual favors from a female motorist and then lying about it."

---

[276] 711 F.3d 998 (9th Cir. 2013).

"Milke's claim was straightforward: She couldn't effectively cross-examine Saldate because the state had failed to disclose significant impeachment evidence." The Court found that the detective's "credibility was crucial to the state's case against Milke. It's hard to imagine anything more relevant to the jury's—or the judge's—determination whether to believe Saldate than evidence that Saldate lied under oath and trampled the constitutional rights of suspects in discharging his official duties."

The Court, therefore, granted the petitioner's writ of habeas corpus and directed that all records pertaining to the detective be turned over to the petitioner. In a sharply worded concurring opinion, Chief Judge Kozinski wrote, "The Phoenix Police Department and Saldate's supervisors there should be ashamed of having given free rein to a lawless cop to misbehave again and again, undermining the integrity of the system of justice they were sworn to uphold."

After the writ was issued, the State of Arizona chose to retry Debra Milke. Not only that, but when she tried to have the charges dismissed, her motion to dismiss was denied. She appealed. Finally, on appeal, the court dismissed the charges due to the "egregious prosecutorial misconduct that raise[d] serious concerns regarding the integrity of our system of justice."[277]

United States v. Bundy[278]

Though this is not a habeas case, it nonetheless is an important case for *Brady* violations. In the section above about self-representation (Sixth Amendment), we referred to the Bundy trials. After the Bundy family refused to pay the federal government for a license to graze their cattle (they argued that they had rights to use the land), the government attempted to seize the family's livestock. At this point, the Bundy

---

[277] *Milke v. Mroz*, 339 P.3d 659, 236 Ariz. 276 (Ct. App. 2014). This case took another interesting twist when Milke's lawsuit against the city of Phoenix was dismissed because she destroyed all of her records and communications about the case. *See Milke v. City of Phoenix*, 497 F. Supp. 3d 442 (D. Ariz. 2020).
[278] 968 F.3d 1019 (9th Cir. 2020).

family put out a call for help, and various militias came to defend them. The court refers to what happened as a "standoff."

The government waited until after the trial began to turn over the *Brady* material. The trial court dismissed the charges due to the government's conduct. The Ninth Circuit Court of Appeals agreed:

> Surveying all of the withheld evidence, we agree with the district court that the defendants suffered not only prejudice, but substantial prejudice. The district court concluded that the defendants specifically suffered prejudice in not being able to prepare their case fully, refine their voir dire strategy, and make stronger opening statements.

Silva v. Brown[279]

In this case, Silva was convicted of murder, kidnapping, robbery, and gun offenses. While there was independent evidence of the kidnapping, robbery, and gun offenses, the evidence for the murder conviction came from the testimony of a co-defendant. As part of the co-defendant's plea agreement, the co-defendant was not allowed to have a psychiatric evaluation until after the trial was completed.

Where was the *Brady* violation? The government did not disclose that part of the plea agreement included a requirement not to undergo a psychiatric evaluation. Apparently, the prosecution had doubts about the mental competence of the co-defendant, who the government intended to use as its witness.

The Court held, "The legitimate question whether Thomas was competent, or perhaps insane, creates, in our minds, a reasonable probability of a different result. In the absence of disclosure of Thomas's questionable mental state to the defense and the jury, the guilty verdict returned on the murder charge is not one worthy of our confidence."

Therefore, the Court vacated the murder conviction. In summing up the case, the Court wrote:

---

[279] 416 F.3d 980 (9th Cir. 2005).

[T]he fact of the prosecution's undisclosed deal with Thomas, had it been presented to the jury, would have put the testimony of this critical witness in a substantially different light, both directly, by casting doubt on the accuracy of Thomas's testimony, and indirectly, by inducing the defense to focus the jury's attention on Thomas's lapses and inconsistencies and by calling into question the prosecutor's faith in the competence of his own witness. With the murder prosecution so heavily dependent on Thomas's testimony, and given the powerful effect the revelation of the prosecution's own doubts about its star witness would likely have had on the jury, we cannot say that, in the absence of this evidence, Silva 'received a fair trial, understood as a trial resulting in a verdict worthy of confidence.' *Kyles*, 514 U.S. at 434.

Browning v. Baker[280]

Earlier, we cited to this case in the section about ineffective assistance of counsel for failure to investigate the facts of the case. Recall that the petitioner's attorney purposefully did not investigate the source of bloody footprints, out of a fear that the footprints belonged to Browning. The Court rebuked the attorney, saying, "Under *Strickland*, counsel's investigation must determine strategy, not the other way around." We now analyze this case for its *Brady* violation.

In this case, Browning argued that bloody footprints (which did not belong to him) were left by the real killer. The prosecution argued that the footprints belonged to paramedics who arrived on the scene, so the bloody footprints did not establish that someone else was the killer. The prosecution, however, failed to disclose that the bloody footprints were there before the paramedics arrived and could, therefore, not have belonged to the paramedics. That the paramedics arrived after the bloody footprints were observed supports the claim that bloody footprints belonged to the real killer.

---

[280] 875 F.3d 444 (9th Cir. 2017).

The prosecution also told the court that they did not cut a deal with a witness. While technically true, the witness was given the understanding that the prosecution would reduce his sentence in another case. The "expectation of a potential benefit in exchange for his testimony—that constituted impeachment evidence that should have been disclosed."

Third, the prosecution (innocently?) distorted a description of the perpetrator given by a witness, so the description matched Browning. The actual words of the witness did not match Browning, and the prosecution did not provide a transcript of the actual testimony.

The Court highlighted that the withheld evidence was material: "The bloody shoeprints were strong evidence that Browning was not the killer." The Court granted the writ of habeas corpus, reasoning that "[t]he strength of the undisclosed evidence is too great, and the remainder of the trial record too weak."

Kyle Rittenhouse

The Rittenhouse trial occurred in state court and is outside the scope of this book. Nonetheless, an interesting potential *Brady* violation came up. Toward the end of the trial, it turned out that the prosecution provided a low-resolution video of the drone footage to the defense, though the prosecution was in possession of high-resolution video of the drone footage. Apparently, the iPhone automatically compresses large video files. Since Rittenhouse was found not guilty, the judge did not issue a ruling about the potential *Brady* violation.

Police Misconduct—Suggestive Witness Identification

Aaron Spolin has written a book devoted to witness identification or, more aptly, witness misidentification.[281] In it, he describes how one factor that leads to witness misidentification is suggestive police techniques.

---

[281] Aaron Spolin (2020), *Witness Misidentification in Criminal Trials: Reforming Identification Procedures to Protect the Innocent.*

Briefly, the general rule is that "the Due Process Clause requires courts to assess, on a case-by-case basis, whether improper police conduct created a 'substantial likelihood of misidentification.'"[282]

In *Browning v. Baker*, which we have discussed a few times already, another problem was present. There were "textbook examples of suggestive techniques" during witness identification. For example, "While Josy identified Browning at trial, it was only after seeing Browning at more than a dozen preliminary hearings, and at each he was presented as the accused."

For a second example, "An officer presented Coe with Browning—who was shirtless and handcuffed—and said, 'We think we have a suspect. Is this him?' At this point, Browning's appearance, the officer's question, and the form of the showup rendered the procedures highly suggestive and any resulting identification of little evidentiary value." It is worth pointing out that the courts are unsympathetic to these types of claims and often deny claims of due process violations based on suggestive witness identification.[283]

Judicial Misconduct—Racial/Ethnic Bias

Due process requires a fair hearing before a fair judge, which means a judge who is not biased.[284] In *Bracy v. Gramley*, the judge presiding over Bracy's conviction was convicted of taking bribes in *other* cases. Bracy argued that the judge was biased against him since the judge "had an interest in a conviction here to deflect suspicion that he was taking bribes in other cases." The court did not grant the writ but allowed Bracy to proceed with obtaining information from the government (discovery) to see if it supported the claim of bias.[285]

---

[282] *Perry v. New Hampshire*, 565 U.S. 228 (2012).

[283] *See Sexton v. Beaudreaux*, 585 U.S. ___, 138 S. Ct. 2555 (2018). *See also Walden v. Shinn,* 990 F.3d 1183 (9th Cir. 2021).

[284] *See Bracy v. Gramley*, 520 U.S. 899 (1997).

[285] In *Bracy v. Schomig*, 286 F.3d 406 (7th Cir. 2002), the Seventh Circuit Court of Appeals affirmed the conviction but vacated the sentence of death and ordered a new

The standard that the court uses is "whether the average judge in her position was likely to be neutral or whether there existed an unconstitutional potential for bias."[286] This standard was applied in *Echavarria v. Filson*, where the judge had been investigated by the same FBI agent who had investigated the petitioner in that case. The court highlighted the *risk of bias* by stating, "The question is whether an average judge in Judge Lehman's position would have feared that the FBI might reopen its investigation or renew its advocacy for state prosecution if he made rulings favorable to Echavarria." Therefore, the court vacated the finding of guilt and ordered a new trial because "[t]he risk of bias in this case deprived Echavarria of the fair tribunal to which he was constitutionally entitled."

Recall that we discussed a situation where an attorney was so biased that he could not properly represent racial minorities.[287] In that case, Ezzard Ellis was convicted of murder with a special circumstance, attempted murder, and robbery, and was sentenced to life without the possibility of parole. In 2020, his conviction was vacated, and he was ordered to be freed or retried. What happens when a judge is biased like the attorney in the *Ellis* case?

Randy Halprin and six of his friends escaped from a Texas prison and went to rob a store. An officer responded to reports of the robbery and was shot and killed by one of the seven robbers. The group is known as the Texas 7. One member of the group committed suicide, and the other six were sentenced to death. Four have been put to death, and two are on death row.

Randy Halprin was the only Jewish member of the group. Fifteen years after his conviction, the judge who presided over the case ran for public office. At this point, stories about the judge's antisemitism began to emerge. The judge used ethnic slurs to refer to

---

death penalty hearing. After that, the governor issued a limited pardon so that Bracy's sentence was commuted to life in prison. *People v. Collins*, 815 N.E.2d 860 (App. Ct. 2004).

[286] *Hurles v. Ryan*, 752 F.3d 768 (9th Cir. 2014).

[287] *Ellis v. Harrison*, 947 F.3d 555 (9th Cir. 2020).

Jews, set up a trust that would have withheld payments to his children if they married non-white non-Christians, and threatened his daughter that he would not pay her law school tuition unless she broke up with her Jewish boyfriend. He was proud to have sentenced Jews and Latinos to death in the Texas 7 case.

The federal court denied Halprin's writ of habeas corpus. However, days before he was to be executed, the Texas Court of Criminal Appeals stayed the execution and ordered a trial to review whether the judge was biased against Halprin.

On October 11, 2021, Judge Lela Lawrence Mays recommended that Halprin receive a new trial. She highlighted that the sentencing judge was biased against Halprin because Halprin was Jewish and that the judge's "anti-Semitic bias motivated his actions." Much evidence of antisemitism was submitted. Judge Mays noted that a significant number of discretionary decisions went against Halprin— decisions that could go either way and are up to the judge to make.

Much earlier, we cited to *Buck v. Davis*,[288] where the petitioner's attorney used an expert witness at sentencing who testified that the petitioner was likely to act violently in the future due to the petitioner's race. The expert's testimony made it more likely that the petitioner would receive the death penalty. The Court granted the writ of habeas corpus due to the ineffective assistance of counsel.

In that case, the Supreme Court noted the "reasonable probability that Buck was sentenced to death in part because of his race. This is a disturbing departure from the basic premise that our criminal law punishes people for what they do, not who they are." Judge Mays cited this line in holding that Halprin was sentenced to death because of who he was, not because of what he did or did not do.

The court concluded that "Halprin's right to a fair proceeding has been violated. A new fair trial is the only remedy." The Texas Court of Criminal Appeals now has to decide whether to accept Judge Mays' sensible recommendation.

---

[288] 580 U.S. ___, 137 S. Ct. 759 (2017).

Juror Misconduct—Racial/Ethnic Bias

After discussing judicial bias, we now turn to juror bias. What happens if it turns out that a juror is biased against a defendant? In *Pena-Rodriguez v. Colorado*,[289] two jurors made negative comments about Hispanic men, which indicated that those jurors voted to convict because of an anti-Hispanic bias.

The Supreme Court held:

[W]here a juror makes a clear statement that indicates he or she relied on racial stereotypes or animus to convict a criminal defendant, the Sixth Amendment requires that the no-impeachment rule give way in order to permit the trial court to consider the evidence of the juror's statement and any resulting denial of the jury trial guarantee.

Though the Court referred to the Sixth Amendment, it did so within the context of the Fourteenth Amendment, which was adopted to "eliminate racial discrimination emanating from official sources in the States."

Juror Misconduct—Improper Influences on the Jury

Enrique Godoy was convicted of second-degree murder and was sentenced to 16 years to life in prison.[290] A member of the jury had a friend who was a judge—not the judge presiding over the trial. The juror asked questions to her judge-friend and reported his answers to the other members of the jury.

Godoy filed a motion for new trial, arguing that his right to a trial by an impartial jury was violated because of improper outside influence. The trial court denied the motion, and the appellate court upheld the conviction and sentence. Godoy then filed a federal writ of habeas corpus, which was denied by the lower court.

The Ninth Circuit Court of Appeals remanded the writ of habeas corpus. The Court highlighted that "due process does not

---

[289] 580 U.S. ___, 137 S. Ct. 855 (2017).
[290] *Godoy v. Spearman*, 861 F.3d 956 (9th Cir. 2017).

tolerate 'any ground of suspicion that the administration of justice has been interfered with' by external influence." Since "no evidentiary hearing on prejudice has yet been held, we remand to the district court to conduct such a hearing."

In a similar case, the Ninth Circuit again remanded for a consideration about whether to hold an evidentiary hearing.[291] In 1995, Clark filed his writ of habeas corpus in federal court (this was before the passage of the AEDPA). After being sent back to state court and then filing numerous amended petitions, the writ was denied in 2014. One juror consulted with his minister, who allegedly told the juror that the death penalty was warranted. The Court remanded this case for determining "whether the contact was 'sufficiently improper' and then determining whether that improper contact had a 'credible risk of influencing the verdict.'"

Prosecutorial Misconduct—Exclusion of Juror Members Due to Race

The exclusion of a juror based on race falls under the Fourteenth Amendment's Equal Protection clause, though we include it in this section about due process violations. During jury selection, the prosecution and defense are allowed to exclude jurors. Jurors can be excluded when there is a good reason ("for cause"). Jurors can also be excluded for no reason at all ("peremptory"). What happens if the prosecution uses its peremptory challenges to exclude minorities?

In *Batson v. Kentucky*,[292] the prosecutor used his peremptory challenges to exclude the four black men who were in the jury pool, and the result was that the jury consisted of only white people. The Court held that "[t]he Equal Protection Clause guarantees the defendant that the State will not exclude members of his race from the jury venire on account of race."

---

[291] *Clark v. Chappell*, 936 F.3d 944 (9th Cir. 2019).
[292] 476 U.S. 79 (1986).

The Court also noted, "The harm from discriminatory jury selection extends beyond that inflicted on the defendant and the excluded juror to touch the entire community. Selection procedures that purposefully exclude black persons from juries undermine public confidence in the fairness of our system of justice." The rule is that a juror cannot be excluded on the basis of the juror's race.

There is a three-part test to determine if a *Batson* violation has occurred:

1. To establish a violation, a petitioner must show enough facts to infer that a juror was dismissed due to the juror's race.
2. Then, the burden shifts to the government to suggest a neutral reason for the exclusion of the juror.
3. If the government is able to do that, then the Court must decide whether the juror was excluded because of the juror's race.

To create an inference that a juror was dismissed due to the juror's race, "statistical disparities," without anything more, is sufficient. "In this case, two-thirds of the black veniremembers not removed for cause were struck by the prosecutor. We have found an inference of discrimination in cases where smaller percentages of minority veniremembers were peremptorily struck."[293] The courts also may compare qualifications of juror members. If a black juror is excluded but a white juror with similar qualifications is allowed to be on the jury, then the court may conclude that a *Batson* violation occurred. For example, in *Shirley v. Yates*, the Court conducted a "comparative juror analysis" and concluded that a "comparative juror analysis here shows that a white juror with a very similar level of 'life experience' was seated." The court granted the writ.

Below are other cases for which courts have granted a writ of habeas corpus due to a *Batson* violation.

---

[293] *Shirley v. Yates*, 807 F.3d 1090 (9th Cir. 2015).

Crittenden v. Chappell[294]

The only black member of the jury pool was given the lowest possible rating by the prosecutor for unjustified reasons. The juror was actually a "model prosecution juror" according to the factors that the prosecution claims it used to select jurors. The court compared the juror to other jurors and found that similar jurors received positive ratings and were seated on the jury.

Currie v. McDowell[295]

Currie's conviction was vacated because of a *Batson* violation. At the retrial, the prosecutor again excluded jurors due to their race. At the third trial, the prosecutor removed a black person from the jury. When the case reached the Ninth Circuit, the court granted the writ of habeas corpus. The court noted that the prosecutor gave various pretextual reasons for the exclusion of the juror, highlighting that comparable jurors were not excluded from the jury pool.

Foster v. Chatman[296]

In this case, all four of the black juror members were excluded by the prosecutor. Using the Georgia Open Records Act, the petitioner requested the prosecutor's records from the trial. The records make clear that the prosecution sought to exclude all potential black jurors. The Supreme Court vacated the conviction, citing a prior Supreme Court case: "If a prosecutor's proffered reason for striking a black panelist applies just as well to an otherwise-similar nonblack [panelist] who is permitted to serve, that is evidence tending to prove purposeful discrimination."

The Court also noted "the shifting explanations, the misrepresentations of the record, and the persistent focus on race in the prosecution's file." The Court concluded, "The State's new argument today does not dissuade us from the conclusion that its prosecutors

---

[294] 804 F.3d 998 (9th Cir. 2015).
[295] 825 F.3d 603 (9th Cir. 2016).
[296] 587 U.S. ___, 136 S. Ct. 1737 (2016).

were motivated in substantial part by race when they struck Garrett and Hood from the jury 30 years ago. *Two peremptory strikes on the basis of race are two more than the Constitution allows* [emphasis added]."

Flowers v. Mississippi[297]

Flowers was tried six times for the murder of four people. The verdicts of guilt from the first three trials were vacated due to either prosecutorial misconduct or to *Batson* violations. The fourth and fifth trials ended with mistrials. At the sixth trial, the prosecutor used peremptory challenges to exclude five of the six black juror members. Flowers was found guilty and was sentenced to death.

The Supreme Court looked to the history of the case, pointing out that "in the six trials combined, the State employed its peremptory challenges to strike 41 of the 42 black prospective jurors that it could have struck."[298] In fact, in the third trial, the prosecutor used all 15 of his peremptory strikes to strike the 15 black prospective jurors!

The Court succinctly summed up what is required. "Equal justice under law requires a criminal trial free of racial discrimination in the jury selection process." The Court also provided factors to look for. What follows is a quote from the case of those factors:

- o statistical evidence about the prosecutor's use of peremptory strikes against black prospective jurors as compared to white prospective jurors in the case;
- o evidence of a prosecutor's disparate questioning and investigation of black and white prospective jurors in the case;
- o side-by-side comparisons of black prospective jurors who were struck and white prospective jurors who were not struck in the case;

---

[297] 588 U.S. ___, 139 S. Ct. 2228 (2019).
[298] *Id.*

- a prosecutor's misrepresentations of the record when defending the strikes during the *Batson* hearing;
- relevant history of the State's peremptory strikes in past cases; or
- other relevant circumstances that bear upon the issue of racial discrimination.

Another factor that the Court focused on is the disparate questioning of the prospective jurors. "The State asked the five black prospective jurors who were struck a total of 145 questions. By contrast, the State asked the 11 seated white jurors a total of 12 questions." By asking so many questions "of the black prospective jurors or conducting additional inquiry into their backgrounds, a prosecutor can try to find some pretextual reason—any reason—that the prosecutor can later articulate to justify what is in reality a racially motivated strike."

In addition to focusing on the jurors as a whole, the Supreme Court focused on a specific juror who was struck. Judging from her answers, one juror appeared to be a good fit from the prosecutor's perspective because she was pro-death penalty and had a connection to law enforcement. She was nonetheless struck, allegedly because she knew some of the witnesses. Typically, knowing the defendant or a witness is a good reason to disqualify a potential juror member. What, then, was the problem here? The problem was that three white prospective jurors also knew some of the witnesses, and the prosecutor did not ask any questions of these three about their connection to the case. "If the State were concerned about prospective jurors' connections to witnesses in the case, the State presumably would have used individual questioning to ask those potential white jurors whether they could remain impartial despite their relationships."

In this case, the Supreme Court granted the petitioner's writ of habeas corpus and vacated the conviction and death penalty sentence. On remand, the prosecutor's office submitted a motion to dismiss the indictment. On September 4, 2020, the court signed the order of dismissal, and Curtis Flowers was a free man after having spent more than 20 years in prison, and after having gone through six trials.

Insufficient Evidence To Convict

While the evidence relied on to convict a petitioner may often be flimsy, arguing insufficient evidence as a basis for a writ of habeas corpus is an uphill battle. "[J]udges will sometimes encounter convictions that they believe to be mistaken, but that they must nonetheless uphold."[299]

In *Cavazos*, a grandmother was convicted of shaking her grandson to death. The prosecutor argued that the baby died from shaken baby syndrome (SBS), while the defense argued that the baby tragically died from sudden infant death syndrome (SIDS). The jury found the defendant guilty. The grandmother filed a writ of habeas corpus, which was granted by the Ninth Circuit under the reasoning that the prosecutor's experts relied on the absence of indicators in the brain to suggest SIDS. The Ninth Circuit then determined that the grandmother was convicted due to an *absence of evidence* and reversed the conviction.

The Supreme Court, however, reinstated the conviction. "Doubts about whether Smith is in fact guilty are understandable. But it is not the job of this Court, and was not that of the Ninth Circuit, to decide whether the State's theory was correct. The jury decided that question, and its decision is supported by the record."

In a move that possibly indicates that the Supreme Court itself was troubled, the Court noted, "It is said that Smith, who already has served years in prison, has been punished enough, and that she poses no danger to society. These or other considerations perhaps would be grounds to seek clemency, a prerogative granted to executive authorities to help ensure that justice is tempered by mercy." It appears that this paragraph was meant to signal to the petitioner, to the parole

---

[299] *Cavazos v. Smith*, 565 U.S. 1 (2011).

board, or to the governor that the petitioner was a suitable candidate for clemency.

The dissent pointed to a significant amount of evidence to suggest that the grandmother was not guilty: (1) grandmothers are usually not perpetrators of shaken baby syndrome; (2) the grandmother had helped raise her other grandchildren without incident; (3) her other grandchildren were sleeping in the same room as the baby; and (4) the baby's mother was asleep in the room next door. The dissent also highlighted much scientific evidence to show that the grandmother was not guilty. The dissent concluded with a strongly worded, "justice is not served by the Court's exercise of discretion to take up this tragic, fact-bound case."

The takeaway from this case is that courts will not second-guess decisions that have some evidence to support the decision. To succeed on a writ due to insufficient evidence, a petitioner must show that "no rational trier of fact could have agreed with the jury."

This rule was applied in *Long v. Johnson*,[300] where the petitioner was convicted of killing her boyfriend. In her writ of habeas corpus, she argued that there was insufficient evidence to convict her. The Ninth Circuit noted that, if they had been sitting on the jury, they may have found the petitioner not guilty, and if they were a state appellate court, they may have reversed the conviction. Since the Ninth Circuit is a federal court that reviews state convictions and must defer to the jury (and, under the AEDPA, to the state courts), the Ninth Circuit affirmed the conviction.

The story, however, does not end there. Kimberly Long filed a state writ, arguing that she had received ineffective assistance of counsel. Her attorney did not consult with an expert about the time of death, which was a main issue in the case. The prosecutor claimed that Kimberly had returned home at 1:20 a.m. and murdered her boyfriend, and she claimed that she had returned around 2:00 a.m. and called 911

---

[300] 736 F.3d 891 (9th Cir. 2013).

a few minutes later. Two time-of-death experts testified that the boyfriend was dead before 1:20 a.m.

> Neither forensic pathologist could give an exact timing of the victim's death. However, both forensic pathologists testified in this court that the victim's death occurred significantly earlier than 1:20 a.m., the earliest time the prosecution could place the petitioner at the scene.

After having her writ granted by the trial court and reversed by the appellate court, the California Supreme Court granted the writ and ordered a new trial.[301] In April 2021, the prosecutor agreed to drop the charges.[302]

> Though not so common, the courts do occasionally grant a writ of habeas corpus when there was insufficient evidence to convict. In *Lucero v. Holland*, the petitioner was convicted of possession of a "dirk or dagger or sharp instrument" while incarcerated.[303] The evidence consisted of a gang expert who testified that gang members were expected to have access to weapons and that the petitioner had access to a weapon. This testimony, however, failed to show that the petitioner *controlled* the weapon, "as California courts have made clear, constructive possession, custody, or control is distinct from aiding and abetting a co-defendant's control and possession." For this reason, the court granted the writ.

Restraints at Trial

A defendant may not be physically restrained in court unless the court orders that the defendant be restrained. This applies to the guilt phase and the penalty phase of a trial.[304] There are three reasons for this rule:

---

[301] *In re Long*, 10 Cal.5th 764 (2020).
[302] Christopher Damien, "*Murder charge against Corona woman dismissed, DA says it can't prove her guilt in new trial*," Palm Springs Desert Sun, April 22, 2021, https://www.desertsun.com/story/news/crime_courts/2021/04/22/kimberly-longs-murder-charge-dropped-riverside-county-district-attorney/7338447002/.
[303] 902 F.3d 979 (9th Cir. 2018).
[304] *Deck v. Missouri*, 544 U.S. 622 (2005).

(1) the presence of restraints undermines the presumption of innocence; (2) an unshackled defendant is better able to assist and communicate with his or her attorney; and (3) the absence of restraints maintains a dignified court room.

Issues with Competence

A defendant has a constitutional right not to be tried while he or she is incompetent. "It has long been accepted that a person whose mental condition is such that he lacks the capacity to understand the nature and object of the proceedings against him, to consult with counsel, and to assist in preparing his defense may not be subjected to a trial."[305] A judge must hold a competency hearing when the judge has a "bona fide doubt" about a defendant's competency.[306]

In *Maxwell v. Roe*, the lower court denied a writ of habeas corpus in which the petitioner alleged that he was incompetent during trial. On appeal, the Court of Appeals for the Ninth Circuit reversed. The court highlighted that it should have been obvious to the state court that the petitioner may have been incompetent, concluding that:

> Maxwell's inability to control himself in court, his suicide attempt, his history of mental illness, his impaired communication with defense counsel, and his 14-day involuntary psychiatric hold during his trial would have raised a bona fide doubt in a reasonable trial judge that he was no longer able to consult with his lawyer with a reasonable degree of rational understanding.[307]

The court then held that a competency hearing years later would reveal little about whether a petitioner had been competent during a trial. Therefore, the writ was granted, and state was ordered to either free the petitioner or provide him with a new trial.

---

[305] *Drope v. Missouri*, 420 U.S. 162 (1975).
[306] *Pate v. Robinson*, 383 U.S. 375 (1966).
[307] 606 F.3d 561 (2010).

H. Conclusion

We have presented a thorough outline of many potential arguments that are available in federal writs of habeas corpus. The arguments presented are for informational purposes and are not intended to be relied upon by a reader in filing his or her own federal writ of habeas corpus. The law changes, and each of the arguments and citations must be checked to determine whether the case is still good law. As we noted in the introduction, the information here is presented as a starting point to provide information to the reader and is not presented as an ending point. Our sincere hope is that the reader has learned about the *substantive* requirements of federal writs of habeas corpus.

Chapter 5
ARGUMENTS THAT SHOULD NOT BE RAISED IN A FEDERAL WRIT OF HABEAS CORPUS

A. Introduction

After presenting a detailed outline about what may be argued in a federal writ of habeas corpus, we now turn to what generally may *not* be argued in a federal writ of habeas corpus. This list is much shorter than the list of what may be argued. The purpose of this chapter is to present to the reader what to avoid in a federal writ of habeas corpus.

B. Fourth Amendment Claims

In the previous chapter, we discussed whether a Fourth Amendment claim may be raised in a federal writ of habeas corpus. The Supreme Court has held that a Fourth Amendment claim typically cannot be raised in a writ of habeas corpus. A quick summary is in order. The Fourth Amendment protects against unlawful searches and seizures. Generally speaking, the police may not walk into someone's home and start looking around.[308] The police are required to obtain a search warrant in order to search private property.

If the police were to illegally search a residence and obtain evidence, and then the prosecution were to seek to use that evidence at trial, the evidence would likely be excluded based on a violation of the Fourth Amendment. Since the exclusion of evidence should normally occur at trial, the Supreme Court held that, "where the State has provided an opportunity for full and fair litigation of a Fourth Amendment claim, the Constitution does not require that a state prisoner be granted federal habeas corpus relief on the ground that

---

[308] There are exceptions that are beyond the scope of this book.

evidence obtained in an unconstitutional search or seizure was introduced at his trial."[309]

We previously noted two possible ways to raise a Fourth Amendment claim in a writ of habeas corpus:

First, there are rare occasions when a defendant sought to exclude the evidence obtained via an illegal search and seizure and, for whatever reasons, the state court did not rule on the issue. In this circumstance, the defendant did not receive "an opportunity for full and fair litigation of a Fourth Amendment claim." Not all federal circuit courts allow for this. The Second Circuit does not, while the Ninth Circuit does.[310]

Second, a defendant may argue that he or she received ineffective assistance of counsel (Sixth Amendment) for trial counsel's failure to exclude the evidence seized in the unlawful search and seizure. To succeed on this claim, the defendant must argue that the evidence should have been suppressed (Fourth Amendment) *and* that the defendant was prejudiced by trial counsel's failure to suppress the evidence (Sixth Amendment). This is a "demanding standard."[311]

Therefore, one argument that is generally unavailable in a writ of habeas corpus is a Fourth Amendment claim for an unlawful search and seizure.

C. New Constitutional Procedural Rules—The Teague Rule

There is a simple yet complex rule about whether new constitutional procedural rules, which did not exist at the time of the defendant's trial, may be used by a defendant in a writ of habeas corpus. The rule is: New constitutional procedural rules do not apply to cases that are

---

[309] *Stone v. Powell*, 428 U.S. 465 (1976).

[310] *See Capellan v. Riley* 975 F.2d 67 (2d Cir. 1992) and *Anderson v. Calderon*, 232 F.3d 1053 (9th Cir. 2000). For a summary of the different approaches, *see Good v. Berghuis*, 729 F.3d 636 (6th Cir. 2013).

[311] *Evans v. Davis*, 875 F.3d 210 (5th Cir. 2017).

already final. Another way of saying this is that new procedural rules are not retroactive.

In *Teague v. Lane*, the Supreme Court held "under the habeas corpus statute as interpreted by this Court, a new rule of criminal procedure ordinarily does not apply retroactively to overturn final convictions on federal *collateral* review."[312] The rationale of this rule is that the "costs imposed upon the States by retroactive application of new rules of constitutional law on habeas corpus thus generally far outweigh the benefits of this application."[313]

The reason that this rule is simple is because it is a bright-line rule that new constitutional rules do not apply to a writ of habeas corpus filed in federal court. The reason that this rule is complex is because it is often difficult to know when a rule is a "new" rule and when a rule is an extension of an old rule.

This question is critical, for a new rule will not apply to a defendant in a writ of habeas corpus, while an old rule will apply to the defendant. The *Teague* decision itself notes that "[i]t is admittedly often difficult to determine when a case announces a new rule." The Court announced that "a case announces a new rule when it breaks new ground or imposes a new obligation on the States or the Federal Government. To put it differently, a case announces a new rule if the result was not dictated by precedent existing at the time the defendant's conviction became final."[314]

In 2021, the Supreme Court pointed out that "in the 32 years since *Teague* … this Court has announced many important new rules of criminal procedure. But the Court has not applied *any* of those new rules retroactively on federal collateral review."[315]

In *Edwards v. Vannoy*, the defendant was convicted of robbery, kidnapping, and rape and was sentenced to life in prison without

---

[312] *Edwards v. Vannoy*, 593 U.S. ___, 141 S. Ct. 1547 (2021) (explaining the holding of *Teague v. Lane*, 489 U.S. 288 (1989)).

[313] *Sawyer v. Smith*, 497 U.S. 227 (1990).

[314] *Teague*, 489 U.S. at 301 (citations omitted).

[315] *Edwards v. Vannoy*, 593 U.S. ___, 141 S. Ct. at 1551–52.

parole. For some of the counts, 11 members of the jury found Edwards guilty, and for other counts, 10 members of the jury found him guilty. At the time, Louisiana allowed for convictions when 10 of the 12 jurors voted to convict.

While Edwards' writ of habeas corpus was pending, the Supreme Court decided that there is a constitutional right to a unanimous jury verdict, meaning that all 12 jurors must vote to convict. In *Edwards v. Vannoy*, the Supreme Court was faced with whether the unanimous jury requirement would apply on collateral review.

The answer to whether Edwards' constitutional rights were violated depends on whether the requirement for a unanimous jury is a "new" rule. If so, Edwards would not be able to rely on this rule in his writ of habeas corpus. The Court noted, "The starkest example of a decision announcing a new rule is a decision that overrules an earlier case."

In *Edwards v. Vannoy*, it was clear that the decision overruled earlier cases, which allowed for non-unanimous jury verdicts. To get around this, the defendant argued that the right to a unanimous jury is part of "the original meaning of the Sixth Amendment's right to a jury trial and the Fourteenth Amendment's incorporation of that right (and others) against the States." Therefore, argued the defendant, the rule is an "old rule," which should apply to his case.

The Supreme Court rejected this argument. According to the Supreme Court, what matters is how the law was *interpreted*. Since the law was interpreted as allowing non-unanimous jury verdicts, the requirement for unanimous verdicts is considered a "new" rule. Due to its interpretation, the Court affirmed the denial of the writ of habeas corpus.

D. The End of the Exception to the Teague Rule

To recap, in *Teague*, the Court noted that a new rule applies retroactively when the new rule changes "our understanding of the

157

bedrock procedural elements essential to the fairness of a proceeding." This is usually referred to as the watershed exception. In theory, these are rules that are *so* important that they *must* be applied retroactively.

The problem with this rule, as noted in *Edwards v. Vannoy*, is that "the Court since *Teague* has rejected *every* claim that a new procedural rule qualifies as a watershed rule." As a case in point, the Supreme Court was not sympathetic to Edwards' argument that a unanimous jury verdict should be considered a "watershed" rule.

After rejecting Edwards' arguments, the Court pointed out the obvious: There is no real watershed exception to the rule against applying new constitutional rules retroactively. "At this point, some 32 years after *Teague*, we think the only candid answer is that none can—that is, no new rules of criminal procedure can satisfy the watershed exception. We cannot responsibly continue to suggest otherwise to litigants and courts."

The Court continued as follows:

Continuing to articulate a theoretical exception that never actually applies in practice offers false hope to defendants, distorts the law, misleads judges, and wastes the resources of defense counsel, prosecutors, and courts. Moreover, no one can reasonably rely on an exception that is non-existent in practice, so no reliance interests can be affected by forthrightly acknowledging reality. It is time—probably long past time—to make explicit what has become increasingly apparent to bench and bar over the last 32 years: New procedural rules do not apply retroactively on federal collateral review [emphasis added]. The watershed exception is moribund. It must "be regarded as retaining no vitality."

Practice tip #1

When a Supreme Court decision may help a defendant in his or her writ of habeas corpus, the defendant should argue that the rule is not a new rule (if possible). This is, however, easier said than done. In *Edwards v. Vannoy*, the defendant did make such an argument, but the

158

Court rejected it. If the rule is found to be a "new" procedural rule, a writ of habeas corpus predicated on the new rule will be denied.

Practice tip #2

If possible, argue that the new rule is a substantive rule and is not a procedural rule. In *Montgomery v. Louisiana*, a 17-year-old was convicted of a 1963 murder and was sentenced to life in prison without parole.[316] In 2012, the Supreme Court held that a mandatory life sentence for a minor is unconstitutional (we discussed this case in the section about arguments that are based on the Eighth Amendment).[317]

What about a minor who had already been convicted and sentenced to a mandatory life sentence? May this person argue that his or her sentence was unconstitutional? As we already saw, if the rule prohibiting mandatory life sentences is a *procedural* rule, it would not apply to someone who was already convicted. The lower courts held that the new rule was not retroactive, so the defendant could not use it to argue that his mandatory sentence was unconstitutional.

The Supreme Court highlighted that a substantive rule may be applied retroactively. How does one know if a rule is procedural or if it is substantive? "[A] procedural rule regulate[s] only the manner of determining the defendant's culpability. A substantive rule, in contrast, forbids criminal punishment of certain primary conduct or prohibits a certain category of punishment for a class of defendants because of their status or offense."[318]

The State of Louisiana argued that the *Miller* rule (which barred mandatory life without parole for youth) is a procedural rule because it governs the process for a sentence of life without parole, and the court must consider the defendant's youth as part of the process. The Supreme Court rejected this, holding that "because *Miller* determined that sentencing a child to life without parole is excessive

---

[316] 577 U.S 136,___ .S. Ct. 718 (2016).
[317] *See Miller v. Alabama*, 567 U.S. 460 (2012).
[318] *Montgomery*, 136 S. Ct. at 732.

for all 'but the rare juvenile offender whose crime reflects irreparable corruption,' it rendered life without parole an unconstitutional penalty for 'a class of defendants because of their status'—that is, juvenile offenders whose crimes reflect the transient immaturity of youth."[319]

Essentially, the case comes down to whether the focus of the *Miller* rule is on the Court considering a defendant's youth before sentencing the minor to life without parole (a procedural rule) or on the effect of the rule—that only in the rarest of cases may a minor be sentenced to life without parole (substantively, minors cannot be sentenced to life without parole).

The Court also emphasized that its decision does not place a big burden on states. There is no need to retry any minor. All that a state must do is allow "juvenile homicide offenders to be considered for parole."

This case illustrates that it is sometimes difficult to know whether a new rule is substantive or procedural. This distinction is crucial and may be the determining factor for whether a writ of habeas corpus is granted or denied. It may be important, therefore, to hire a competent and knowledgeable attorney to write the writ of habeas corpus. A good attorney may also be able to think of creative arguments to argue that certain laws appearing on the surface to be procedural are really substantive. After all, as *Montgomery v. Louisiana* illustrates, it is sometimes hard to tell the difference between a procedural law and a substantive law.

E. The Future of the Teague Doctrine

In *Teague*, the Supreme Court held that rules of criminal procedure do not apply retroactively. *Teague* contained an exception, the watershed exception, which allowed for the retroactive application of a procedural rule when the new rule changes "our understanding of the bedrock procedural elements essential to the fairness of a proceeding."

---

[319] Citations omitted.

In practice, the Court never identified such a watershed rule, and the watershed exception was abolished in *Edwards v. Vannoy*. The *Teague* doctrine only applies to procedural rules, not to substantive rules.

There are calls to abolish the *Teague* doctrine itself, which would then allow new procedural rules to be applied retroactively on habeas corpus. In a 2021 law review article, Jeffrey G. Ho argues, "In light of the weighty remedial interests—not just in accuracy but in human dignity and judicial integrity—a revised retroactivity framework should be more generous about granting retroactivity remedies for violations of constitutional rights."[320]

This is something to take into consideration for a defendant for whom a new procedural law would render his or her conviction or sentence unconstitutional, but the *Teague* doctrine prevents the defendant from relying on the new procedural rule. A defendant should consider asking the Court to revisit the *Teague* doctrine.

Justice Gorsuch wrote in his concurring opinion in *Edwards v. Vannoy*, regarding the watershed exception, "Nor is it only *Teague*'s results that mystify. The test itself has been fraught with contradictions from the start." Jeffrey G. Ho argues that the whole *Teague* doctrine must be reconsidered. Defendants should keep abreast of the law, as a change to the *Teague* doctrine could benefit may defendants and may appear in the future.

F. Conclusion

In this chapter, we have presented what arguments are typically *not available* for a federal writ of habeas corpus. This list is much shorter than the arguments that are available for a writ of habeas corpus. We have also presented ways for a defendant to argue these violations in a writ of habeas corpus, including:

---

[320] Jeffrey G. Ho, *"Finality, Comity, and Retroactivity in Criminal Procedure: Reimagining the Teague Doctrine After* Edwards v. Vannoy," 73 Stan. L. Rev. 1551 (2021).

- Argue a Fourth Amendment violation under the Sixth Amendment's right to effective assistance of counsel.
- Argue that a new rule is really a substantive rule, not a procedural rule.
- Argue that the *Teague* doctrine should be reconsidered.

In the next chapter, we will address claims of actual innocence, which do not appear in our chapter on arguments that may be raised in a federal writ of habeas corpus and also do not appear in this chapter about arguments that should not be made in a federal writ of habeas corpus.

Chapter 6
CLAIMS OF ACTUAL INNOCENCE

A. May a Defendant Argue Actual Innocence in a Federal Writ of Habeas Corpus?

The reader may have noticed that we did not include actual innocence in our chapter about arguments that are appropriate for a federal writ of habeas corpus. The reader may have also noticed that we did not include actual innocence in our chapter about arguments that should not be made in a federal writ of habeas corpus.

Why did we not discuss claims of actual innocence earlier? There is good reason for this. A claim of actual innocence is in its own category. Over and over again, the federal courts note that it has never been established that a claim for actual innocence exists for the purposes of a federal writ of habeas corpus.

For example, the Ninth Circuit has written, "We have not resolved whether a freestanding actual innocence claim is cognizable in a federal habeas corpus proceeding in the non-capital context, although we have assumed that such a claim is viable."[321]

The Supreme Court has made clear that claims of actual innocence can serve as a "gateway" to raising other constitutional violations. In Chapter 3, we discussed *McQuiggin v. Perkins* in relation to the one-year deadline.[322] In that case, the Court held that "actual innocence, if proved, serves as a gateway through which a petitioner may pass whether the impediment is a procedural bar, as it was in *Schlup* and *House*, or, as in this case, expiration of the statute of limitations."

What about a "free standing" claim of actual innocence? May this be argued in a federal writ of habeas corpus? The Supreme Court has avoided answering this question.

---

[321] *Jones v. Taylor*, 763 F.3d 1242 (9th Cir. 2019).
[322] 569 U.S. 383 (2013).

Why do claims of actual innocence fall into a gray area? On the one hand, claims made in a federal writ of habeas corpus must allege a violation of the Constitution. If you recall, we discussed this in our introductory chapters. A federal writ must allege a "violation of the Constitution or laws or treaties of the United States."[323] The Supreme Court noted, "Claims of actual innocence based on newly discovered evidence have never been held to state a ground for federal habeas relief absent an independent constitutional violation occurring in the underlying state criminal proceeding."[324]

The Court also noted that "the principle that federal habeas courts sit to ensure that individuals are not imprisoned in violation of the Constitution—not to correct errors of fact." Simply put, claims of actual innocence do not fall within any constitutional amendment. For this reason, the Supreme Court labels the actual innocence argument a "gateway," in that allows the defendant to overcome procedural impediments.[325]

On the other hand, the concurring opinion in *Herrera* noted that there is a "fundamental legal principle that executing the innocent is inconsistent with the Constitution ... the execution of a legally and factually innocent person would be a constitutionally intolerable event."

To summarize, in *McQuiggin v. Perkins*, the Supreme Court writes, "We have not resolved whether a prisoner may be entitled to habeas relief based on a freestanding claim of actual innocence." In a concurring opinion in *Herrera*, Justice Scalia took the position that "[t]here is no basis in text, tradition, or even in contemporary practice (if that were enough) for finding in the Constitution a right to demand judicial consideration of newly discovered evidence of innocence brought forward after conviction." Justice Scalia expressed hope by

---

[323] 28 U.S.C. § 2254(a).

[324] *Herrera v. Collins*, 506 U.S. 390 (1993).

[325] *See Herrera v. Collins*, 506 U.S. 390 (1993); *see also McQuiggin v. Perkins*, 569 U.S. 383 (2013).

adding, "With any luck, we shall avoid ever having to face this embarrassing question again." It appears that he was wrong. There appear to be more arguments of actual innocence than ever before.

B. How Different Circuit Courts Answer the Question

Most Circuit courts do not allow independent claims of actual innocence to be made in a federal writ of habeas corpus. For example, "[t]he Fifth Circuit does not recognize freestanding claims of actual innocence on federal habeas review."[326]

The Fifth Circuit is not the only federal circuit court to hold this way. The First, Third, Fourth, Sixth, Seventh, Eighth, Tenth, and Eleventh circuits all hold that a claim for actual innocence cannot be independently raised in a federal writ of habeas corpus. For another example, the Seventh Circuit writes, "For claims based on newly discovered evidence to state a ground for federal habeas relief, they must relate to a constitutional violation independent of any claim of innocence."[327]

The Ninth Circuit, in contrast, assumes without deciding that there is an independent actual innocence claim that may be raised in a federal writ of habeas corpus.[328]

The Second Circuit has referred to this as an "open question" and assumed that a freestanding claim of actual innocence exists, for the purposes of deciding the case that was before it.[329] A New York district court noted, "While refusing to accept the justiciability of a

---

[326] *In re Swearingen*, 556 F.3d 344 (5th Cir. 2009).

[327] *Johnson v. Bett*, 349 F.3d 1030 (7th Cir. 2003). *See also David v. Hall*, 318 F.3d 343 (1st Cir. 2003); *Fielder v. Varner*, 379 F.3d 113 (3d Cir. 2004); *Rouse v. Lee*, 339 F.3d 238 (4th Cir. 2003); *Cress v. Palmer*, 484 F.3d 844 (6th Cir. 2007); *Burton v. Dormire*, 295 F.3d 839 (8th Cir. 2002); *LaFevers v. Gibson*, 238 F.3d 1263 (10th Cir. 2001); *Rozzelle v. Florida Dept. of Corrections*, 672 F.3d 1000 (11th Cir. 2012).

[328] *See Jones v. Taylor*, 763 F.3d 1242 (9th Cir. 2019).

[329] *See Friedman v. Rehal*, 618 F.3d 142 (2d Dept. 2010).

freestanding claim of actual innocence, the Court of Appeals for the Second Circuit has come close."[330]

Though denying the writ due to lack of proof of actual innocence, the court in *DiMattina* wrote:

> The rising tide supporting recognition of an avenue for habeas relief based on actual innocence is sound. Developments in science and our better understanding of topics such as false confessions and false identifications militate in favor of adjudicating freestanding claims of innocence.

The court also pointed to the following rationale:

> Having been entrusted with the power to rein in arbitrary executive detainment of prisoners, the judiciary must be authorized to issue a writ of habeas corpus where the executive, or an official acting at the behest of the executive, detains an innocent person in prison

The takeaway is that, until the Supreme Court resolves this key question, defendants in the First, Third, Fourth, Sixth, Seventh, Eighth, Tenth, and Eleventh circuits are limited to using actual innocence as a gateway to avoid a procedural default and must argue that their incarceration violates the Constitution. Defendants in the Ninth Circuit, and possibly the Second Circuit, may argue that actual innocence is itself a basis upon which to grant a federal writ of habeas corpus.

C. The Standard for Actual Innocence

For the circuits that allow independent claims of actual innocence and for actual innocence claims that may be used to avoid a procedural default, the Supreme Court has noted that actual innocence cases are "rare."

---

[330] *DiMattina v. United States*, 949 F. Supp. 2d 387 (E.D.N.Y. 2013). Other Second Circuit decisions, however, lean toward the view that actual innocence is a gateway to a valid constitutional claim that was procedurally barred. *See Rivas v. Fischer*, 687 F.3d 514 (2d Cir. 2012); *Hyman v. Brown*, 927 F.3d 639 (2d Cir. 2019).

In *McQuiggin v. Perkins*, the Supreme Court wrote:

> We caution, however, that tenable actual-innocence gateway
> pleas are rare: "[A] petitioner does not meet the threshold
> requirement unless he persuades the district court that, in light
> of the new evidence, no juror, acting reasonably, would have
> voted to find him guilty beyond a reasonable doubt."[331]

In the Ninth Circuit:

> The standard for establishing a freestanding claim of actual
> innocence is extraordinarily high and … the showing for a
> successful claim would have to be truly persuasive. We have
> held that, at a minimum, the petitioner must go beyond
> demonstrating doubt about his guilt, and must affirmatively
> prove that he is probably innocent.[332]

The Second Circuit requires evidence of "factual innocence, not mere
legal insufficiency."[333]

Many people are under the misconception that, if a witness
recants, then that is sufficient to show actual innocence. While that
may work in a rare case, courts have made it clear that affirmative
evidence of innocence is required. As one court wrote, a "later
recantation of his trial testimony does not render his earlier testimony
false."[334] Another court wrote, "when, as here, a witness is recanting
prior sworn testimony supporting a conviction, we expect district
courts to look upon the recantation with the utmost suspicion."[335] In
Hyman, the court explained:

> The district court should consider not only the recantation, but
> the motives that may have prompted it, the timing of the
> submission, any possible motive for the original testimony, any

---

[331] *McQuiggin v. Perkins*, 569 U.S. 383 (2013) (*citing Schlup*, 513 U.S. at 329;
House, 547 U.S. at 538) (emphasizing that the *Schlup* standard is "demanding" and
seldom met).

[332] *Jones v. Taylor*, 763 F.3d 1242 (9th Cir. 2014).

[333] *Hyman v. Brown*, 927 F. 3d 639 (2d Cir. 2019) (citations omitted).

[334] *Allen v. Woodford*, 395 F.3d 979 (9th Cir. 2005).

[335] *Hyman v. Brown*, 927 F. 3d 639 (2d Cir. 2019) (citations omitted).

inconsistencies in the witness's account or between that account and other evidence, the plausibility or implausibility of inferences or assumptions that crediting the recantation would require, as well as all other factors generally considered in assessing witness credibility.

Ideally, what is needed is either new witnesses or other independent evidence of innocence. For example, in *Hyman*, the court held that the defendant failed to make a showing of actual innocence because, even if the witness lied about what she saw, this "means she cannot inculpate petitioner (or anyone else), but neither can she exonerate him. She simply has no eyewitness evidence bearing on either petitioner's guilt or his innocence." In that case, the court pointed to other evidence that implicated the defendant and acknowledged that the decision does not "foreclose the possibility that, in some circumstances, a recanted identification based on an admitted lack of knowledge, might so thoroughly undermine the evidence supporting the jury's verdict as to support the probability determination required by *Schlup*."

Practice Tip

When possible, actual innocence claims should be supported by independent evidence of actual guilt. This may include new witnesses, scientific evidence, or strong proof that someone else was guilty. Ideally, actual innocence claims should not be premised on recanted testimony, which is viewed suspiciously.

D. Sample Cases Involving Claims of Actual Innocence

In *Jones v. Taylor*, the Ninth Circuit noted the standard for claims of actual innocence.[336] To succeed, a defendant must show that "in light of new evidence, it is more likely than not that no reasonable juror would have found [the] petitioner guilty beyond a reasonable

---

[336] 763 F.3d 1242 (9th Cir. 2014).

doubt."[337] The court held that proof "in the form of recantation testimony, uncorroborated by any other evidence" is not enough to establish actual innocence.

The *Jones v. Taylor* decision leaves open the possibility that witness and victim recantations may show actual innocence if:

- The witnesses are disinterested (i.e., not family members or other people with a vested interested in the outcome of the case);
- There is a good reason for the recantation; or
- The recantations do not appear to be coordinated with each other.

The Court in *Taylor* highlighted, "Evidence that merely undercuts trial testimony or casts doubt on the petitioner's guilt, but does not affirmatively prove innocence [emphasis added], is insufficient to merit relief on a freestanding claim of actual innocence."

We now present a few cases where a defendant successfully argued actual innocence, though in these cases the defendant used the actual innocence argument to avoid a procedural default for a constitutional violation.

House v. Bell[338]

In this case, a defendant was found guilty of murder. In his writ of habeas corpus, the defendant was able to show that much of the scientific evidence (DNA and blood evidence) was either unreliable or showed that he was innocent. For example, a DNA test showed that semen found on the victim did not belong to the defendant. The defendant also presented compelling evidence that the victim's husband was the murderer. Two witnesses had heard the victim's husband admit that he had killed his wife.

---

[337] Citations omitted.
[338] 547 U.S. 518 (2006).

The defendant requested that the Court grant his writ of habeas corpus. Incredibly, the Court held that "whatever burden a hypothetical freestanding innocence claim would require, this petitioner has not satisfied it." The Court, however, allowed the defendant to present his claims to the federal court, using the claim of actual innocence as a gateway to allow the defendant to present a constitutional claim when he otherwise would not have been able to.

Reeves v. Fayette SCI[339]

Reeves confessed to robbery and murder, though there was significant evidence that linked other individuals to the crime. In this case, the police had absolutely no reason to think that Reeves was guilty, had strong evidence that implicated others, and probably knew that Reeves was lying. Nevertheless, the police extracted a confession from Reeves.

Reeves argued that he had received ineffective assistance of counsel (Sixth Amendment) because his counsel had failed to present all the evidence that pointed to Reeves' innocence. Though Reeves waited too long to file his federal writ of habeas corpus, the Court allowed him to file it, using the actual innocence claim as a gateway to the assertion of the Sixth Amendment claim.

Floyd v. Vannoy[340]

Floyd was convicted of murder and filed a writ of habeas corpus 23 years after he was convicted. Normally, his writ would have been denied because the limitations period is one year. However, Floyd successfully got around his procedural default by using an actual innocence argument. He argued that he was convicted only due to his testimony, and new DNA evidence and fingerprint analysis show that he could not have been the murderer. Therefore, "it is more than likely a reasonable, informed juror would reasonably doubt the credibility of Floyd's confessions."

---

[339] 897 F.3d 154 (3rd Cir. 2018).
[340] 894 F.3d 143 (5th Cir. 2018).

After allowing Floyd to use the actual innocence claim to avoid the one-year statute of limitations, the court focused on his claim of a *Brady* violation. Floyd argued that the state never turned over the report that indicated that the fingerprints did not belong to him. The district court granted the writ of habeas corpus, and the Fifth Circuit affirmed.

The dissent accused the majority of playing fast and loose with the *Brady* rule to justify the granting of the writ. To the dissent, the majority wanted to grant the writ because of actual innocence but was precluded by law from doing so. In the Fifth Circuit, there is no freestanding claim of actual innocence. To the dissent, the actual innocence argument was correctly made, but the decision on the *Brady* claim was incorrect.

According to the dissenting opinion, the conclusion here is that Floyd is actually innocent but is not entitled to a writ of habeas corpus. This is precisely what happens when actual innocence may be used as a gateway but not as a freestanding claim—the defendant is technically innocent but cannot use a writ of habeas corpus to challenge the incarceration.

Rivas v. Fischer[341]

This was a murder case. For five years, this was a cold case, until a new district attorney asked the medical examiner to review the case. The murder was thought to have occurred on March 27 or 28, 1988. For those dates, Rivas had an "unchallenged" alibi. When the case was reviewed five years later, the medical examiner concluded that the murder had occurred on March 26, 1988. Rivas did not have an alibi for that date and was convicted of murder.

In his writ, Rivas submitted an affidavit and testimony from one of the foremost experts of forensic science, who showed that it was *impossible* for the murder to have occurred on March 26 and that the murder had occurred sometime on March 27. Since Rivas had an

---

[341] 687 F.3d 514 (2d Cir. 2012).

unchallenged alibi for March 27, he could not have been the murderer. The Second Circuit used the actual innocence claim to allow Rivas to proceed with a writ of habeas corpus, even though the writ was filed after the one-year deadline.

E. It May Be Possible to Argue Actual Innocence in a State Writ of Habeas Corpus

As a reminder, the focus of this book is on *federal* writs of habeas corpus. Even if claims of actual innocence are used as a "gateway" to raise other constitutional violations in a *federal* writ of habeas corpus, this does prevent a defendant from raising claims of actual innocence in a *state* writ of habeas corpus, if possible.

All fifty states allow for post-conviction DNA testing.[342] States also have a wide range of procedures available for raising other claims of innocence. For example, California Penal Code section 1473.7 allows for the filing of a state writ of habeas corpus when "[n]ewly discovered evidence of actual innocence exists that requires vacation of the conviction or sentence as a matter of law or in the interests of justice."

In another example, New York allows for a motion to vacate judgment when:

> (g) New evidence has been discovered since the entry of a judgment based upon a verdict of guilty after trial, which could not have been produced by the defendant at the trial even with due diligence on his part and which is of such character as to create a probability that had such evidence been received at the trial the verdict would have been more favorable to the defendant; provided that a motion based upon such ground

---

[342] John M. Leventhal, *"A Survey of Federal and State Courts' Approaches to a Constitutional Right of Actual Innocence: Is There a Need for a State Constitutional Right in New York in the Aftermath of CPL § 440.10(1)(G-1)?,"* 76 Alb. L. Rev. 1453 (2013).

must be made with due diligence after the discovery of such alleged new evidence; or

(g-1) Forensic DNA testing of evidence performed since the entry of a judgment, (1) in the case of a defendant convicted after a guilty plea, the court has determined that the defendant has demonstrated a substantial probability that the defendant was actually innocent of the offense of which he or she was convicted, or (2) in the case of a defendant convicted after a trial, the court has determined that there exists a reasonable probability that the verdict would have been more favorable to the defendant.[343]

Therefore, a defendant with a claim of actual innocence is encouraged to learn about the state procedures that may be available to raise a claim of innocence.

F. Conclusion

A few years ago, Diane P. Wood, Chief Judge of United States Court of Appeals for the Seventh Circuit, wrote a law review article titled, "The Enduring Challenges for Habeas Corpus."[344] In her article, she argued that innocence "should stand at the top of the hierarchy of reasons for granting relief, even at such a late stage as a collateral petition—well above a claim of a violation of *Miranda* rights, or a complaint that Confrontation Clause rights were violated, or even a claim that the jury did not reflect a fair cross-section of the community." She suggested that the Supreme Court and Congress have stopped short of allowing for standalone claims of actual innocence because they are concerned that the courts will be inundated with claims of actual innocence. She calls for the adoption of a

---

[343] CPL § 440.10.

[344] Diane P. Wood, *"The Enduring Challenges for Habeas Corpus,"* 95 Notre Dame L. Rev. 1809 (2020). For a different perspective, see William H. Pryor Jr., *"The Great Writ and Federal Courts: Judge Wood's Solution in Search of a Problem,"* 95 Notre Dame L. Rev. 1835 (2020).

standard that allows for claims of actual innocence, but with a high enough threshold of proof to keep out cases that are clearly not actual innocence cases.

From the Supreme Court's frequent avoidance of this question, it appears that the Court does not want to answer the question. Nonetheless, the question about whether claims of actual innocence could be raised independently, or whether they are a "gateway" to other valid constitutional claims, is a question that the reader should keep in the back of his or her mind. Sooner or later, there will have to be an answer to this question.

Chapter 7
EXHAUSTION OF CLAIMS IN STATE COURT

A. What Is "Exhaustion"?

Earlier, in the chapter about statutes of limitations, we briefly referred to a concept known as "exhaustion." We noted that the general rule is that only claims that were "exhausted" in state court may be brought in federal court. Typically, to exhaust a claim, one must seek review of that claim in the highest state court available. We will now address the exhaustion requirement in greater detail.

According to 28 U.S.C. § 2254(b)(1)(A), a defendant is required to have "exhausted the remedies available in the courts of the State" before filing a writ of habeas corpus in federal court. Exhaustion means that all claims raised in the writ of habeas corpus were presented to the highest state court before filing a writ of habeas corpus in federal court.

The rationale of this requirement is that the state should have the "opportunity to pass upon and correct alleged violations of its prisoners' federal rights."[345] This is known as "comity." Not only must a claim be presented to the State court, but the claim must be "fairly presented" to the State court.

B. Presented to the Highest State Court

A claim must be presented to the highest state court available. It is not enough to present a claim to an appellate court. For example, in California, a claim must be presented to the California Supreme Court before a defendant can file a writ of habeas corpus in federal court. Later in this chapter, we will focus on how to exhaust claims in California, New York, and Texas.

---

[345] *Duncan v. Henry*, 513 U.S. 364, 365 (1995) (citation omitted).

A claim does not always have to be presented in a state *writ of habeas corpus*. To understand this better, it is important to consider at which point a defendant will be making his or her arguments of a constitutional violation. Some types of claims typically cannot be raised on appeal because those claims depend on facts that are outside the trial court record. For example, under many circumstances, a claim of ineffective assistance of counsel depends on facts that are not in the trial record. Therefore, such a claim would not be made on appeal. A claim for ineffective assistance of counsel is often made in a state writ of habeas corpus.

In contrast, a claim that exists in the trial record can be raised on appeal. If, for example, the prosecution were to use a confession that the defense counsel objects to on the grounds that the defendant's *Miranda* rights were violated, and the trial court decides to admit the confession as evidence, the defendant may argue on appeal that his Fifth Amendment *Miranda* rights were violated. If the defendant makes this argument on appeal and then seeks review of the appellate decision in the highest state court, this defendant can then file a writ of habeas corpus in federal court. The defendant would not have to file a state writ of habeas corpus since the defendant already presented his or her arguments to the state court.

In Chapter 4, about appropriate arguments to be raised in a federal writ of habeas corpus, we discussed *Garcia v. Long*.[346] There, we discussed the merits of the case. Garcia told the police officers that he did not want to talk to them, and the police nevertheless continued to ask him questions. He was found guilty and sentenced to 35 years to life. The federal court granted Garcia's writ of habeas corpus and reversed his conviction.

Now, we will discuss the procedural aspects of the case. Garcia sought to suppress his confession, arguing that his *Miranda* rights were violated. The judge denied the motion to suppress. On appeal, he again argued that his Fifth Amendment rights were violated. The

---

[346] 808 F.3d 771 (9th Cir. 2015).

California appellate court disagreed and affirmed the conviction. Then, Garcia petitioned the California Supreme Court for review, and the Court denied the petition.

Thus, Garcia had "exhausted" his state remedies. He timely presented his claim to the California Supreme Court, which is the state's highest court. Consequently, Garcia did not need to file a writ of habeas corpus in state court since his claims were already exhausted during the appellate process.

Discretionary Review

In many states, there is no automatic right to have the state's highest court review a case. In those states, a defendant must request that the state's supreme court agree to hear the case. The odds of having a case accepted are quite low:

- In California, less than 5 percent of cases are accepted for review by the California Supreme Court.
- In New York, the Court of Appeals (New York's highest court) received 1,824 criminal leave applications in 2020 and granted leave in 29 of the cases.

Given the low chances of a case being heard there, one could, perhaps, be forgiven for thinking that one would not have to seek review in the state's highest court. Yet, when confronted with this problem, the Supreme Court held that "a state prisoner must present his claims to a state supreme court in a petition for discretionary review in order to satisfy the exhaustion requirement."[347] In that case, the Supreme Court held that exhaustion "turns on an inquiry into what procedures are 'available' under state law." Each state has different procedures. We will now examine the procedures of California, New York, and Texas.

---

[347] *O'Sullivan v. Boerckel*, 526 U.S. 838 (1999).

California

For a defendant who is able to argue on appeal in state court that a federal right was violated, this defendant would have to file a petition for review with the California Supreme Court. If the court denies the petition, the defendant may file a writ of habeas corpus in federal court.

For a defendant who did not make his or her claims on appeal, the defendant has two options. First, the defendant could file a writ of habeas corpus in California state trial court, then file it in the California appellate court, and then either file the writ of habeas corpus in the California Supreme Court or file a petition for review with the California Supreme Court.

The second option is a Petition for Review to Exhaust State Remedies. Rule 8.508 of the California Rules of Court allows for the filing of a petition directly with the California Supreme Court in order for a defendant to exhaust his or her remedies in state court. However, the defendant must still make sure to adequately present all claims. We will address this later in the chapter.

New York

For a defendant who is able to argue on appeal that a federal right was violated, this defendant would have to file an application for leave to appeal to the Court of Appeals. If the court denies the motion, the defendant may file a writ of habeas corpus in federal court.

Section 440.10 of the Criminal Procedure Law allows a defendant to file an Article 440 motion to vacate judgment. The statute lists many grounds for this motion, including that "[t]he judgment was obtained in violation of a right of the defendant under the constitution of this state or of the United States." Other sections overlap with various constitutional claims.

If an Article 440 motion is denied, a defendant can request that the appellate division (intermediate court of appeals) accept the case. If the intermediate court denies the request, then a defendant's arguments are considered as if they were presented to the highest available court, and the defendant is free to file a writ of habeas corpus in federal court.

     If the appellate court accepts the case and denies the CPL 440 motion, the defendant must seek leave to appeal in the Court of Appeals (New York's highest court). If the Court of Appeals denies leave, then the defendant may file a writ of habeas corpus in federal court. A defendant should be aware of the various deadlines involved for requesting leave to appeal to the appellate court/Court of Appeals.

     In most cases, defendants in New York who seek to challenge their conviction or sentence must file a CPL 440 motion. A state writ of habeas corpus may be filed for pre-trial issues, such as issues involving bail or delay in prosecuting. A state writ may also be filed for a limited number of post-conviction issues, such as a miscalculation of sentence that, upon the correct calculation, would result in immediate release from prison. A New York defendant who alleges constitutional violations would typically file an Article 440 motion.

Texas

In Texas, a claim must be presented to the Texas Court of Criminal Appeals (highest court in Texas) before the claim can be included in a federal writ of habeas corpus.

     For a defendant who raised constitutional claims on appeal, the defendant would have to file a petition for discretionary review with the Texas Court of Criminal Appeals.[348] Like California and New York, there is no automatic right to have the Texas Court of Criminal Appeals accept a case. If the petition for discretionary review is denied, or if the court accepts the case but affirms the judgment, a defendant may thereafter file a writ of habeas corpus in federal court.

     Article 11.07 of the Texas Code of Criminal Procedure allows for the filing of a post-conviction writ of habeas corpus. The writ is

---

[348] Tex. R. App. P. 68.1.

filed in the trial court, which reviews the petition. The trial court decides whether the petition should be dismissed or a hearing should be scheduled. The trial court makes findings of fact, which it forwards to the Texas Court of Criminal Appeals. The Court of Criminal Appeals ultimately decides whether to grant or deny the petition. Once the Court of Criminal Appeals issues its decision, the claim is considered "exhausted," and the defendant may file a writ of habeas corpus in federal court.

C. How to Exhaust a Claim

After discussing *where* to present a claim—the highest court in the state—the next question is *how* to exhaust a claim in state court. The answer to this question is that a defendant must "fairly present" the claims to the state court. The rationale for this is: "If state courts are to be given the opportunity to correct alleged violations of prisoners' federal rights, they must surely be alerted to the fact that the prisoners are asserting claims under the United States Constitution." The Court continued, "If a habeas petitioner wishes to claim that an evidentiary ruling at a state court trial denied him the due process of law guaranteed by the Fourteenth Amendment, he must say so, not only in federal court, but in state court."[349]

What emerges is that a defendant must inform the state court that his or her incarceration is in violation of federal law. In *Baldwin v. Reese*, a defendant's writ of habeas corpus alleged ineffective assistance of counsel, but the defendant did not refer to the Constitution. The Supreme Court highlighted this omission: "The petition refers to provisions of the Federal Constitution in respect to other claims but not in respect to this one. The petition provides no citation of any case that might have alerted the court to the alleged federal nature of the claim." The Supreme Court held that the

---

[349] *Duncan v. Henry*, 513 U.S.364 (1995).

ineffective assistance of counsel claim was not exhausted in state court and, therefore, could not be raised in a federal writ of habeas corpus.

To fairly present a claim, the best practice is to cite to the Constitution. For example, instead of writing "the petitioner received ineffective assistance of counsel," write:

- "The petitioner's Sixth Amendment right to effective assistance of counsel was violated;" or
- "The petitioner received ineffective assistance of counsel, in violation of the Sixth Amendment to the Constitution."

There is no question that citing to the Constitution is the best way to fairly present a federal claim to the state court. If a defendant does not cite to the Constitution, then the defendant must, at the very least, cite to federal cases that interpret the Constitution. "Citing a specific constitutional provision or relying on federal constitutional precedents alerts state courts of the nature of the claim."[350]

A Second Circuit case lists the ways in which a state writ of habeas corpus makes clear that it is raising violations of federal law:

(a) reliance on pertinent federal cases employing constitutional analysis,

(b) reliance on state cases employing constitutional analysis in like fact situations,

(c) assertion of the claim in terms so particular as to call to mind a specific right protected by the Constitution, and

(d) allegation of a pattern of facts that is well within the mainstream of constitutional litigation.[351]

Some courts are more generous than others in finding that a defendant exhausted the federal issues in a state writ of habeas corpus. For example, the Second Circuit held that a claim was fairly presented when the "state and federal claims share the same legal standard." In that case, the court held, "Jackson exhausted his federal claim because, in this case, the legal standards for his federal and state claims were so

---

[350] *Jones v. Vacco*, 126 F.3d 408 (2d Cir. 1997).
[351] *Daye v. Attorney General*, 696 F.2d 186 (2d Cir. 1982).

similar that by presenting his state claim, he also presented his federal claim."[352]

Nonetheless, the position the defendant found himself in, in *Jackson v. Edwards*, is not a position that most defendants would want to be in. A defendant does not want to have his or her federal petition for writ of habeas corpus opposed on the ground that the claim was not exhausted in state court. A defendant does not want to be in a position where he or she has to argue that the federal claim was exhausted in state court and then have wait for the court to decide the issue. Obviously, the best practice is to cite to federal violations when filing a state writ of habeas corpus.

Fair Presentation of the Facts

A defendant must also fairly present the facts of the case to state court. "[F]or purposes of exhausting state remedies, a claim for relief in habeas corpus must include reference to a specific federal constitutional guarantee, *as well as a statement of the facts that entitle the petitioner to relief* [emphasis added]."[353] This does not mean that a defendant must present every single fact that supports the writ of habeas corpus. "Rather, to exhaust the factual basis of the claim, the petitioner must only provide the state court with the operative facts, that is, all of the facts necessary to give application to the constitutional principle upon which [the petitioner] relies."[354]

In *Robinson v. Schriro*, the court held that a claim was fairly presented to state court when:

> Robinson clearly raised the constitutional issue by citing to a federal case that held that the application of the especially cruel, heinous, or depraved aggravating factor to the petitioner violated the Eighth and Fourteenth Amendments of the U.S. Constitution. He also specifically noted his lack of

---

[352] *Jackson v. Edwards*, 404 F.3d 612 (2d Cir. 2005).
[353] *Gray v. Netherland*, 518 U.S. 152 (1996).
[354] *Davis v. Silva*, 511 F.3d 1005 (9th Cir. 2008).

participation in the shooting in support of his claim. He thus presented the same claim he does now—that, given his lack of participation in the murder, a finding of especial cruelty, heinousness and depravity violated his rights.[355]

In summation, to make a "fair presentation," a defendant must:

- Cite to a violation of a federal right. Ideally, this should include a citation to a specific Amendment of the Constitution.
- Present enough facts to make out a violation of federal law.

If a defendant does not exhaust his remedies in state court, the likely result is that the Court will dismiss the writ of habeas corpus and give the defendant the chance to file a writ in state court. Due to the one-year deadline to file a writ of habeas corpus in federal court, a defendant who has to re-file will have to move very quickly or risk the passing of the one-year deadline.

D. Exceptions to the Exhaustion Rule

There are a limited number of exceptions to the exhaustion rule. These exceptions are not something that a defendant should plan to rely on. Courts routinely deny the application of exception to the exhaustion rule. Only in a rare case will a court hold that an exception to the exhaustion rule applies.

There are three exceptions to the exhaustion rule. Two of the exceptions are codified in 28 U.S.C. § 2254(b) as noted below:

1. Waiver: Theoretically, exhaustion is not jurisdictional, and it may be waived.[356] This means that if the state does not argue that the claims were not exhausted, then a petitioner could proceed in federal court with an unexhausted claim.
   i. However, in practice, the AEDPA changed things: "A State shall not be deemed to have waived the exhaustion

---

[355] 595 F.3d 1086 (9th Cir. 2010).
[356] See *Granberry v. Greer*, 481 U.S. 129 (1987).

requirement or be estopped from reliance upon the
requirement unless the State, through counsel, expressly
waives the requirement."[357] Now, the state must expressly
waive the exhaustion issue. Therefore, if the state does
not raise the defense of exhaustion, the state does not
waive the issue.

    ii. Even if the State does not argue that the claims were not
exhausted, the Court on its own may deny the writ of
habeas corpus due to lack of exhaustion of remedies in
state court.[358]

   iii. If it is clear to the federal court that the claims lack merit,
the federal court may deny the writ of habeas corpus,
even if the issues were not exhausted in state court.[359]

2. <u>No state proceeding is available</u>: The first exception, found
in 28 U.S.C. § 2254(b)(1)(B)(i), is when "there is an
absence of available State corrective process."

    i. One example of an absence of available state relief occurs
when there is no state procedure for certain types of
claims. For example, a Texas prisoner who seeks to
challenge a prison disciplinary hearing is barred by Texas
law from bringing a state writ of habeas corpus.
Therefore, such a defendant may file a federal claim

---

[357] 28 U.S.C. § 2254(b)(3)

[358] *See Stone v. San Francisco*, 968 F.2d 850 (9th Cir. 1992)

[359] "An application for a writ of habeas corpus may be denied on the merits,
notwithstanding the failure of the applicant to exhaust the remedies available in the
courts of the State." 28 U.S.C. § 2254(b)(2). *See also Cassett v. Stewart*, 406 F.3d
614 (9th Cir. 2005) ("We now join our sister circuits in adopting the *Granberry*
standard and hold that a federal court may deny an unexhausted petition on the
merits only when it is perfectly clear that the applicant does not raise even a
colorable federal claim").

    The Second Circuit appears to apply a lower standard, to allow a dismissal
if the claim is "plainly meritless." *See Abuzaid v. Mattox*, 726 F.3d 311 (2d Cir.
2013).

without exhausting his or her claims in state court, since the state court refuses to hear these types of claims.[360]

ii. Some federal courts consider an "inordinate delay" in state court to be the equivalent of an absence of an available state corrective process.[361] Other courts are less clear if they would agree with this.[362]

iii. Overall, there are not many situations for which a state proceeding is unavailable.

3. Futility: The second exception, found in 28 U.S.C. § 2254(b)(1)(B)(ii), is when "circumstances exist that render such process ineffective to protect the rights of the applicant." Courts sometimes refer to this as "futility." It means that it would have been a waste of everyone's time if a defendant were required to pursue a claim in state court.

i. Theoretically, it would be futile to make a claim when a state supreme court has already ruled on the issue involved. The reason this is true is because the state supreme court already decided the operative issue.

ii. In practice, however, there is much debate about whether the futility exception is still valid.[363]

iii. In one case where the futility doctrine was considered, the Ninth Circuit wrote that "the California Supreme Court has not definitively rejected the claim Alfaro now raises in her petition for habeas relief. Therefore, even assuming that futility persists as a potential exception to AEDPA's exhaustion requirement, it does not excuse

---

[360] *See, e.g., Anthony v. Johnson*, 177 F.3d 978 (5th Cir. 1999)

[361] *See Lee v. Stickman*, 357 F.3d 338 (3rd Cir. 2004)

[362] *See Hopes v. Davis*, 761 F. App'x 307 (5th Cir. 2019)

[363] *See Alfaro v. Johnson*, 862 F.3d 1176 (9th Cir. 2017). For example, one Court wrote, "Our sister Circuits that have considered the issue have similarly concluded that the exhaustion requirement is not excused merely because a petitioner's claim will likely be denied on the merits in state court." *Parker v. Kelchner*, 429 F.3d 58, 63 (3rd Cir. 2005)

Alfaro's failure to exhaust her state court remedies in this instance."[364]

iv. In *Selsor v. Workman*, on the other hand, the court held that it would have been futile to file a writ in state court when the state's supreme court "consistently upheld admission of similar evidence."[365]

As mentioned above, these exceptions rarely apply. A defendant is, therefore, cautioned to exhaust all remedies in state court.

E. Mixed Petitions

If a claim must be presented to the state court before presenting the claim to the federal court, what happens if a federal writ contains some exhausted claims and some claims that are not exhausted? This is known as a "mixed petition" because it contains a mix of exhausted and unexhausted claims.

We discussed a mixed petition in Chapter 3 in relation to deadlines because mixed petitions often involve deadline issues. While the reader is referred back to that chapter for a more detailed analysis of these options, we summarized the options available as follows:

(1) File a federal writ with the exhausted claims and forget about the unexhausted claim.

(2) Voluntarily dismiss the federal writ until the state claims are exhausted and then file the writ in federal court with all of the claims.

(3) File a "mixed petition" with the exhausted and unexhausted claims and file a "stay and abeyance," asking the federal court to stay the federal writ. This requires a showing of "good cause."

(4) File a "mixed petition" and then amend the petition to delete the unexhausted claims and ask the court to stay the

---

[364] *Alfaro v. Johnson*, 862 F.3d 1176 (9th Cir. 2017).
[365] 644 F.3d 984 (10th Cir. 2011).

federal writ. Then, after exhausting the claims in state court, file an amended petition. The new claims may face timeliness issues.

F. Conclusion

To sum up this chapter, all issues must be exhausted in state court. This means that:

- A defendant must cite federal law.
- A defendant must present facts that fit into a federal violation.
- A defendant must present his or her claims to the highest state court.

The issue of exhaustion leads to a related issue, known as a "procedural default," which we will discuss in the next chapter.

Chapter 8
PROCEDURAL DEFAULTS

In the previous chapter, we discussed the issue of exhaustion. Briefly, this means that potential arguments a defendant wants to use in his or her federal writ of habeas corpus must first be presented to the state court before the arguments may be presented to federal court. This is due to *comity*, which means that the state court should be given the first opportunity to correct any mistakes that it may have committed. Unexhausted claims are almost always dismissed and occasionally denied outright. There are extremely limited exceptions to the exhaustion requirement, which we presented in the previous chapter.

What happens if a defendant presents a claim to the state court, but the state court holds that the defendant failed to satisfy the state procedural requirements for the claim. In other words, the state court refuses to adjudicate the *merits* of the claim because a state *procedural* rule was violated. May the defendant thereafter file a claim in federal court? The short answer is no. In this chapter, we will discuss the details of what is known as a "procedural default."

A. What Is a Procedural Default?

A procedural default occurs when a defendant does not follow a state's procedures for raising his or her claims in state court. For example, some claims may only be raised on appeal, or some claims can only be raised if a trial attorney objected at trial. If a defendant fails to raise the issue on appeal, or if the attorney fails to object at trial, then the defendant *procedurally defaulted* on the issue. Similarly, if the state has a time frame for filing a state writ of habeas corpus, a defendant will have procedurally defaulted if he or she files the writ after the state's deadline.

In *Jackson v. Giurbino*, the prosecutor pointed out that the defendant chose to remain silent. A prosecutor cannot comment about a defendant invoking his or her constitutional right to remain silent.

188

Because Jackson's attorney did not object when this happened at trial, Jackson was barred from raising the issue on appeal due to the state procedural rule. The federal court denied the claim on the grounds that the defendant procedurally defaulted.[366]

The rationale for the rule is that the federal courts "will not review a question of federal law decided by a state court if the decision of that court rests on a state law ground that is independent of the federal question and adequate to support the judgment."[367] "The procedural default doctrine thus advances the same comity, finality, and federalism interests advanced by the exhaustion doctrine."[368]

One thing that the federal court will review is the adequacy of the state rule, meaning that "the state procedural bar must be clear, consistently applied, and well-established at the time of the petitioner's purported default."[369] If a state law is not clear, or if it is not consistently applied, then the federal court will not use the procedural default as a bar to filing a federal writ of habeas corpus.

In *Melendez*, the Court gave a few examples of procedural rules that were not adequate. In one case, there was "no procedural default because Oregon Supreme Court's practice of declining to consider claims not explicitly raised in petition [was] not consistently enforced." The reader is cautioned that the adequacy of state rules is bound to change over time.[370] Thus, a rule that is inadequate at a

---

[366] 364 F.3d 1002 (9th Cir. 2004). The court granted the writ for a different reason: The police failed to give a *Miranda* warning to the defendant. The court vacated the defendant's first-degree murder conviction and ordered a new trial.

[367] *Coleman v. Thompson*, 501 U.S. 722 (1991).

[368] *Davila v. Davis*, 582 U.S. 521 (2017) (holding that because the "Constitution does not guarantee the right to counsel" in habeas proceedings, ineffective habeas counsel generally "cannot supply cause to excuse a procedural default").

[369] *Melendez v. Pliler*, 288 F.3d 1120 (9th Cir. 2002).

[370] *See Ybarra v. McDaniel*, 656 F.3d 984 (9th Cir. 2011) ("a procedural rule's adequacy is not necessarily determined by our court once and for all time. The rule's adequacy as to any particular petitioner must be assessed as of the date of that petitioner's purported default.").

certain point in time may become adequate at a later point in time. The court must look to adequacy at the time of default.

Procedural Default vs. Exhaustion Part 1

When a claim is presented to state court, the claim is considered exhausted. This is true even if the state court dismisses the claim for a procedural reason. The procedural default doctrine allows the federal court to dismiss a writ of habeas corpus when the issue is exhausted in state court but is procedurally defaulted.

Procedural Default vs. Exhaustion Part 2

When the federal court denies a writ due to exhaustion, the defendant can return to state court to exhaust the issue. When the federal court denies a writ because of a procedural default, the writ will be dismissed, and the defendant cannot subsequently raise those issues anymore.[371]

B. What are the Ramifications of a Procedural Default?

The answer to this question is straightforward. "Federal habeas courts reviewing convictions from state courts will not consider claims that a state court refused to hear based on an adequate and independent state procedural ground."[372]

---

[371] In *Sandgathe v. Maass*, 314 F.3d 371 (9th Cir. 2002), the Court wrote: "The practical difference between the two is that when a defendant merely fails to exhaust, he may still be able to return to state court to present his claims there. When a defendant's claim is procedurally defaulted, either the state court was presented with the claim but declined to reach the issue for procedural reasons, or it is clear that the state court would hold the claim procedurally barred" (citation omitted).

[372] *Davila v. Davis*, 582 U.S. 521 (2017).

C. Are There any Exceptions to a Procedural Default?

Exception #1: The "Cause and Prejudice" Exception

An exception to the procedural default rule exists if a defendant can show "cause for the noncompliance and some showing of actual prejudice resulting from the alleged constitutional violation."[373] Thus, there are two requirements: (1) cause and (2) actual prejudice. These are sometimes referred to as the "cause and prejudice" standard.

What Is Cause?
The Supreme Court held, "[W]e think that the existence of cause for a procedural default must ordinarily turn on whether the prisoner can show that some objective factor external to the defense impeded counsel's efforts to comply with the State's procedural rule."[374]

Though "attorney error is an objective external factor providing cause for excusing a procedural default only if that error amounted to a deprivation of the constitutional right to counsel," this is only true when there is a constitutional right to counsel.[375] In Chapter 2, Overview of Requirements, we noted that there is no constitutional right to an attorney for filing a writ of habeas corpus. It follows, then, that a procedural default due to ineffective assistance of habeas counsel is *not* valid cause to excuse a procedural default.[376]

There is one exception. If a state requires claims of ineffective assistance of counsel to be raised in a writ of habeas corpus, not on direct appeal, then a procedural default due to ineffective assistance of counsel will be considered "cause" to allow a defendant to raise a procedurally defaulted claim in a federal writ.[377]

This exception was extended a year later to situations where "state procedural framework, by reason of its design and operation,

---

[373] *Wainwright v. Sykes*, 433 U.S. 72 (1977).
[374] *Murray v. Carrier*, 477 U.S. 478 (1986).
[375] *Davila v. Davis*, 582 U.S. 521 (2017).
[376] *Id.*
[377] *See Martinez v. Ryan*, 566 U.S. 1 (2012).

makes it highly unlikely in a typical case that a defendant will have a meaningful opportunity to raise a claim of ineffective assistance of trial counsel on direct appeal."[378] This is known as the *Martinez/Trevino* rule.

In *Davila v. Davis*, the Court was faced with whether to extend the *Martinez/Trevino* rule. The Court ruled that the limited exception is available only for claims that *trial* counsel provided ineffective assistance of counsel, and only when it is unlikely that such a claim can be made on direct appeal. In those circumstances, a procedural default of counsel may be considered to be sufficient "cause" to allow a defendant to proceed with a federal writ.

In *Davila*, the court refused to extend this holding to claims of ineffective assistance of counsel for *appellate* counsel. If post-conviction counsel does not raise the issue that the appellate counsel was ineffective, the claim is procedurally defaulted. The Court presented numerous technical reasons for not extending the exception.

In summary, the cause prong may be met if post-conviction counsel fails to argue that trial counsel was ineffective, and the state requires claims of writ of habeas corpus to be raised in a collateral proceeding (or the typical situation is that such claims are made in a collateral proceeding).

What Is Prejudice?
The second prong of the exception to procedural defaults is prejudice. To satisfy this prong, the ineffective assistance of counsel must be substantial. "To overcome the default, a prisoner must also demonstrate that the underlying ineffective-assistance-of-trial-counsel claim is a substantial one, which is to say that the prisoner must demonstrate that the claim has some merit."[379]

---

[378] *Trevino v. Thaler*, 569 U.S. 413 (2013).
[379] *Martinez v. Ryan*, 566 U.S. 1 (2012).

"There is considerable overlap between these requirements, since each considers the strength and validity of the underlying ineffective assistance claim."[380]

A Case That Satisfied the "Cause and Prejudice" Standard
An example of how these factors play out is seen in *Ramirez v. Ryan*.[381] In this case, Ramirez was convicted of murder and sentenced to death. Ramirez's trial counsel did not investigate or present mitigating evidence, which would have included that Ramirez's IQ likely fell within the range of what could be considered mental retardation and that Ramirez had grown up in an abusive household. It was trial counsel's first capital case.

The court held that trial counsel was aware that Ramirez had an IQ of 70–77 yet "failed to investigate further or present a claim of mental impairment, and instead relied on Dr. McMahon's conclusion that Ramirez was 'well within the average range of intelligence.'"

After concluding that the prejudice standard was met, the court turned to the "cause" prong. Ramirez's post-conviction counsel did not argue that the trial attorney provided ineffective assistance of trial counsel. The court reasoned that:

> Post-conviction counsel possessed evidence that indicated that Ramirez could have an intellectual disability, and knew that trial counsel failed to present or pursue evidence of an intellectual disability. Had post-conviction counsel performed effectively, by reviewing the record, trial counsel's failure to present evidence of Ramirez's intellectual disability would have readily revealed itself.

Therefore, the court concluded that Ramirez was prejudiced, and excused Ramirez's procedural default. Ramirez was allowed to argue ineffective assistance of counsel in his federal writ of habeas corpus, even though the claim was procedurally defaulted.

---

[380] *Djerf v. Ryan*, 931 F.3d 870 (9th Cir. 2019).
[381] 937 F.3d 1230 (9th Cir. 2019).

In this case, the Supreme Court granted certiorari on the issue of whether a defendant may use new evidence in federal court when the defendant procedurally defaulted in state court. Oral arguments were heard on December 8, 2021. As of yet, a decision has not been issued.

Exception #2: The State Procedural Law Is Not Independent of Federal Law

For a claim to be procedurally defaulted, it must be due to a *state* procedural law. If the state procedural law is related to a federal law, then the claim will *not* be procedurally defaulted.[382]

While this may be confusing in theory, in practice it is clearer. In *Cooper v. Neven*, the Ninth Circuit held that a claim was not procedurally defaulted when "the Nevada Supreme Court explicitly relied on its federal *Brady* analysis as controlling the outcome of its state procedural default analysis."[383] If the state court has to engage in any sort of federal analysis, then the possibility of an exception to the procedural default doctrine may exist.

Exception #3: Fundamental Miscarriage of Justice

The fundamental miscarriage of justice exception applies almost exclusively to claims of actual innocence. If a defendant has a claim of actual innocence, the defendant may raise this claim in a federal writ of habeas corpus, even if the claim is procedurally defaulted.

We discussed this in Chapter 6, Claims of Actual Innocence. There, we noted that an actual innocence argument is a gateway to allow a defendant to overcome procedural impediments to a federal writ of habeas corpus. We cautioned that actual innocence cases are rare and require independent evidence of actual innocence. Evidence

---

[382] *See La Crosse v. Kernan*, 244 F.3d 702 (9th Cir. 2001) ("For a state procedural rule to be 'independent,' the state law basis for the decision must not be interwoven with federal law.").
[383] 641 F.3d 322 (9th Cir. 2011).

that casts doubt on a defendant's guilt is usually not enough. The reader is encouraged to refer to the chapter about actual innocence for more details.

D. How to Know if There is a Procedural Default

For there is to be a procedural default, "it must be clear from the face of the opinion that the state court's decision rest[ed] on a state procedural bar."[384] If there is a doubt or any ambiguity, "courts should presume that the state court adjudicated the claim on the merits."[385]

Sometimes, it is unclear if the state denied a writ of habeas corpus on the merits or because of a procedural default, but:

- If the state court cites only to a state case that discusses procedural requirements, that likely means that the writ was denied on state procedural grounds.
- If the state court cites a procedural rule and also denies a claim on the merits, the claim will be procedurally defaulted.[386]

The Supreme Court has established that there is a presumption that a state denial is on the merits unless indicated otherwise: "When a federal claim has been presented to a state court and the state court has denied relief, it may be presumed that the state court adjudicated the claim on the merits in the absence of any indication or state-law procedural principles to the contrary."[387]

---

[384] *Garner v. Lee*, 908 F.3d 845 (2d Cir. 2018) (citation omitted).

[385] *Id.*

[386] *See Loveland v. Hatcher*, 231 F.3d 640 (9th Cir. 2000) ("if the state court's reliance upon its procedural bar rule was an independent and alternative basis for its denial of the petition, review on the merits of the petitioner's federal constitutional claims in federal court is precluded."). *See also Ayala v. Chappell*, 829 F.3d 1081 (9th Cir. 2016).

[387] *Harrington v. Richter*, 562 U.S. 86 (2011).

The takeaway is that a defendant must be very careful to follow the state's procedural laws, or the defendant will risk having the federal court deny his or her writ of habeas corpus.

Chapter 9
SUCCESSIVE WRITS

A significant limitation of federal writs of habeas corpus is that a defendant generally may only file one writ of habeas corpus. A second writ, known as a "successive writ," will typically be denied. This means that all potential claims must be included in a defendant's first writ of habeas corpus. If a defendant does not include an argument, there is a strong likelihood that the defendant will no longer be able to do so in the future. For this reason, an experienced post-conviction attorney is recommended. The attorney will have the knowledge and experience to know what arguments are available and what arguments are potentially available. In this chapter, we will focus on the complexities of the rule against "successive writs."

A. The Rule for When a Successive Writ Is Filed

According to 28 U.S.C. § 2244, there are two limitations on successive writs. First, "[a] claim presented in a second or successive habeas corpus application under section 2254 that was presented in a prior application shall be dismissed." This means that once a claim was already presented, it cannot be presented a second time.

Second, "[a] claim presented in a second or successive habeas corpus application under section 2254 that was not presented in a prior application shall be dismissed." This means that a claim that was not presented in a first writ cannot be presented in a second writ.

These two rules can be summarized as follows: A claim raised in a prior writ must be dismissed, and a claim *not* raised in a prior writ must also be dismissed.

Where, then, does that leave a defendant? If claims raised and not raised in a prior writ must be dismissed, can a defendant *ever* file a second writ of habeas corpus? The answer is yes.

There are two exceptions under 28 U.S.C. § 2244. The first exception applies when "the applicant shows that the claim relies on a new rule of constitutional law, made retroactive to cases on collateral review by the Supreme Court, that was previously unavailable." The second exception applies when:

> (i) the factual predicate for the claim could not have been discovered previously through the exercise of due diligence; and
>
> (ii) the facts underlying the claim, if proven and viewed in light of the evidence as a whole, would be sufficient to establish by clear and convincing evidence that, but for constitutional error, no reasonable factfinder would have found the applicant guilty of the underlying offense.

The Supreme Court has summarized these rules as follows:

> Title 28 U.S.C. § 2244(b), the so-called gatekeeping provision of the Antiterrorism and Effective Death Penalty Act of 1996 (AEDPA), governs federal habeas proceedings. Under AEDPA, a state prisoner is entitled to one fair opportunity to seek federal habeas relief from his conviction. Section 2244(b), however, sets stringent limits on second or successive habeas applications. Among those restrictions, a prisoner may not reassert any claims "presented in a prior application," § 2244(b)(1), and may bring a new claim only in limited situations.[388]

We will discuss these exceptions later in the chapter. The takeaway message is that *all* claims *must* be presented in a defendant's first writ of habeas corpus. If not, the defendant risks waiving his or her claims.

B. How to Define a Successive Writ

A successive writ is not simply defined as a second writ of habeas corpus. The Supreme Court has referred to a successive writ as a "term

---

[388] *Banister v. Davis*, ___ U.S. ___, 140 S. Ct. 1698 (2020).

of art,"[389] and it "is not self-defining."[390] Thus, it is difficult to pinpoint a precise definition for what is considered a successive writ.

Nonetheless, the Court has provided some guidance to answer this question. It is helpful to look at what is *not* considered a successive writ. The first situation that is not considered a successive writ is when the federal court dismisses an unexhausted claim. In *Slack v. McDaniel*, the Court considered where a dismissal due to unexhausted claims results in a subsequent federal writ being considered a successive writ. The Court held that "a habeas petition which is filed after an initial petition was dismissed without adjudication on the merits for failure to exhaust state remedies is not a 'second or successive' petition as that term is understood in the habeas corpus context."[391]

The second situation where a second writ is not considered a successive writ occurs when the second writ challenges a new judgment. In *Magwood v. Patterson,* the Court rejected the State's claim that a defendant is entitled to *one opportunity* to file a writ of habeas corpus and held that a defendant is entitled to a writ of habeas corpus each time there is a new judgment.[392] For example, in *Magwood v. Patterson*, the defendant was convicted of murder and sentenced to death. After the state courts denied the defendant's appeals and writs of habeas corpus, he filed a writ in federal court. The federal court granted the writ as to the sentence only (not as to the finding of guilt) and ordered the State to either release the defendant or to resentence him. The State decided to resentence the defendant, and Magwood was once again sentenced to death.

After being sentenced to death at the resentencing, the defendant again filed a writ of habeas corpus in federal court. The Court of Appeals for the Eleventh Circuit held that the defendant was

---

[389] *See Slack v. McDaniel*, 529 U.S. 473 (2000).
[390] *See Panetti v. Quarterman*, 551 U.S. 930 (2007).
[391] *Slack v. McDaniel*, 529 U.S. 473 (2000).
[392] 561 U.S. 320 (2010).

barred by the rule against successive writs and denied the writ. To this, the Supreme Court held that a defendant may file a second writ to challenge a new judgment or sentence. "Because Magwood's habeas application challenges a new judgment for the first time, it is not 'second or successive' under § 2244(b)."[393]

What happens if an amended judgment amends *some* of the convictions or sentence but does not change the conviction and sentence on other counts? In this situation, the Ninth Circuit and the Second Circuit hold that a defendant may file another writ of habeas corpus when the "amended judgment left the convictions and sentences on the two remaining counts unchanged, and the second petition challenges those unaltered components of the judgment."[394]

The Ninth Circuit, in fact, goes so far as to hold that "a state court's alteration of the number of presentence credits to which a prisoner was entitled under California law constitutes a new, intervening judgment."[395] In that case, the defendant's presentence credits were changed from 533 days to 554 days. The Ninth Circuit looked to California state law, which holds that "only a sentence that awards a prisoner all credits to which he is entitled is a legally valid one." Therefore, "a state trial court's alteration of the number of presentence credits to which a prisoner is entitled is a legally significant act: it replaces an invalid sentence with a valid one." Consequently, the defendant was allowed to file a writ of habeas corpus based on the new sentence.

---

[393] In 2011, the Eleventh Circuit confirmed that the defendant was not eligible for the death penalty. *See Magwood v. Warden, Alabama Dept. of Corrections*, 664 F.3d 1340 (11th Cir. 2011).

[394] *Wentzell v. Neven*, 674 F.3d 1124 (9th Cir. 2012). *See also Johnson v. United States*, 623 F.3d 41 (2d Cir. 2010). This is also the rule in the Third, Fourth, Sixth and Eleventh Circuits. *See In re Gray*, 850 F.3d 139 (4th Cir. 2017); *King v. Morgan*, 807 F.3d 154 (6th Cir. 2015); *Insignares v. Sec'y, Fla. Dep't of Corr.*, 755 F.3d 1273 (11th Cir. 2014).

[395] *Gonzalez v. Sherman*, 873 F.3d 763 (9th Cir. 2017).

The Fifth Circuit, in contrast, has a rule that is more limited. In *In re Lampton*, the Fifth Circuit held that a sentence that is vacated in part is not considered to be a "new sentence."[396] In the Fifth Circuit, a new sentence only occurs when the entirety of a sentence is vacated, and the defendant is resentenced. In the Fifth Circuit, a *partial* vacatur of a sentence does not entitle the defendant to file a second writ of habeas corpus.

The third situation where a second writ is not considered a successive writ occurs when a claim is not ripe to be raised in the first writ. This rule emerged from *Panetti v. Quarterman*.[397] In that case, the defendant was found guilty of murder and was sentenced to death. His state and federal writs of habeas corpus were denied. He then filed another writ of habeas corpus, arguing that his mental capacity had deteriorated to the point that he was not mentally competent to be put to death. The Court held that the defendant was allowed to file a second writ of habeas corpus based on a claim that was not ripe for his first writ of habeas corpus. The Court reasoned as follows:

> We conclude, in accord with this precedent, that Congress did not intend the provisions of AEDPA addressing "second or successive" petitions to govern a filing in the unusual posture presented here: a § 2254 application raising a *Ford*-based incompetency claim filed as soon as that claim is ripe.

Essentially, since the claim did not exist at the time of the earlier writ, the claim is not barred from being raised in a later writ.

In summary, a defendant may not file a "successive writ." This phrase is a term of art and is difficult to define. It generally means a second writ. There are, however, three situations that allow a second writ not to be considered a successive writ:

1. A writ that was dismissed for failure to exhaust claims.
2. A writ based on a new or amended sentence/judgment.

---

[396] 667 F.3d 585 (5th Cir. 2012).
[397] 551 U.S. 930 (2007).

3. A writ based on a claim that was not ripe to be filed in the first writ.

C. Situations in Which a Successive Writ is Allowed

We now turn to situations in which a writ is considered to be successive, yet a defendant is allowed to file the writ. As noted earlier, 28 U.S.C. § 2244 contains two exceptions to the rule against successive writs. The first exception applies when there is a new constitutional rule that was made retroactive. The second exception applies when:

(i) the factual predicate for the claim could not have been discovered previously through the exercise of due diligence; and

(ii) the facts underlying the claim, if proven and viewed in light of the evidence as a whole, would be sufficient to establish by clear and convincing evidence that, but for constitutional error, no reasonable factfinder would have found the applicant guilty of the underlying offense.

We will focus first on the second exception, for newly discovered evidence that shows actual innocence, and then turn to the first exception. Both exceptions rarely apply, and the defendant is cautioned to try his or her very best to include all potential arguments in the first federal writ of habeas corpus.

Newly Discovered Evidence

Due Diligence

To file a second writ of habeas corpus pursuant to the newly discovered evidence exception, a defendant must show *due diligence* in discovering the evidence. In short, this means that the defendant must have done all that he or she could have done to obtain the evidence. For example, in *Solorio v. Muniz*, the Ninth Circuit held that a defendant did not exercise due diligence when he had reason to believe that the prosecutor did not turn over evidence as required by the *Brady* rule, yet the defendant did not make a request for the prosecution's records (*see* California Penal Code § 1054.9).[398]

In *Solorio*, the Ninth Circuit highlighted that due diligence depends on what a defendant should have known. "A petitioner must exercise due diligence in investigating new facts where he is on notice that new evidence *might* exist. He cannot escape the due diligence requirement simply by showing he did not know of the new evidence earlier."

In this case, the Court denied the defendant's successive writ, reasoning that "Solorio concedes that he knew at the time of trial that Memo was a confidential police informant and that Fonseca's interview was taped. Solorio's knowledge of Memo's informant status and the existence of Fonseca's taped interviews was sufficient to put him on notice to investigate further."

Actual Innocence

As we noted in Chapter 6 about actual innocence, this phrase means "factual innocence, not mere legal insufficiency."[399] In *Solorio*, the Ninth Circuit held that the evidence that was not turned over "pales when set against the balance of inculpatory evidence presented at trial."

Both the due diligence and actual innocence prongs are difficult to establish. Together, it is exceedingly difficult for a defendant to show that a second writ of habeas corpus may be filed based on newly discovered evidence of actual innocence.

New Constitutional Rule

While it may be rare to file a second writ based on new evidence of actual innocence, it is possible to file a second writ based on a new constitutional rule, pursuant to which a defendant would not have been convicted at trial.

---

[398] 896 F.3d 914 (9th Cir. 2018).
[399] *See King v. Trujillo*, 638 F.3d 726 (9th Cir. 2011).

For example, in 2002, the Supreme Court held that it is unconstitutional to execute those with intellectual disabilities.[400] In *In re Campbell*, the defendant's attorney requested evidence of intelligence tests and was told by the State that the defendant had taken an IQ test and had an IQ of 84. The State, however, "never disclosed that it was in possession of evidence of three intelligence tests suggesting that Campbell was intellectually disabled," including one IQ test that showed an IQ of 68.

In that case, the court held that the *Atkins* rule against executing those who are intellectually disabled applied retroactively. When Campbell filed his first federal writ of habeas corpus in 2000, the *Atkins* decision had not yet been decided. The Fifth Circuit held, "The evidence in the record before us is more than sufficient to satisfy Campbell's burden of making out a prima facie showing of intellectual disability sufficient to warrant a successive habeas petition."[401] On May 13, 2014, the date that Campbell was scheduled to be executed, the Fifth Circuit stayed the execution and allowed Campbell to proceed on his successive writ, which alleged that he was mentally incompetent and, therefore, could not be sentenced to death.

In another case, the Ninth Circuit summarized what is required and referred to these as "demanding requirements":

- a new rule of constitutional law,
- made retroactive to cases on collateral review by the Supreme Court,
- that was previously unavailable.[402]

In *Henry v. Spearman*, Henry argued that he was convicted pursuant to a law that is unconstitutionally vague, as determined by a 2015 Supreme Court case. In 2016, the Supreme Court held that the

---

[400] *See Atkins v. Virginia*, 536 U.S. 304 (2002).
[401] 750 F.3d 523 (5th Cir. 2014).
[402] *Henry v. Spearman*, 899 F.3d 703 (9th Cir. 2018).

2015 decision was retroactive.[403] Therefore, the court allowed the defendant to file a successive writ of habeas corpus.

In contrast, in another Ninth Circuit case, the Court held, "Here, Young has not shown that the Supreme Court made *Riley* retroactive. *Riley* does not itself hold that it is retroactive, 573 U.S. at 386, 134 S. Ct. 2473, nor does Young offer a string of cases 'logically dictat[ing]' that conclusion. *Garcia*, 923 F.3d at 1246."[404]

The "Watershed" Exception

We previously noted that there used to be a "watershed" exception to the rule against applying new constitutional procedural rules retroactively. In 2021, the Supreme Court eliminated this exception:

> Continuing to articulate a theoretical exception that never actually applies in practice offers false hope to defendants, distorts the law, misleads judges, and wastes the resources of defense counsel, prosecutors, and courts. Moreover, no one can reasonably rely on an exception that is non-existent in practice, so no reliance interests can be affected by forthrightly acknowledging reality. It is time—probably long past time—to make explicit what has become increasingly apparent to bench and bar over the last 32 years: New procedural rules do not apply retroactively on federal collateral review. The watershed exception is moribund. It must "be regarded as retaining no vitality."[405]

Therefore, there is no longer an exception for procedural rules that may be applied retroactively since "[n]ew procedural rules do not apply retroactively on federal collateral review."

---

[403] *Welch v. United States*, 578 U.S. 120 (2016).

[404] *Young v. Pfeiffer*, 933 F.3d 1123 (9th Cir. 2019). In another case, the Ninth Circuit similarly denied a request for a successive petition on the grounds that the defendant did not show that the constitutional rule was made retroactive. *See Garcia v. United States*, 923 F.3d 1242 (9th Cir. 2019).

[405] *Edwards v. Vannoy*, 593 U.S. ___, 141 S. Ct. 1547 (2021).

Should the Court Consider the Statute of Limitations When Deciding Whether To Allow a Successive Writ?

Title 28 U.S.C. § 2244(d)(1)(D) establishes that a writ of habeas corpus must be filed within one year of "the date on which the factual predicate of the claim or claims presented could have been discovered through the exercise of due diligence." Thus, even if a defendant has no actual knowledge of a claim at the time of the first writ of habeas corpus, the court will look to the point when the defendant "could have discovered" the factual predicate for the claim.

In one case, a defendant was found to be mentally competent to stand trial when he had an IQ of 70.[406] At the time, the diagnostic manual provided that 70 was the cut-off for intellectual disability. The new diagnostic manual changed the criteria for determining intellectual disability:

> The new diagnostic guidelines included significant changes in the diagnosis of intellectual disability, which changed the focus from specific IQ scores to clinical judgment. The DSM-5 recognizes that an individual with an IQ score over 70 may still qualify as intellectually disabled. The previous diagnostic manual, in effect when Johnson filed his initial federal habeas petition, did not classify Johnson as intellectually disabled because of his IQ. Further bolstering that his claim was unavailable until now, Johnson under a current full-scale IQ testing scored 70, within the *Atkins* range.

If one had to predict what would happen in *In re Johnson*, one would predict that the Fifth Circuit would allow the successive writ. This is because *Atkins* applies retroactively and because Johnson submitted strong evidence of intellectual disability.

While the Fifth Circuit granted authorization to file a successive writ, the Fifth Circuit noted that the new diagnostic manual was published on May 18, 2013, and Johnson filed his writ more than one year later. The court did not address whether the statute of

---

[406] *In re Johnson*, 935 F.3d 284 (5th Cir. 2019).

limitations should be equitably tolled and determined that the lower court would be a better place to address equitable tolling. The Court did note that "Campbell has brought forth a viable basis for equitable tolling that merits further factual development."

The Ninth Circuit, in contrast, does not focus on other procedural issues when addressing whether to authorize a successive writ of habeas corpus. In one case, the Ninth Circuit rejected the State's argument on the grounds that "[t]his is the type of complicated analysis that courts of appeals are to avoid when performing their gatekeeping function under § 2244(b). The requirement of a mere prima facie showing render[s] irrelevant other possible grounds for dismissal such as ultimate lack of merit, nonexhaustion, procedural default, and the like."[407]

To summarize, some circuit courts will only look to whether there is a constitutional rule that applies retroactively (28 U.S.C. § 2244(b)). Other courts will also consider the statute of limitations (28 U.S.C. § 2244(d). The Third Circuit summarized this split as follows:

> Our sister circuits are split on the scope of our gatekeeping review. Three circuits limit that review to the § 2244(b) requirements. *In re McDonald*, 514 F.3d 539, 543-44 (6th Cir. 2008); *Henry v. Spearman*, 899 F.3d 703, 710 (9th Cir. 2018) (citing *McDonald* approvingly in dictum); *Ochoa v. Sirmons*, 485 F.3d 538, 542-44 (10th Cir. 2007). Five others sometimes consider § 2244(d)'s timeliness requirement. *In re Vassell*, 751 F.3d 267, 271 (4th Cir. 2014); *In re Campbell*, 750 F.3d 523, 533-34 (5th Cir. 2014); *Johnson v. Robert*, 431 F.3d 992, 992-93 (7th Cir. 2005) (per curiam); *In re Hill*, 437 F.3d 1080, 1083 (11th Cir. 2006) (per curiam); *In re Williams*, 759 F.3d 66, 68-69 (D.C. Cir. 2014).[408]

---

[407] *Henry v. Spearman*, 899 F.3d 703 (9th Cir. 2018).
[408] *In re Rosado*, 7 F.4th 152 (3d Cir. 2021).

D. A Cautionary Tale

Due to the nature of the rule against successive writs, there are situations in which a defendant may have a potentially meritorious claim but is not allowed to raise the claim in a writ of habeas corpus. This is what occurred in *Brown v. Muniz*.[409]

Gregory Brown was convicted of attempted murder and other charges and was sentenced to 56 years to life in prison. Brown appealed his conviction and then filed a writ of habeas corpus in federal court, which was denied in 1998. In 2010, Brown learned that there was impeachment evidence for three of the police officers who were involved in his case, which had not been provided to his attorney. Under the *Brady* rule, the prosecutor must turn over exculpatory and impeaching evidence.[410]

In this case, the Ninth Circuit held that a *Brady* violation occurred at the time of trial, and the issue was, therefore, considered "ripe" (theoretically) for a first writ of habeas corpus. Consequently, if a defendant files a writ of habeas corpus and later learns of a *Brady* violation, the courts will address the *Brady* writ as a successive writ. Why does this matter? As noted by the court, "A different and more demanding standard governs most second-in-time federal habeas petitions." The court cited the rules that we discussed above:

> [A]bsent a showing of intervening constitutional law, a second or successive habeas petitioner must overcome two obstacles to invoke the district court's jurisdiction: he must (1) show that the factual predicate for his habeas claim reasonably could not have been discovered at the time of his initial habeas petition, and (2) demonstrate that the previously undiscovered facts, if

---

[409] 889 F.3d 661 (9th Cir. 2018).
[410] The reader is referred to our section about *Brady* violations, located in Chapter 4 about appropriate arguments for a federal writ of habeas corpus.

shown to be true in a habeas action, suffice to prove his innocence by clear and convincing evidence.

Consequently, Gregory Brown was required to show due diligence in obtaining the *Brady* material and that the *Brady* material could prove his innocence by clear and convincing evidence. The court concluded that Brown did not show actual innocence and denied the writ.

Mindful of the harsh result, the court in *Brown v. Muniz* blamed Congress for its "legislative choice to prioritize state-federal comity and the finality of criminal proceedings over affording petitioners multiple opportunities to invoke the federal courts' jurisdiction under the same standard of review.... That a petitioner's burden is higher under these circumstances may seem inequitable, but that is a policy, not a legal, objection."

First Writ vs. Successive Writ

For a *Brady* violation that is raised in a first writ, the defendant must show that "there is a reasonable probability that, had the evidence been disclosed, the result of the proceeding would have been different."[411] In a successive writ, a defendant must show that the evidence shows actual innocence. The difference in these two standards highlights why it is so important to include all potential arguments in a first writ of habeas corpus.

E. Permission for a Successive Writ

According to 28 U.S.C. § 2244(b)(3), a defendant is required to obtain permission from the court of appeals to file a successive writ. The court is supposed to decide within 30 days whether to allow the successive writ.

Earlier in this chapter, we discussed whether the courts should consider other procedural issues, such as the statute of limitations, when deciding whether to allow a defendant to proceed with a

---

[411] *Strickler v. Greene*, 527 U.S. 263 (1999).

successive writ. In one case, the court focused on the 30-day time frame, "which suggests that [we] do not have to engage in ... difficult legal analysis in our gatekeeping role."[412]

A denial of permission for a successive writ is not appealable. "The grant or denial of an authorization by a court of appeals to file a second or successive application shall not be appealable and shall not be the subject of a petition for rehearing or for a writ of certiorari."[413]

Henry v. Spearman also focused on this factor, "which counsels greater caution before denying an authorization than before granting one because an erroneously denied motion cannot be corrected, while an erroneously filed petition can still be denied on its merits."

F. Conclusion

This chapter is best summed up with a sentence from a 2011 Ninth Circuit case. "Few applications to file second or successive petitions ... survive these substantive and procedural barriers."[414]

There are four situations in which a defendant may file a second writ of habeas corpus:
- There is a new or amended judgment.
- The issue raised in the second writ was not ripe to be raised in the first writ.
  - Example—mental health issues that develop after the defendant filed a first writ of habeas corpus;
  - *Brady* violations—these are ripe to have been raised in a first writ, even if the defendant is unaware of the *Brady* violation.
- Newly discovered evidence of actual innocence.

---

[412] *Henry v. Spearman*, 899 F.3d 703 (9th Cir. 2018).
[413] 28 U.S.C. § 2244(b)(3)(E).
[414] *King v. Trujillo*, 638 F.3d 726 (9th Cir. 2011).

- A new constitutional rule of law that is applied retroactively.

These four situations lead to two conclusions:

- A defendant must do absolutely everything possible to include all potential arguments in a first writ of habeas corpus.
- A defendant must keep abreast of the law to learn when the Supreme Court issues new constitutional rules of law that are applied retroactively. If a defendant files a writ 10 years after the Supreme Court makes a new constitutional rule, the writ will likely be denied. A defendant must act promptly.

An experienced attorney will be able to review a file and determine not only whether a claim exists on the face of the record but also what *potential* claims may exist. A good attorney may be the difference between having the court review a writ to see if a defendant was prejudiced (a lower standard of proof) or if a defendant is actually innocent (a higher standard of proof).

Chapter 10
WRITS OF HABEAS CORPUS FILED AFTER A GULTY PLEA

After dealing with the procedural and substantive components of a federal writ of habeas corpus, we will now discuss writs of habeas corpus for an individual who pleaded guilty. According to a report by the National Association of Criminal Defense Lawyers, approximately 95 percent of criminal convictions are due to a plea. The other 5 percent are found guilty at trial.[415] Another report, by the Pew Research Center, found that 90 percent of federal defendants pleaded guilty, 8 percent had their charges dismissed, and 2 percent went to trial.[416]

The Pew report noted that "jury trials accounted for fewer than 3% of criminal dispositions in 22 jurisdictions with available data, including Texas (0.86%), Pennsylvania (1.11%), California (1.25%), Ohio (1.27%), Florida (1.53%), North Carolina (1.66%), Michigan (2.12%) and New York (2.91%)."

Clark Neily, senior vice president for legal studies at the Cato Institute, believes that "coercive plea bargaining" explains why so few cases go to trial. He explains:

> Though physical torture remains off limits, American prosecutors are equipped with a fearsome array of tools they can use to extract confessions and discourage people from exercising their right to a jury trial. These tools include charge-stacking (charging more or more serious crimes than the conduct really merits), legislatively-ordered mandatory-minimum sentences, pretrial detention with unaffordable bail, threats to investigate and indict friends or family members, and

---

[415] https://www.nacdl.org/Document/TrialPenaltySixthAmendmentRighttoTrial NearExtinct
[416] https://www.pewresearch.org/fact-tank/2019/06/11/only-2-of-federal-criminal-defendants-go-to-trial-and-most-who-do-are-found-guilty/

the so-called trial penalty—what the National Association of Criminal Defense Lawyers calls the "substantial difference between the sentence offered prior to trial versus the sentence a defendant receives after a trial."[417]

As most cases end with a guilty plea, it is crucial to consider how a guilty plea impacts a defendant's ability to file a federal writ of habeas corpus.

Unfortunately, when a defendant pleads guilty, there are limited arguments available for a federal writ of habeas corpus. Someone who pleaded guilty generally cannot challenge a deprivation of constitutional rights that occurred prior to the plea.[418] There are, however, three types of arguments available for a person who pleads.

A. Ineffective Assistance of Counsel

In our section about effective assistance of counsel, we discussed at length the right to effective assistance of counsel during plea negotiations.[419] This right is broad. The Ninth Circuit held "that although freestanding constitutional claims are unavailable to habeas petitioners who plead guilty, claims of pre-plea ineffective assistance of counsel are cognizable on federal habeas review when the action, or inaction, of counsel prevents petitioner from making an informed choice whether to plead."[420] The rationale for this is that the decision to plead guilty must be made knowingly and voluntarily. If an attorney renders ineffective assistance of counsel, which affects that calculus of a defendant's decision-making, it may not be said that a defendant's decision to plead guilty was knowing and voluntary.

Since ineffective assistance of counsel is a broad constitutional right, some constitutional violations may be raised through ineffective

---

[417] https://www.nbcnews.com/think/opinion/prisons-are-packed-because-prosecutors-are-coercing-plea-deals-yes-ncna1034201

[418] *See Tollett v. Henderson*, 411 U.S. 258 (1973).

[419] *See Hill v. Lockhart*, 474 U.S. 52 (1985); *Lafler v. Cooper*, 566 U.S. 156 (2012).

[420] *Mahrt v. Beard*, 849 F.3d 1164 (9th Cir. 2017).

assistance of counsel, even when a defendant pleads guilty. For example, in *Mahrt v. Beard*, the Ninth Circuit cited to numerous federal courts that allow claims of ineffective assistance of counsel due to a failure to file a motion to suppress when there is a guilty plea. In *Mahrt v. Beard*, however, because the Ninth Circuit, applying the AEDPA standard, found that the state court's denial of the writ of habeas corpus was not unreasonable.

B. Arguments That Challenge the Power of the State to Charge the Defendant with a Crime

There are other potential arguments for a defendant who pleads guilty. Generally, these arguments challenge "the very power of the State to bring the defendant into court to answer the charge brought against him."[421] A defendant who pleads guilty may have arguments that, "if successful, would mean that the government cannot prosecute the defendant *at all*."[422] These are situations in which "the government lacked the power to bring the indictment."[423] Some examples include:

- Unconstitutional statute—A defendant who pleads guilty may argue that the criminal statute is unconstitutional.[424]
- Double jeopardy—A double jeopardy claim may be raised.[425]
- Prosecutorial vindictiveness—In one case, a defendant was found guilty of committing a misdemeanor and sentenced to six months in prison. When the defendant appealed, the prosecutor indicted the defendant for the same conduct but this time charged the defendant with a felony. The defendant pleaded guilty and was sentenced to five to seven years. The Supreme Court allowed the defendant to argue

---

[421] *Blackledge v. Perry*, 417 U.S. 21 (1974).
[422] *United States v. Chavez-Diaz*, 949 F.3d 1202 (9th Cir. 2020).
[423] *United States v. Montilla*, 870 F.2d 549 (9th Cir. 1989).
[424] *Class v. United States* , 583 U.S. ___, 138 S. Ct. 798 (2018).
[425] *Menna v. New York*, 423 U.S. 61 (1975).

that his due process rights were violated due to prosecutorial vindictiveness.[426]

C. Where the State Court Allows the Defendant to Make a Constitutional Argument After Pleading Guilty

The last exception occurs when a state allows a defendant to make constitutional arguments after a guilty plea. In such a situation, the defendant may file a federal writ of habeas corpus based on those arguments.[427] For example, in New York, a defendant who pleaded guilty may appeal an adverse decision on a pretrial motion to suppress evidence.[428] Thus, theoretically, this claim may be raised in a federal writ.[429]

---

[426] *Blackledge v. Perry*, 417 U.S. 21 (1974).

[427] *Lefkowitz v. Newsome*, 420 U.S. 283, 293 (1975).

[428] New York CPL § 710.70(2).

[429] I write "theoretically" because a Fourth Amendment claim cannot be raised in a federal writ of habeas corpus. As previously discussed, it could be raised, however, within a Sixth Amendment right to effective counsel claim.

Chapter 11
FILING A WRIT OF HABEAS CORPUS

Now that the reader knows what types of arguments go into a federal writ of habeas corpus, and what procedural rules exist for filing a federal writ of habeas corpus, we turn to *how* to file the writ.

Probably the safest course of action would be to hire an attorney who knows the procedures for filing a writ in federal district court. After all, an individual can only file one federal writ, with rare exceptions, and it would be a shame to file it incorrectly and then discover that the writ was lost due to some technical issue. For example, filing a writ in the wrong court before the deadline but then filing it in the correct court after the deadline would likely result in a denied writ. With that being said, some defendants do not want or cannot afford to hire an attorney, and for these individuals it would be far better to file their own writs than to give up at this late stage.

A. Who to Name as the Respondent in the Writ of Habeas Corpus

The first question we address is who to name as the respondent in the writ. Though we have presented a writ of habeas corpus as a criminal matter in this book and have referred to the person filing the writ as the *defendant*, a writ of habeas corpus is technically a civil matter. Consequently, there must be a person named as a respondent in the writ of habeas corpus.

Habeas corpus is a Latin phrase that roughly translates to "bring a body before the court." A writ of habeas corpus is an order from the court to the government official who is acting on behalf of the State to incarcerate the defendant. Since the warden of the jail where the defendant is incarcerated is the person who is acting on behalf of the State, the warden is the one who is named as the respondent in the writ. For someone who is not incarcerated, the respondent should be the person with legal responsibility for custody.

This is sometimes the Attorney General and at other times may be the Parole Board. Most of the time, however, the person filing a writ is in custody and should name the warden as the respondent in the writ of habeas corpus.

In California, for example, either the warden of the prison or the California Secretary of Corrections and Rehabilitation may be named as the respondent.

B. In Which Court Should the Writ Be Filed?

According to 28 U.S.C. § 2241(d), the writ should be filed as follows:
- If there is only one federal district court in the state, then the writ is filed in that court. Approximately 50 percent of the states have only one district court.
- If there is more than one district court, the writ may be filed in:
  o The district where the defendant is held in custody, *or*
  o The district in which the state court found the defendant guilty.
- If there is more than one district court where the writ may be filed, and the defendant chooses to file the writ in one of the courts, that court, "in the exercise of its discretion and in furtherance of justice may transfer the application to the other district court for hearing and determination."

C. The Standard Form

A pro se defendant must use the form that is made available for free by the government. These forms are generally updated by the courts from time to time and are straightforward, although they are somewhat more constraining than the more free-form memorandums that are allowed with attorney submissions.

When completing the form, refer to these important reminders:
- Don't forget to sign the writ.

- Read the rules—The Rules Governing Section 2254 Cases and Section 2255 Proceedings apply to all federal courts, and each court also has its own local rules, which govern filings in that particular court. The rules are in the appendix to this book.
- Know how many copies to file—Rule 3a requires the filing of the original writ plus (2) copies. It is important to check the local rules to learn the specific requirements for each court.

D. The Fee

The fee to file a writ of habeas corpus is $5.00. *See* 28 U.S. Code § 1914(a).

E. What Happens After the Writ is Filed?

After a writ is filed in federal court, the judge assigned to the writ has two options: (1) dismissal; or (2) issue an order to show cause. If the judge determines that there is no merit to the writ, then the judge will dismiss the writ. Often, at this stage, a determination that there is no merit is based on a procedural impediment. Remember all the procedural issues that we discussed at length, such as exhaustion, statute of limitations, etc.? If a judge determines that a writ is procedurally barred, the judge will dismiss the writ at this stage.

As per Rule 4, "[i]f it plainly appears from the petition and any attached exhibits that the petitioner is not entitled to relief in the district court, the judge must dismiss the petition and direct the clerk to notify the petitioner." The court typically gives notice to the defendant, prior to dismissal, to allow the defendant to respond to the issues that the court has identified.

If there are no procedural issues, and a defendant writes facts that show a possibility of obtaining habeas relief, the court will typically issue an order to show cause. An order to show cause is directed to the respondent, who must show why the habeas relief should *not* be granted. What this means is that the respondent must argue why the defendant is not entitled to habeas relief.

The respondent files what is called an answer. In the answer, the respondent may raise procedural grounds for dismissal (or may file a motion to dismiss based on those grounds). The respondent will seek to challenge the defendant's facts and/or interpretation of the law. Rule 5c requires the respondent to "attach to the answer parts of the transcript that the respondent considers relevant." The respondent must also file the briefs that were submitted on appeal and the appellate decision(s).

In response, the defendant may file a traverse. Here, the defendant opposes the respondent's answer. The defendant should show that the respondent is incorrect, either in the respondent's assertion of the facts or in the respondent's understanding of the law.

At this point, the judge has each side's arguments before her. Typically, the judge will then decide whether to grant the writ or not. There are occasions when a judge will order an evidentiary hearing, such as if the fact-finding of the state court was defective or deficient.[430] When this happens, Rule 8c requires the judge to appoint an attorney for the defendant.

Prior to an evidentiary hearing, a defendant may request the appointment of an attorney. The court will look to whether the "interests of justice" require an attorney and will specifically look at how complex the case is, including "the legal complexity of the case, the factual complexity of the case, and the petitioner's ability to investigate and present his claims, along with any other relevant factors."[431]

If the federal court grants the writ, then the court typically will order the state to release the defendant from confinement or to retry the defendant. If the court denies the writ, for a procedural reason or

---

[430] *See, e.g., Jones v. Ryan*, 1 F.4th 1179 (9th Cir. 2021).
[431] *Hoggard v. Purkett*, 29 F.3d 469 (8th Cir. 1994).

on the merits, a defendant has an option to request permission to appeal.

F. How to Appeal a Denial of a Writ of Habeas Corpus

There is no automatic right to appeal a denial of a federal writ of habeas corpus. A defendant must obtain a certificate of appealability. A defendant obtains this by filing an application for a certificate of appealability in the district court, together with a notice of appeal. If the district court denies the request, it can be submitted to the circuit court. If the circuit court denies the request, a defendant may then submit the request to the Supreme Court.[432] There is a short deadline for filing a notice of appeal; a defendant must check the rules to know these deadlines.

When determining whether to issue a certificate of appealability, the courts look to whether "the applicant has made a substantial showing of the denial of a constitutional right."[433] "A petitioner satisfies this standard by demonstrating that jurists of reason could disagree with the district court's resolution of his constitutional claims or that jurists could conclude the issues presented are adequate to deserve encouragement to proceed further."[434]

In one recent example, the Ninth Circuit issued "a certificate of appealability limited to the issue of 'whether [Silveira's] guilty plea was not knowing and voluntary due to the ineffective assistance of counsel.'"[435] In a second case, the Fifth Circuit "granted a certificate of appealability on a single issue: Whether the district court abused its discretion in denying equitable tolling."[436]

---

[432] In *Edwards v. Vannoy*, 593 U.S. ___, 141 S. Ct. 1547 (2021), the district and circuit courts denied the certificate of appealability. Edwards then filed a writ of certiorari with the Supreme Court, which agreed to take the case.
[433] 28 U.S.C. § 2253(c)(2).
[434] *Miller-El v. Cockrell*, 537 U.S. 322 (2003).
[435] *United States v. Silveira*, 997 F.3d 911 (9th Cir. 2021).
[436] *Jones v. Lumpkin*, No. 19-10079 (5th Cir. Jan. 5, 2022).

Chapter 12
CONCLUSION: *BROWN V. DAVENPORT* AND THE FUTURE OF WRITS OF HABEAS CORPUS

We conclude this legal journey by returning to President Clinton's words that the AEDPA would not change the standards for adjudicating writs of habeas corpus. In April 2022, the Supreme Court addressed a situation where there were two competing standards for adjudicating a writ of habeas corpus. One standard, the "equitable standard," comes from *Brecht v. Abrahamson*.[437] In that case, the Court held that a writ may be granted upon a claim of constitutional error when the error had a "substantial and injurious effect or influence in determining the jury's verdict." On the other hand, the AEDPA standard requires a showing that the state court decision was an unreasonable application of federal law.

In *Brown v. Davenport*,[438] Davenport was convicted of first-degree murder. He argued that his constitutional rights were violated due to the fact that he was restrained at trial. As we explained in Chapter 4 about potential arguments, a defendant may not be physically restrained in court, unless the court orders that the defendant be restrained. This applies to the guilt phase and the penalty phase of a trial.[439] There are three reasons for this rule: (1) restraints undermine the presumption of innocence; (2) an unshackled defendant is better able to assist and communicate with his attorney; and (3) the absence of restraints maintains a dignified court room. After an evidentiary hearing about whether the error was harmless, the state court concluded that shackling Davenport was harmless, and the conviction stood.

---

[437] 507 U.S. 619 (1993).

[438] No. 20-826 (Apr. 21, 2022). The quotations in this chapter are from this decision.

[439] *Deck v. Missouri*, 544 U.S. 622 (2005).

Davenport then filed a writ of habeas corpus in federal court. The district court (trial level court) denied the writ. The Sixth Circuit Court of Appeal, however, granted the writ. Relying solely on *Brecht*, the Sixth Circuit determined that Davenport was able to "show that the error had a 'substantial and injurious effect or influence' on the outcome of his trial."

The Supreme Court disagreed. The Court held that *both* standards must be met:

> Today, then, a federal court must deny relief to a state habeas petitioner who fails to satisfy either this Court's equitable precedents or AEDPA. But to grant relief, a court must find that the petitioner has cleared both tests. The Sixth Circuit erred when it held Mr. Davenport to just one of these burdens. It granted relief after finding for him on *Brecht*. But it failed to ask the further question whether he satisfied AEDPA.

The Court then provided two differences between *Brecht* and the AEDPA:

> (1) "where AEDPA asks whether every fairminded jurist would agree that an error was prejudicial, *Brecht* asks only whether a federal habeas court *itself* harbors grave doubt about the petitioner's verdict."
>
> (2) AEDPA focuses on whether a court unreasonably applied federal law, as determined by the *Supreme Court*. Under *Brecht*, "a federal habeas court may consult and draw on the whole body of law," including "circuit case law."

By focusing only on *Brecht*, the Sixth Circuit "granted relief to Mr. Davenport after concluding that it harbored grave doubts about the jury's verdict. It did not claim that every reasonable jurist would share its doubts. Nor did it purport to hold that the Michigan state courts had acted contrary to or unreasonably applied a decision of this Court." In a 6-3 decision, the Supreme Court reversed the granting of the writ of habeas corpus and denied the writ.

The reader may be wondering why we chose to conclude our book with a relatively mundane discussion about an unlikely situation where a defendant does not argue the AEDPA standard. The answer comes from the dissent. The majority set forth an abridged history of the writ of habeas corpus, which the dissent called "a from-Blackstone-onward theory of habeas practice." Among other things, the majority noted:

- "At the same time, even this writ had its limits. Usually, a prisoner could not use it to challenge a final judgment of conviction issued by a court of competent jurisdiction."
- "Instead, a habeas court could examin[e] only the power and authority of the court to act, not the correctness of its conclusions."

The dissent accused the majority of "hoping that the seeds it sows now will yield more succulent fruit in cases to come." In a concurring opinion in 2021, Justice Gorsuch argued that, historically, a prisoner could not use the writ of habeas corpus to challenge a conviction. In 2022, this historical argument was included in a majority opinion.

In an article on SCOTUSBlog, a prominent website that covers the Supreme Court, Eve Brensike Primus explains the dissent: "Gorsuch laid out his vision (joined by five other justices) of a much narrower federal habeas writ in the hopes of limiting the scope of the writ in future cases." She continues, "Whose view of the history will prevail in future cases remains to be seen, but it is significant that Gorsuch has now managed to get his more constricted view of the scope of the Great Writ into a majority decision."[440]

What is the future of the writ of habeas corpus? Both the majority and dissent agree that the writ has developed over the course of American history, though they disagree about the extent of this evolution. The writ of habeas corpus looked different in 1800 than it did in 1900 and looked different in 1900 than it did in 2000. It stands

---

[440] Eve Brensike Primus, "*In rejecting a prisoner's post-conviction claim, court plants seeds for narrowing habeas relief*," SCOTUSBlog (Apr. 22, 2022, 10:35 AM), https://www.scotusblog.com/2022/04/in-rejecting-a-prisoners-post-conviction-claim-court-plants-seeds-for-narrowing-habeas-relief/.

to reason that it will look different in 2100 than it did in 2000. It is important to remember that many of the changes to the writ of habeas corpus happened due to specific people with specific facts who did not give up on their claims of constitutional violations, and with the assistance of a hard-working and dedicated attorney.

In other words, the law has changed and continues to change because lawyers and defendants have looked *beyond* the law, fighting for what the law should be, not merely what it has been. This evolution is slow and painstaking, but it will undoubtably cause the continued evolution of our nation's "Great Writ."

APPENDIX A: Rules Governing Section 2254 Cases in the United States District Courts and Rules Governing Section 2255 Proceedings for the United States District Courts

RULES GOVERNING
SECTION 2254 CASES IN THE UNITED STATES DISTRICT COURTS

and

RULES GOVERNING
SECTION 2255 PROCEEDINGS FOR THE UNITED STATES DISTRICT COURTS

Effective Feb. 1, 1977, as amended to Dec. 1, 2019

TABLE OF CONTENTS

RULES GOVERNING SECTION 2254 CASES IN THE UNITED STATES DISTRICT COURTS

Effective Feb. 1, 1977, as amended to Dec. 1, 2019

Rule 1. Scope

(a) Cases Involving a Petition under 28 U.S.C. § 2254. These rules govern a petition for a writ of habeas corpus filed in a United States district court under 28 U.S.C. § 2254 by:

(1) a person in custody under a state-court judgment who seeks a determination that the custody violates the Constitution, laws, or treaties of the United States; and

(2) a person in custody under a state-court or federal-court judgment who seeks a determination that future custody under a state-court judgment would violate the Constitution, laws, or treaties of the United States.

(b) Other Cases. The district court may apply any or all of these rules to a habeas corpus petition not covered by Rule 1(a).

Rule 2. The Petition

(a) Current Custody; Naming the Respondent. If the petitioner is currently in custody under a state-court judgment, the petition must name as respondent the state officer who has custody.

(b) Future Custody; Naming the Respondents and Specifying the Judgment. If the petitioner is not yet in custody - but may be subject to future custody - under the state-court judgment being contested, the petition must name as respondents both the officer who has current custody and the attorney general of the state where the judgment was entered. The petition must ask for relief from the state-court judgment being contested.

(c) Form. The petition must:

(1) specify all the grounds for relief available to the petitioner;

(2) state the facts supporting each ground;

(3) state the relief requested;

(4) be printed, typewritten, or legibly handwritten; and

(1)

(5) be signed under penalty of perjury by the petitioner or by a person authorized to sign it for the petitioner under 28 U.S.C. § 2242.

(d) Standard Form. The petition must substantially follow either the form appended to these rules or a form prescribed by a local district-court rule. The clerk must make forms available to petitioners without charge.

(e) Separate Petitions for Judgments of Separate Courts. A petitioner who seeks relief from judgments of more than one state court must file a separate petition covering the judgment or judgments of each court.

Rule 3. Filing the Petition; Inmate Filing

(a) Where to File; Copies; Filing Fee. An original and two copies of the petition must be filed with the clerk and must be accompanied by:

(1) the applicable filing fee, or

(2) a motion for leave to proceed in forma pauperis, the affidavit required by 28 U.S.C. § 1915, and a certificate from the warden or other appropriate officer of the place of confinement showing the amount of money or securities that the petitioner has in any account in the institution.

(b) Filing. The clerk must file the petition and enter it on the docket.

(c) Time to File. The time for filing a petition is governed by 28 U.S.C. § 2244(d).

(d) Inmate Filing. A paper filed by an inmate confined in an institution is timely if deposited in the institution's internal mailing system on or before the last day for filing. If an institution has a system designed for legal mail, the inmate must use that system to receive the benefit of this rule. Timely filing may be shown by a declaration in compliance with 28 U.S.C. § 1746 or by a notarized statement, either of which must set forth the date of deposit and state that first-class postage has been prepaid.

(2)

Rule 4. Preliminary Review; Serving the Petition and Order

The clerk must promptly forward the petition to a judge under the court's assignment procedure, and the judge must promptly examine it. If it plainly appears from the petition and any attached exhibits that the petitioner is not entitled to relief in the district court, the judge must dismiss the petition and direct the clerk to notify the petitioner. If the petition is not dismissed, the judge must order the respondent to file an answer, motion, or other response within a fixed time, or to take other action the judge may order. In every case, the clerk must serve a copy of the petition and any order on the respondent and on the attorney general or other appropriate officer of the state involved.

Rule 5. The Answer and the Reply

(a) When Required. The respondent is not required to answer the petition unless a judge so orders.

(b) Contents: Addressing the Allegations; Stating a Bar. The answer must address the allegations in the petition. In addition, it must state whether any claim in the petition is barred by a failure to exhaust state remedies, a procedural bar, non- retroactivity, or a statute of limitations.

(c) Contents: Transcripts. The answer must also indicate what transcripts (of pretrial, trial, sentencing, or post-conviction proceedings) are available, when they can be furnished, and what proceedings have been recorded but not transcribed. The respondent must attach to the answer parts of the transcript that the respondent considers relevant. The judge may order that the respondent furnish other parts of existing transcripts or that parts of untranscribed recordings be transcribed and furnished. If a transcript cannot be obtained, the respondent may submit a narrative summary of the evidence.

(d) Contents: Briefs on Appeal and Opinions. The respondent must also file with the answer a copy of:

(3)

(1) any brief that the petitioner submitted in an appellate court contesting the conviction or sentence, or contesting an adverse judgment or order in a post-conviction proceeding;

(2) any brief that the prosecution submitted in an appellate court relating to the conviction or sentence; and

(3) the opinions and dispositive orders of the appellate court relating to the conviction or the sentence.

(e) Reply. The petitioner may file a reply to the respondent's answer or other pleading. The judge must set the time to file unless the time is already set by local rule.

Rule 6. Discovery

(a) Leave of Court Required. A judge may, for good cause, authorize a party to conduct discovery under the Federal Rules of Civil Procedure and may limit the extent of discovery. If necessary for effective discovery, the judge must appoint an attorney for a petitioner who qualifies to have counsel appointed under 18 U.S.C. § 3006A.

(b) Requesting Discovery. A party requesting discovery must provide reasons for the request. The request must also include any proposed interrogatories and requests for admission, and must specify any requested documents.

(c) Deposition Expenses. If the respondent is granted leave to take a deposition, the judge may require the respondent to pay the travel expenses, subsistence expenses, and fees of the petitioner's attorney to attend the deposition.

Rule 7. Expanding the Record

(a) In General. If the petition is not dismissed, the judge may direct the parties to expand the record by submitting additional materials relating to the petition. The judge may require that these materials be authenticated.

(4)

(b) Types of Materials. The materials that may be required include letters predating the filing of the petition, documents, exhibits, and answers under oath to written interrogatories propounded by the judge. Affidavits may also be submitted and considered as part of the record.

(c) Review by the Opposing Party. The judge must give the party against whom the additional materials are offered an opportunity to admit or deny their correctness.

Rule 8. Evidentiary Hearing

(a) Determining Whether to Hold a Hearing. If the petition is not dismissed, the judge must review the answer, any transcripts and records of state-court proceedings, and any materials submitted under Rule 7 to determine whether an evidentiary hearing is warranted.

(b) Reference to a Magistrate Judge. A judge may, under 28 U.S.C. § 636(b), refer the petition to a magistrate judge to conduct hearings and to file proposed findings of fact and recommendations for disposition. When they are filed, the clerk must promptly serve copies of the proposed findings and recommendations on all parties. Within 14 days after being served, a party may file objections as provided by local court rule. The judge must determine de novo any proposed finding or recommendation to which objection is made. The judge may accept, reject, or modify any proposed finding or recommendation.

(c) Appointing Counsel; Time of Hearing. If an evidentiary hearing is warranted, the judge must appoint an attorney to represent a petitioner who qualifies to have counsel appointed under 18 U.S.C. § 3006A. The judge must conduct the hearing as soon as practicable after giving the attorneys adequate time to investigate and prepare. These rules do not limit the appointment of counsel under § 3006A at any stage of the proceeding.

(5)

RULES GOVERNING SECTION 2254 CASES AND SECTION 2255 PROCEEDINGS

Rule 9. Second or Successive Petitions

Before presenting a second or successive petition, the petitioner must obtain an order from the appropriate court of appeals authorizing the district court to consider the petition as required by 28 U.S.C. § 2244(b)(3) and (4).

Rule 10. Powers of a Magistrate Judge

A magistrate judge may perform the duties of a district judge under these rules, as authorized under 28 U.S.C. § 636.

Rule 11. Certificate of Appealability; Time to Appeal

(a) Certificate of Appealability. The district court must issue or deny a certificate of appealability when it enters a final order adverse to the applicant. Before entering the final order, the court may direct the parties to submit arguments on whether a certificate should issue. If the court issues a certificate, the court must state the specific issue or issues that satisfy the showing required by 28 U.S.C. § 2253(c)(2). If the court denies a certificate, the parties may not appeal the denial but may seek a certificate from the court of appeals under Federal Rule of Appellate Procedure 22. A motion to reconsider a denial does not extend the time to appeal.

(b) Time to Appeal. Federal Rule of Appellate Procedure 4(a) governs the time to appeal an order entered under these rules. A timely notice of appeal must be filed even if the district court issues a certificate of appealability.

(6)

Rule 12. Applicability of the Federal Rules of Civil Procedure

The Federal Rules of Civil Procedure, to the extent that they
are not inconsistent with any statutory provisions or these rules,
may be applied to a proceeding under these rules.

* * * * *

RULES GOVERNING SECTION 2255 PROCEEDINGS
FOR THE UNITED STATES DISTRICT COURTS

Effective Feb. 1, 1977, as amended to Dec. 1, 2019

Rule 1. Scope

These rules govern a motion filed in a United States district court
under 28 U.S.C. § 2255 by:

(a) a person in custody under a judgment of that court who
seeks a determination that:

(1) the judgment violates the Constitution or laws of the
United States;

(2) the court lacked jurisdiction to enter the judgment;

(3) the sentence exceeded the maximum allowed by law;
or

(4) the judgment or sentence is otherwise subject to collateral review; and

(b) a person in custody under a judgment of a state court or
another federal court, and subject to future custody under a judgment of the district court, who seeks a determination that:

(1) future custody under a judgment of the district court
would violate the Constitution or laws of the United States;

(2) the district court lacked jurisdiction to enter the judgment;

(3) the district court's sentence exceeded the maximum
allowed by law; or

(4) the district court's judgment or sentence is otherwise
subject to collateral review.

Rule 2. The Motion

(a) Applying for Relief. The application must be in the form
of a motion to vacate, set aside, or correct the sentence.

(b) Form. The motion must:

(8)

(1) specify all the grounds for relief available to the moving party;

(2) state the facts supporting each ground;

(3) state the relief requested;

(4) be printed, typewritten, or legibly handwritten; and

(5) be signed under penalty of perjury by the movant or by a person authorized to sign it for the movant.

(c) Standard Form. The motion must substantially follow either the form appended to these rules or a form prescribed by a local district-court rule. The clerk must make forms available to moving parties without charge.

(d) Separate Motions for Separate Judgments. A moving party who seeks relief from more than one judgment must file a separate motion covering each judgment.

Rule 3. Filing the Motion; Inmate Filing

(a) Where to File; Copies. An original and two copies of the motion must be filed with the clerk.

(b) Filing and Service. The clerk must file the motion and enter it on the criminal docket of the case in which the challenged judgment was entered. The clerk must then deliver or serve a copy of the motion on the United States attorney in that district, together with a notice of its filing.

(c) Time to File. The time for filing a motion is governed by 28 U.S.C. § 2255 para. 6.

(d) Inmate Filing. A paper filed by an inmate confined in an institution is timely if deposited in the institution's internal mailing system on or before the last day for filing. If an institution has a system designed for legal mail, the inmate must use that system to receive the benefit of this rule. Timely filing may be shown by a declaration in compliance with 28 U.S.C. § 1746 or by a notarized statement, either of which must set forth the date of deposit and state that first-class postage has been prepaid.

(9)

RULES GOVERNING SECTION 2254 CASES AND SECTION 2255 PROCEEDINGS

Rule 4. Preliminary Review

(a) Referral to a Judge. The clerk must promptly forward the motion to the judge who conducted the trial and imposed sentence or, if the judge who imposed sentence was not the trial judge, to the judge who conducted the proceedings being challenged. If the appropriate judge is not available, the clerk must forward the motion to a judge under the court's assignment procedure.

(b) Initial Consideration by the Judge. The judge who receives the motion must promptly examine it. If it plainly appears from the motion, any attached exhibits, and the record of prior proceedings that the moving party is not entitled to relief, the judge must dismiss the motion and direct the clerk to notify the moving party. If the motion is not dismissed, the judge must order the United States attorney to file an answer, motion, or other response within a fixed time, or to take other action the judge may order.

Rule 5. The Answer and the Reply

(a) When Required. The respondent is not required to answer the motion unless a judge so orders.

(b) Contents. The answer must address the allegations in the motion. In addition, it must state whether the moving party has used any other federal remedies, including any prior post- conviction motions under these rules or any previous rules, and whether the moving party received an evidentiary hearing.

(c) Records of Prior Proceedings. If the answer refers to briefs or transcripts of the prior proceedings that are not available in the court's records, the judge must order the government to furnish them within a reasonable time that will not unduly delay the proceedings.

(d) Reply. The moving party may file a reply to the respondent's answer or other pleading. The judge must set the time to file unless the time is already set by local rule.

Rule 6. Discovery

(a) Leave of Court Required. A judge may, for good cause, authorize a party to conduct discovery under the Federal Rules of Criminal Procedure or Civil Procedure, or in accordance with the practices and principles of law. If necessary for effective discovery, the judge must appoint an attorney for a moving party who qualifies to have counsel appointed under 18 U.S.C. § 3006A.

(b) Requesting Discovery. A party requesting discovery must provide reasons for the request. The request must also include any proposed interrogatories and requests for admission, and must specify any requested documents.

(c) Deposition Expenses. If the government is granted leave to take a deposition, the judge may require the government to pay the travel expenses, subsistence expenses, and fees of the moving party's attorney to attend the deposition.

Rule 7. Expanding the Record

(a) In General. If the motion is not dismissed, the judge may direct the parties to expand the record by submitting additional materials relating to the motion. The judge may require that these materials be authenticated.

(b) Types of Materials. The materials that may be required include letters predating the filing of the motion, documents, exhibits, and answers under oath to written interrogatories propounded by the judge. Affidavits also may be submitted and considered as part of the record.

(c) Review by the Opposing Party. The judge must give the party against whom the additional materials are offered an opportunity to admit or deny their correctness.

(11)

RULES GOVERNING SECTION 2254 CASES AND SECTION 2255 PROCEEDINGS

Rule 8. Evidentiary Hearing

(a) Determining Whether to Hold a Hearing. If the motion is not dismissed, the judge must review the answer, any transcripts and records of prior proceedings, and any materials submitted under Rule 7 to determine whether an evidentiary hearing is warranted.

(b) Reference to a Magistrate Judge. A judge may, under 28 U.S.C. § 636(b), refer the motion to a magistrate judge to conduct hearings and to file proposed findings of fact and recommendations for disposition. When they are filed, the clerk must promptly serve copies of the proposed findings and recommendations on all parties. Within 14 days after being served, a party may file objections as provided by local court rule. The judge must determine de novo any proposed finding or recommendation to which objection is made. The judge may accept, reject, or modify any proposed finding or recommendation.

(c) Appointing Counsel; Time of Hearing. If an evidentiary hearing is warranted, the judge must appoint an attorney to represent a moving party who qualifies to have counsel appointed under 18 U.S.C. § 3006A. The judge must conduct the hearing as soon as practicable after giving the attorneys adequate time to investigate and prepare. These rules do not limit the appointment of counsel under § 3006A at any stage of the proceeding.

(d) Producing a Statement. Federal Rule of Criminal Procedure 26.2(a)—(d) and (f) applies at a hearing under this rule. If a party does not comply with a Rule 26.2(a) order to produce a witness's statement, the court must not consider that witness's testimony.

Rule 9. Second or Successive Motions

Before presenting a second or successive motion, the moving party must obtain an order from the appropriate court of appeals

(12)

authorizing the district court to consider the motion, as required
by 28 U.S.C. § 2255, para. 8.

Rule 10. Powers of a Magistrate Judge

A magistrate judge may perform the duties of a district judge
under these rules, as authorized by 28 U.S.C. § 636.

Rule 11. Certificate of Appealability; Time to Appeal

(a) Certificate of Appealability. The district court must issue or deny a certificate of appealability when it enters a final order adverse to the applicant. Before entering the final order, the
court may direct the parties to submit arguments on whether a certificate should issue. If the court issues a certificate, the court must
state the specific issue or issues that satisfy the showing required
by 28 U.S.C. § 2253(c)(2). If the court denies a certificate, a party
may not appeal the denial but may seek a certificate from the court
of appeals under Federal Rule of Appellate Procedure 22. A motion to reconsider a denial does not extend the time to appeal.

(b) Time to Appeal. Federal Rule of Appellate Procedure
4(a) governs the time to appeal an order entered under these rules.
A timely notice of appeal must be filed even if the district court
issues a certificate of appealability. These rules do not extend the
time to appeal the original judgment of conviction.

Rule 12. Applicability of the Federal Rules of Civil Procedure and the Federal Rules of Criminal Procedure

The Federal Rules of Civil Procedure and the Federal Rules
of Criminal Procedure, to the extent that they are not inconsistent
with any statutory provisions or these rules, may be applied to a
proceeding under these rules.

* * * * *

(13)

APPENDIX B: List of Helpful Cases for Commonly Argued Constitutional Violations

List of Helpful Cases for Commonly Argued Constitutional Violations

Miranda Rights (5th Amendment)
- *Garcia v. Long*, 808 F.3d 771 (9th Cir. 2015)
- *Hurd v. Terhune*, 619 F.3d 1080 (9th Cir. 2010)
- *Jackson v. Conway*, 763 F. 3d 115 (2d Cir. 2014)

Double Jeopardy (5th Amendment)
- *US v. Chilaca*, 909 F. 3d 289 (9th Cir. 2017) (appeal)
- *US v. Voris*, 964 F. 3d 864 (9th Cir. 2020) (appeal)
- *US v. Zalapa*, 509 F. 3d 1060 (9th Cir. 2007) (appeal)

Confrontation Clause (6th Amendment)
- *Barajas v. Wise*, 481 F. 3d 734 (9th Cir. 2007)
- *Howard v. Walker*, 406 F. 3d 114 (2d Cir. 2005)
- *Ocampo v. Vail*, 649 F. 3d 1098 (9th Cir. 2011)
- *Orlando v. Nassau Cty. Dist. Attorney's Office*, 915 F.3d 113 (2d Cir. 2019)
- *Ortiz v. Yates*, 704 F. 3d 1026 (9th Cir. 2012)
- *US v. Carter*, 907 F. 3d 1199 (9th Cir. 2018) (appeal)
- *U.S. v. Rodriguez* 880 F.3d 1151 (9th Cir. 2018) (appeal)

Ineffective Assistance of Counsel (6th Amendment)
- *Andrews v. Davis*, 944 F.3d 1092 (9th Cir. 2019)
- *Andrus v. Texas*, 140 S. Ct. 1875 (2020)
- *Browning v. Baker*, 875 F.3d 444 (9th Cir. 2017) (also *Brady* violation)
- *Buck v. Davis*, 137 S. Ct. 759 92017)
- *Cannedy v. Adams*, 706 F.3d 1148 (9th Cir. 2013)
- *Cornell v. Kirkpatrick*, 665 F.3d 369 (2d Cir. 2011)
- *Doe v. US*, 915 F. 3d 905 (2d Cir. 2019) (coram nobis based on ineffective assistance of counsel)
- *Ellis v. Harrison,* 947 F.3d 555 (9th Cir. 2020)
- *Garza v. Idaho*, 139 S. Ct. 738 (2019)
- *Howard v. Clark*, 608 F.3d 563 (9th Cir. 2010) (remand for factual hearing)
- *Jones v. Ryan*, No. 18-99005 (9th Cir. June 28, 2021)

242

- *Lee v. US,* 137 S. Ct. 1958 (2017)
- *Lockhart v. Terhune,* 250 F. 3d 1223 (9th Cir. 2001)
- *Noguera v. Davis,* No. 17-99010 (9th Cir. July 20, 2021)
- *Porter v. McCollum,* 558 U.S. 30 (2009)
- *Rompilla v. Beard,* 545 U.S. 374 (2005)
- *Seidel v. Merkle,* 146 F.3d 750 (9th Cir. 1998)
- *US v. Engel,* 968 F.3d 1046 (9th Cir. 2020)
- *US v. Gordon,* 156 F.3d 376 (2d Cir. 1998)
- *US v. Nolan,* 956 F.3d 71 (2d Cir. 2020)
- *Vega v. Ryan,* 757 F.3d 960 (9th Cir. 2014)
- *Weeden v. Johnson,* 854 F.3d 1063 (9th Cir. 2017)
- *Zapata v. Vasquez,* 788 F.3d 1106 (9th Cir. 2015)

Speedy Trial (6th Amendment)
- *McNeely v. Blanas,* 336 F. 3d 822 (9th Cir. 2003)
- *US v. Black,* 918 F.3d 243 (2d Cir. 2019)
- *US v. Tigano,* 880 F. 3d 602 (2d Cir. 2018) (appeal)

Eighth Amendment
- *Gonzalez v. Duncan,* 551 F.3d 875 (9th Cir. 2009)
- *Graham v. Florida,* 560 U.S. 48 (2010)
- *Miller v. Alabama,* 567 U.S. 460 (2012)

Brady Violation (Fifth and Fourteenth Amendments)
- *Fuentes v. Griffin,* 829 F.3d 233 (2d Cir. 2016)
- *Floyd v. Vannoy,* 894 F. 3d 143 (5th Cir. 2018) (also actual innocence)
- *Milke v. Ryan,* 711 F.3d 998 (9th Cir. 2013)
- *Silva v. Brown,* 416 F.3d 980 (9th Cir. 2005)
- *Smith v. Cain,* 565 U.S. 72 (2012)
- *US v. Bundy,* 968 F.3d 1019 (9th Cir. 2020)

Due Process (Fifth and Fourteenth Amendments)
- *Browning v. Baker,* 875 F.3d 444 (9th Cir. 2017)
- *Dow v. Virga,* 729 F.3d 1041 (9th Cir. 2013)
- *Godoy v. Spearman,* 861 F.3d 956 (9th Cir. 2017) (remand)
- *Echavarria v. Filson,* 896 F.3d 1118 (9th Cir. 2018)

- *Maxwell v. Roe*, 606 F.3d 561 (9th Cir. 2010)
- *Milke v. Ryan*, 711 F.3d 998 (9th Cir. 2013)
- *Silva v. Brown*, 416 F.3d 980 (9th Cir. 2005)
- *United States v. Velazquez*, No. 19-50099 (9th Cir. June 23, 2021)

Equal Protection
- *Crittenden v. Chappell*, 804 F.3d 998 (9th Cir. 2015)
- *Currie v. McDowell*, 825 F. 3d 603 (9th Cir. 2016)
- *Foster v. Chatman*, 136 S. Ct. 1737 (2016)
- *Flowers v. Mississippi*, 139 S. Ct. 2228 (2019)
- *Shirley v. Yates*, 807 F. 3d 1090 (9th Cir. 2015)

Sufficiency of Evidence
- *Lucero v. Holland*, 902 F.3d 979 (9th Cir. 2018)

PUBLICATION DATA

Copyright 2023
Published through Amazon KDP

Caitlin Dukes and Aaron Spolin
Spolin & Dukes P.C.
11500 W. Olympic Blvd., Suite 400
Los Angeles, CA 90064

(310) 424-5816

Made in the USA
Las Vegas, NV
06 December 2023

82191299R00144